Recognizing Child Abuse

Praise for
Recognizing Child Abuse: A Guide for the Concerned

"The book offers straight-forward, thorough coverage of a complex subject for a wide range of readers including professionals, parents, and all individuals interested in reducing the incidence of child abuse and neglect."
>—David S. Liederman
>Executive Director, Child Welfare League of America

"This up-to-date guide is loaded with vital information about the devastating reality of child abuse in our society. Any person with an interest in knowing more about child maltreatment in America today, or becoming involved in any way with the complex system which deals with child protection will find *Recognizing Child Abuse* to be a valuable resource."
>—Lawrence C. Brown
>Executive Director, American Humane Association

"*Recognizing Child Abuse* is both a practical guide for the professional service provider and a basic source of information for the concerned lay person. In too many cases, the professional service providers, as well as concerned friends or relatives, have inadequate training in recognizing, understanding, and confronting children who are maltreated. Besharov's book should answer basic questions about child maltreatment and should be a useful reference in improving interventions in child protection efforts."
>—Evelyn K. Moore
>Executive Director, National Black Child Development Institute

"Douglas Besharov provides for the layperson, as well as the experienced professional, in clear, understandable language, the information necessary to identify, report, and investigate child abuse. While this handbook clarifies the legal requirements, it also helps the reader appreciate and deal with the human aspects of cases of child abuse."
>—Herbert A. Sohn
>Executive Director, American Orthopsychiatric Association

"A clearly written, informative book and a valuable resource for a wide-ranging audience. Besharov is both persuasive in encouraging reporting by the police, other professionals who work with children, and citizens, and helpful in guiding their decisions on when and how to do so."
>—Hubert Williams
>President, Police Foundation

"A nuts-and-bolts manual for the people who must make life-and-death decisions. *Recognizing Child Abuse* will be extraordinarily useful for child protective workers and other social workers who need to understand the legal obligations and potential liabilities for everyone."
>—Mark G. Battle
>Executive Director, National Association of Social Workers

Recognizing Child Abuse

A Guide for the Concerned

DOUGLAS J. BESHAROV

THE FREE PRESS
A Division of Macmillan, Inc.
NEW YORK

Collier Macmillan Canada
TORONTO

Maxwell Macmillan International
NEW YORK   OXFORD   SINGAPORE   SYDNEY

The Free Press
A Division of Macmillan, Inc.
866 Third Avenue, New York, N.Y. 10022

Collier Macmillan Canada, Inc.
1200 Eglinton Avenue East
Suite 200
Don Mills, Ontario M3C 3N1

Printed in the United States of America

printing number
1 2 3 4 5 6 7 8 9 10

Library of Congress Cataloging-in-Publication Data

Besharov, Douglas J.
    Recognizing child abuse: a guide for the concerned/Douglas J.
Besharov.
        P.   cm.
    Includes bibliographical references.
    ISBN 0–02–903081–1:   ISBN 0–02–903082–X (pbk.)
    1. Child abuse—United States—Investigation.   I. Title.
HV8079.C46B48   1990   89–25638
362.7'68—dc20   CIP

To Carol,
who brightened and guided our lives.

Contents

PART THREE
The Reporting Process

PART FOUR
A Word to Parents

Charts

Illustrations

Acknowledgments

A number of people helped make this book possible, and their assistance should be acknowledged. An immense amount of library research was required, so I first want to express deep appreciation to my research assistants, Sonya A. Adamo, Krista Peterson, and Wende Wrubel.

Many of the materials in this book, however, cannot be found in any library. Thus, much of the book's richness comes from the generosity of people who shared their experience, training curricula, case materials, and other documents with me. Too many people helped to list them all, but some deserve individual mention: Jean Bower, director, Counsel for Child Abuse and Neglect of the D.C. Superior Court; Norman Ellerstein, associate professor of pediatrics, Buffalo (New York) Children's Hospital; Vincent J. Fontana, MD, medical director, New York Foundling Hospital; Robert Horowitz, staff director, National Legal Resource Center on Child Advocacy and Protection, American Bar Association; David W. Lloyd, project director, National Resource Center for Child Sexual Abuse; Herbert A. Sohn, executive director of the American Orthopsychiatric Association and former child abuse consultant, Ontario Ministry for Community and Social Services; Betty Stewart, Assistant Commissioner for Children, Youth and Families, U.S. Department of Health and Human Services; and Susan Weber, director, U.S. National Center on Child Abuse and Neglect. Special thanks go to Jose D. Alfaro, director of Research and Training, Children's Aid Society of the City of New York and, for many years, director of the New York City Mayor's Task Force on Child Abuse and Neglect, who graciously served as a friendly but critical sounding board for ideas and arguments.

The American Bar Association's Center on Children and the Law, Cornell University's Family Life Development Center, the Friends of the D.C. Superior Court, and the Ontario Centre for the Prevention of Child Abuse provided funds for training materials on child abuse and neglect that, in modified form, are used in this book. Other materials in this book appeared in a book I wrote for the National Association of Social Workers, *The Vulnerable Social Worker: Liability for Serving Children and Families* (1985), and a pamphlet I wrote for the American Bar Association, *Child Abuse: A Police Guide* (1987).

The policy framework for this book is based on *Child Abuse and Neglect Reporting and Investigation: Policy Guidelines for Decision Making*,[1] a report issued by a national group of 38 child protective professionals from 19 states. Meeting for three days at Airlie House, Virginia, under the auspices of the American Bar Association's National Legal Resource Center for Child Advocacy and Protection in association with the American Public Welfare Association and the American Enterprise Institute, the "Airlie House group," as it has come to be called, developed policy guidelines for decision making about reporting and investigating child abuse. (I was the "rapporteur" for the effort.) One of the group's major conclusions was that there should be better guidelines for public and professional education about what should be reported (and what should not be). This book seeks to help fulfill that recommendation.

I would also like to thank the CIBA-GEIGY Corporation for permitting the use of the photographs and sketches that appear at different points in this book. These illustrations help explain, in a way that words cannot, what it means to say that a child may be abused or neglected.

I am especially indebted to the work of Dr. Barton Schmitt of the C. Henry Kempe National Center for the Prevention and Treatment of Child Abuse and Neglect. Much of the material on "suspicious injuries" and their assessment is based on his work that appears in two outstanding books: B. Schmitt, ed., *The Child Protection Team Handbook: A Multidisciplinary Approach to Managing Child Abuse and Neglect* (1978) and N. Ellerstein, ed., *Child Abuse and Neglect: A Medical Reference* (1981).

References to the number of states that have one or another provision are not footnoted, so the reader should know that in describing the states' reporting laws, I relied on the legal summaries and analyses prepared by the Information Clearinghouse of the U.S. National Center on Child Abuse and Neglect.[2]

Carrie Wooten and Sally Holland efficiently typed the manuscript for this book. Vincent J. Cannato, John C. Povejsil, and Paul N. Tramontozzi helped edit the final draft. Gregory M. Besharov spent many evenings helping to proofread the typescript. Eleanor C. Besharov provided indispensable and always cheerful administrative and paper-processing assistance. Kelty L. Barber helped in so many ways that to give her proper credit, the closest I can come is to say that she cheerfully made sure this book came together.

Susan H. Besharov, my wife, gets final but greatest thanks. As a therapist, a former sponsor of a Parents' Anonymous group, and a some-time reporter of suspected child abuse, she lent her wisdom to this book.

D. J. B.

1

You Can
Make a Difference

"Mom Held in Child's Scald Death"
New York, New York

"Pair Sentenced for Closeting Girl, 8"
Princess Anne, Maryland

"2 Get 99 Years in Tot's Torture Death"
Athens, Tennessee

"Starving Girl Freed by Police"
Long Beach, California

News stories daily remind us that children are brutally maltreated by their parents—the very persons who should be giving them love and protection. Children are beaten until their bodies no longer heal, they are scalded with boiling water, they are starved and so dehydrated that their skin shrivels around their fragile bones, they are sexually assaulted and forced to perform all sorts of perverted acts, and they are locked in closets or tied to bed posts for days on end. Abused and neglected children are in urgent need of protection—protection that can be provided only if individual citizens are willing to help.

ONE MILLION VICTIMS

It is a personal tragedy when a parent—in a fit of uncontrolled fear, frustration, or rage—flings a child against the floor. But when multiplied by tens of thousands of similar situations in which parents seriously harm their children, such individual episodes become a social problem of the greatest magnitude.

Although all statistics concerning what happens in the privacy of the home must be approached with great care, we know that each year, over one million children are abused or neglected by their parents. According to the Study of National Incidence and Prevalence of Child Abuse and Neglect (hereafter referred to as the national incidence study), conducted for the federal government in 1986, about 300,000 are physically abused, another 140,000 are sexually abused, and 700,000 are neglected or otherwise maltreated.[1] Estimates vary, but it appears that at least 1,100 children die each year as a result of maltreatment.[2] This figure would make maltreatment the sixth largest cause of death for children under age fourteen.[3]

Children who live through years of assault, degradation, and neglect bear emotional scars that can last for years. We all pay the price of their suffering. Maltreated children often grow up to vent on their own children—and others—the violence and aggression their parents visited on them. Some strike out against their parents, as Wayne did:

> Wayne D. suffered extensive physical and emotional abuse at the hands of his father, a prominent Washington, D.C. area attorney. Wayne endured numerous beatings and witnessed many acts of sadism throughout his childhood including watching his father riddle with bullets a paper bag containing a newborn litter of kittens. Referred by his school to a learning diagnostic center, Wayne was diagnosed as suffering from an eye ailment which affected his reading ability and from emotional difficulties which impaired his ability to learn. His parents refused to have either condition treated, telling their son that he was lazy. Neither the school nor the center inquired as to why treatment was not sought. Nor did the police ask questions when they returned Wayne home when he frequently ran away, or when they were called to the home when the father's violent outbursts became dangerous. Although the severe beatings inflicted on his mother were well known in the community, and the bizarre sex parties hosted by the couple were often the subject of gossip, no one asked questions. Wayne's tortured childhood ended when, at fifteen, he shot his parents to death. He was tried and convicted of his father's murder.[4]

Even when maltreated children do not become violent or socially destructive adults, they may have emotional deficits and learning problems that make them a continuing burden on a community's welfare, social service, and mental health systems.[5]

Sexually abused children have special problems. They often feel at fault for the abuse they suffered, which leads to intense feelings of shame, degradation, and worthlessness. As a result, they have difficulty entering into close and trusting relationships, especially with those of the opposite sex. Many have unhappy and short-lived marriages and are more easily exploited by others. (Clinical evidence suggests that sexually abused women often marry abusive men.)

WHAT YOU CAN DO

You can help fight child abuse. Whether you are a friend, a relative, or a professional, you can make a difference. Reporting suspected abuse and neglect is an indispensable first step in protecting endangered children.

Adults who are attacked or otherwise wronged can go to the authorities for protection and the redress of their grievances. But the victims of child abuse and neglect are usually too young or too frightened to obtain protection for themselves. Helpless children can be protected only if a concerned individual—like you—recognizes the danger and reports it to the proper authorities.

Reporting begins the process of protection. Billy Smith (not his real name) might still be alive if any one of a number of people had called the authorities:*

Kansas City, Mo. (UPI) Police investigators said that they could hardly remember a case worse than Billy Smith's. Two- and three-inch strips of flesh had been torn from his face, arms, back, buttocks and stomach; a purple bruise covered his chest; blood soaked his shirt and pants by the time his stepfather brought him to the emergency room.

Mr. Smith, twenty, was charged with second-degree murder and is being held on $500,000 bond. He signed a statement saying he hit Billy with his hand and a belt because he had not learned his ABCs.

Mrs. Smith, twenty-two, was charged with manslaughter by culpable negligence for her son's death. Her bond was set at $250,000.

Those who knew Billy often heard his cries and those of his two-year-old half-sister coming from the family's apartment. But they never thought, until too late, that he would die.

* Quoted in J. Garbarino, "Introduction," in Garbarino, S. H. Stocking, and Associates, *Protecting Children from Abuse and Neglect* (San Francisco: Jossey-Bass, 1981), pp. 1, 12–13. Names were changed or deleted for reasons of confidentiality and readability. Reprinted with permission of United Press International, Copyright 1980.

A string of "what if's" and "only if's" marred Billy's case.

- If neighbors had known about the twenty-four hour toll-free answering service in the state capital for reporting child abuse.
- If the children's grandmother had not been rebuffed by state welfare officials for three months while trying to gain custody of the two children.
- If Mr. A, the postman, who lived above the family, had been more persistent when he told Mr. Smith not to beat the children. "He told me it was his kid 'and I'll do what I want.' I didn't bother him after that."
- If the mother's sisters, who knew that she was being severely beaten by her husband, had not been afraid of stirring up trouble by checking on the children.

You have a moral duty to report suspected child abuse. If someone like you does not report, who will? And, if no one reports, how will the child protective agency know that the child needs help?

Furthermore, you may be *legally mandated* to report. Under threat of criminal and civil sanctions, all states now require a wide array of professionals—including physicians, nurses, dentists, mental health professionals, social workers, teachers (and other school officials), day care or child care workers, and law enforcement personnel—to report suspected child abuse and neglect. About twenty states require all citizens to report, regardless of their professional status or relation to the child. And, of course, all states *allow* any person to report.

USING THIS BOOK

Deciding whether to report suspected child abuse can be one of the most agonizing decisions you make. Failing to report may expose the child to serious injury—and even death—and may expose you to criminal and civil liability. On the other hand, you do not want to seem like a busybody. Any report and the investigation it triggers can be deeply traumatic to all members of the family. And inappropriate reports unnecessarily increase the burdens on already chronically understaffed agencies so that they are less able to take effective action when children are in real danger.

Unfortunately, professionals and lay persons alike often make the wrong decision—either in favor of a report when the child is not in danger or against a report when the child needs protection. Few people fail to

Chart 1–1 **Checklist for Suspicious Situations**

- Is there reasonable cause to suspect that the child was seriously injured or sexually abused?
- Is there reasonable cause to suspect that the child is in substantial danger of serious injury or sexual abuse? That is, is there reasonable cause to suspect that the parent has already engaged in seriously harmful behavior or that the parent suffers from a serious mental disability that would make future maltreatment likely?
- Does the child require prompt medical treatment?
- Should the child be placed in protective custody?
- Are the police needed?
- Should photographs or X rays be taken?
- Is there physical evidence that should be preserved?
- Do your records adequately document the situation?
- Should the child, the parents, or both be told about the report?
- Is a written report also needed?

---

report because they do not care about endangered children. Instead, they may not recognize the danger the child faces or be aware of the protective procedures that are available. Likewise, few inappropriate or unfounded reports are deliberately false statements. Most involve an honest desire to protect children, coupled with confusion about what conditions are reportable.

This confusion, in turn, is largely caused by the vagueness of reporting laws—aggravated by the failure of child protective authorities to provide realistic guidance about reporting responsibilities. As the Airlie House group of experts concluded: "Better public and professional materials are needed to obtain more appropriate reporting."[6] The group recommended that "educational materials and programs should: (1) clarify the legal definitions of child abuse and neglect, (2) give general descriptions of reportable situations (including specific examples), and (3) explain what to expect when a report is made."

This book is designed to give you practical advice about how to make these life-and-death decisions. It explains—in specific, concrete terms—*when* to report and when *not* to report. It describes the most common reasons for a report and the evidence most frequently available to support them. It also lays out the other steps you should take after making a report. (See Chart 1–1.)

Parents who feel that they are losing control, who are reported for suspected child abuse, or who fear that someone else is abusing their child also need advice. Thus, this book seeks to give them practical and supportive advice about how to get legal and therapeutic help for themselves and their children.

The general public, agency administrators, legislators, and other policy-makers who are concerned about the maltreatment of children should also find this book helpful. By describing how to improve the identification and reporting of maltreated children, it provides a framework for legislative and programmatic reform.

This book can be used as a basic resource, a training aid, and a handy desk reference to be consulted in individual cases. It summarizes the reporting laws in all fifty states, on the basis of various technical publications of the U.S. National Center on Child Abuse and Neglect.[7] Heavy emphasis is also placed on court decisions because the decision to report is, ultimately, based on the legal definition of child maltreatment.

The discussion reflects my analysis of the reporting laws of the fifty states and is, therefore, somewhat generalized. Moreover, space limitations preclude a discussion of every situation that may arise. More detailed information about state reporting laws in general is contained in the comprehensive publications of the U.S. National Center on Child Abuse and Neglect. To learn more about the law in your state, you should refer directly to it or consult with your local child protective agency. The agency should also be able to answer your questions about the law, the procedures that implement it, and whether a particular situation should be reported. (Appendix B lists each state's child protective agency.) Information about promising prevention and treatment programs can be obtained from the many fine books on the subject, as well as from the national organizations listed in Appendix A.

2

A Balanced Approach

Abused and neglected children are dying because they are not being reported to the authorities and because the wrong children are being reported. Thus, efforts to encourage more complete reporting must be joined with efforts to reduce the harmfully high rate of inappropriate and unfounded reports. Otherwise, increasing the number of reports will only increase the number and proportion of children who are ineffectually and harmfully processed through the system.

PAST INDIFFERENCE

Until the 1960s, child abuse and child neglect remained largely hidden problems, handled by poorly funded and uncoordinated agencies that were far from public view. If recognized at all, they were seen only in terms of a few isolated cases. People might have known that particular parents were "pretty hard on their children," but they did not realize that there were tens of thousands of such parents.

It was easy to underestimate the magnitude of child abuse or neglect. Few maltreated children were reported to the authorities. Even children with serious—and suspicious—injuries went unreported. A 1968 study in Rochester, New York, for example, revealed that 10 percent of all the children under age five who were treated in a hospital emergency room were abused and another 10 percent were neglected. The researchers concluded that had it not been for their study, most of these cases would have gone unreported.[1] Two years later, a study in nearby Auburn, New York, determined that of 195 hospital emergency room cases, 26 (or approximately 13 percent) involved children with "suspicious injuries" that should have been reported. None were.[2] Children often died because their glaring injuries were not reported:

Two year old Larry was brought to the hospital by his mother for treatment of a broken arm. According to the hospital record, Larry's body was marked and scarred. But no report of suspected abuse was made and there is no record that anyone in the hospital questioned Larry's mother about these injuries.

A week later, Larry's parents again brought him to the hospital. This time, he had multiple bruises over many parts of his body, scars on his buttocks, and healing lesions on his upper and lower legs. Less than an hour after Larry arrived at the hospital, he died.

The medical examiner reported the cause of death to be internal injuries caused by numerous beatings.[3]

Reporting was so haphazard that even the murder of children was sometimes not reported as child abuse. A 1972 study by the New York City Department of Social Services, for example, found that the deaths of many children who had been suspected by the Medical Examiner's Office to be victims of child abuse had not been reported to the official register of child abuse and neglect cases.[4] This is not simply an issue of keeping statistics. When fatalities go unreported, the siblings of these dead children are left unprotected.

There were many reasons for this seeming indifference to child maltreatment. As late as 1966, social worker Elizabeth Elmer of Pittsburgh's Children's Hospital wrote of the "social taboo" surrounding child maltreatment: "We resent evidence that vindictive impulses exist in others and may therefore exist in ourselves. Hence, the 'cloak of silence' and the determined actions to eliminate or disregard the evidence."[5]

Some people simply did not want to "get involved." They did not want to subject themselves to complaints (and possibly lawsuits) from angry parents, to become enmeshed in time-consuming interviews and court proceedings, or to seem critical of people with whom they frequently had close personal relationships.

Ignorance was another reason for nonreporting. To a large extent, professionals as well as laypersons were unaware of the problem and the need to report. Child abuse and child neglect were hardly ever mentioned in professional schools. They were not "considered important enough to be included in the curricula of medical schools" and had "not been given notice in any of the major pediatric textbooks."[6] As a result, diagnostic capacities, even in major hospitals, were rudimentary.

Frustration with the inadequacy of the agencies' handling of prior reports also discouraged reporting; potential reporters frequently concluded that a report was pointless, since nothing would be done anyway. (This is still a major problem.) Moreover, it was not easy to make a report. Procedures were often complex and obscure, requiring the potential reporter's perseverance and ingenuity.

REPORTING LAWS

In the early 1960s, a small group of physicians, led by Dr. C. Henry Kempe, became convinced that the only way to break this pattern of indifference was to *mandate* certain professionals to report. In 1963, they persuaded the U.S. Children's Bureau to publish a model law that required physicians to report children with a "serious physical injury or injuries inflicted . . . other than by accidental means."[7] In the short span of four legislative years, all fifty states enacted reporting laws that were patterned after the model law. "In the history of the United States, few legislative proposals have been so widely adopted in so little time," wrote the late University of Virginia Law School Dean Monrad Paulsen.[8]

Initially, mandatory reporting laws applied only to physicians and they only required reports of "serious physical injuries" or "nonaccidental injuries." In the ensuing years, though, increased public and professional attention, sparked, in part, by the number of abused children revealed by these reporting laws, led many states to expand their reporting laws. Now, almost all states have laws that require the reporting of *all* forms of suspected child maltreatment, including physical abuse, sexual abuse and exploitation, physical neglect, and emotional maltreatment. Under a threat of civil and criminal penalties, these laws require most professionals who serve children to report suspected child abuse and neglect. About twenty states require all citizens to report. But in all states, any citizen is allowed to report.

These reporting laws and the associated public awareness campaigns have been strikingly effective. In 1963, about 150,000 children came to the attention of public authorities because of suspected abuse or neglect.[9] By 1976, an estimated 669,000 children were reported annually. And, in 1987, almost 2.2 million children were reported—more than fourteen times the number reported in 1963. (See Chart 2–1.)

Many people ask whether this vastly increased reporting signals a rise in the incidence of child maltreatment. Although some observers believe that deteriorating economic and social conditions have contributed to a rise in the level of abuse and neglect, there is no way to tell for sure. So many maltreated children previously went unreported that earlier reporting statistics do not provide a reliable baseline against which to make comparisons. However, one thing is clear: The great bulk of reports

Chart 2–1 **Child Abuse and
Neglect Reporting, 1976–87**[10]

Year	Number of Children Reported
1976	669,000
1977	838,000
1978	836,000
1979	988,000
1980	1,154,000
1981	1,225,000
1982	1,262,000
1983	1,477,000
1984	1,727,000
1985	1,928,000
1986	2,100,000
1987	2,178,000

These statistics are based on information supplied by the states to the American Humane Association. They include "unfounded" reports, which are now an estimated 55 to 65 percent of all reports.

now received by child protective agencies would not have been made but for the passage of mandatory reporting laws and the media campaigns that accompanied them.

Child protective programs still have major problems, some of which are discussed in this book. Nevertheless, one must be impressed with the results of this twenty-year effort to upgrade them. Specialized "child protective agencies" have been established to receive reports (usually via highly publicized hotlines) and then to investigate them. And treatment services for maltreated children and their parents have been expanded substantially.

As a result, many thousands of children have been saved from death and serious injury. The best estimate is that over the past twenty years, deaths from child abuse and neglect have fallen from over 3,000 a year (and perhaps as many as 5,000) to about 1,100 a year.[11] In New York State, for example, within five years of the passage of a comprehensive reporting law that also created specialized investigative staffs, there was a 50 percent reduction in child fatalities, from about 200 a year to under 100.[12] Similarly, Drs. Ruth and C. Henry Kempe, well-known leaders in the field, reported that "in Denver, the number of hospitalized abused children who die from their injuries has dropped from 20 a year (between 1960 and 1975) to less than one a year."[13]

UNREPORTED CASES

Despite this progress, a large number of obviously endangered children are still not reported to the authorities. According to the national incidence study, in 1986, professionals still failed to report half the maltreated children *whom they saw.*

Professionals did not report almost 40 percent of the sexually abused children they saw. Nearly 30 percent of the fatal or serious physical abuse cases (defined as life threatening or requiring professional treatment to prevent long-term impairment) were not reported. And almost 50 percent of the moderate physical abuse cases (defined as bruises, depression, emotional distress, or other symptoms lasting more than 48 hours) were not reported. The situation was even worse in neglect cases: About 70 percent of fatal or serious physical neglect cases and about three-quarters of the moderate physical neglect cases were not reported.[14] These percentages mean that in 1986, nearly 50,000 sexually abused children went unreported, about 60,000 children with observable physical injuries severe enough to require hospitalization were not reported, and almost 184,000 children with moderate physical injuries were not reported.

Nonreporting can be fatal to children. A study in Texas revealed that during one three-year period, over 40 percent of the approximately 270 children who died as a result of maltreatment had not been reported to the authorities—even though they were being seen by a public or private agency (such as a hospital) at the time of death or had been seen within the past year.[15] Sometimes two or three children in the same family are killed before someone makes a report.[16]

What can be done to encourage people to report endangered children? Although the fear of getting involved continues to be a major problem, ignorance and misunderstanding about reporting procedures and requirements are the major obstacles to fuller reporting. A study of nonreporting among teachers, for example, blamed their "lack of knowledge for detecting symptoms of child abuse and neglect."[17]

The tragic death of a young child and the sensational publicity that follows often lead to a temporary increase in reporting. But a young

life is too high a price to pay for such a short-lived "improvement."
Communities must conduct continuing educational and public-awareness
campaigns to achieve better reporting, and many do so. However, these
efforts need a much better focus, for the problem of nonreporting is
now compounded by the problem of inappropriate reporting.

UNFOUNDED REPORTS

At the same time that many seriously abused children go unreported,
there is an equally serious problem that further undercuts efforts to
prevent the maltreatment of children: The nation's child protective agencies are being inundated by "unfounded" reports. Although rules, procedures, and even terminology vary (some states use the phrase
"unfounded," while others use "unsubstantiated" or "not indicated"),
in essence, an "unfounded" report is one that is dismissed after an investigation finds insufficient evidence on which to proceed.

The emotionally charged desire to "do something" about child abuse,
fanned by repeated and often sensational media coverage, has led to an
understandable but counterproductive overreaction by professionals and
citizens who report suspected child abuse. Depending on the community,
as many as 65 percent of all reports are closed after an initial investigation reveals no evidence of maltreatment.[18] This situation is in sharp
contrast to 1975, when only about 35 percent of all reports were unfounded.[19]

New York State has one of the highest rates of unfounded reports in
the nation, and its experience illustrates how severe the problem has
become. Between 1979 and 1983, while the number of reports received
by the Department of Social Services increased by about 50 percent
(from 51,836 to 74,120), the percentage of substantiated reports fell
about 16 percent (from 42.8 percent to 35.8 percent). In fact, the
absolute number of substantiated reports actually fell by about 100. Thus,
almost 23,000 additional families were investigated, but fewer children
were aided.[20]

These statistics should not be surprising. Potential reporters are frequently told to "take no chances" and to report any child for whom
they have the slightest concern. There is a recent tendency to tell people
to report children whose behavior suggests that they may have been
abused—even in the absence of any other evidence of maltreatment.
These "behavioral indicators" include, for example, children who are
unusually withdrawn or shy, as well as children who are unusually

friendly to strangers. However, as explained in Chapter 7, only a small minority of children who exhibit such behaviors have actually been maltreated.

Ten years ago, when professionals were narrowly construing their reporting obligations to avoid taking action to protect endangered children, this approach may have been needed. Now, though, all it does is to ensure that child abuse hotlines will be flooded by inappropriate and unfounded reports. For example, a child has a minor bruise and, whether or not there is evidence of parental assault, he is reported as abused.

Many hotlines accept reports even when the caller cannot give a reason for suspecting that the child's condition is due to the parent's behavior. This writer observed one hotline accept a report that a seventeen-year-old boy was found in a drunken stupor. That the boy, and perhaps his family, might benefit from counseling is not disputable. But that hardly justifies the initiation of an involuntary child protective investigation. As Chris Mouzakitis, a professor of social work, concluded: "Much of what is reported is not worthy of follow up."[21]

There is a deeper problem. Across the nation, child protective agencies are being pressed to accept categories of cases that traditionally have not been considered their responsibility and for which their skills do not seem appropriate. In community after community, the dearth of family-oriented social services is pushing child protective agencies to broaden their role from that of a highly focused service for children in serious danger to that of an all-encompassing child welfare service.

In essence, child protective agencies are paying the price for their past successes. People know that a report of possible maltreatment will result in action. As a result, child abuse hotlines are being barraged by reports that, at base, really involve the truancy, delinquency, school problems, and sexual acting out of adolescents—not abuse or neglect. Other inappropriate reports involve children who need specialized education or residential placement; parent-child conflicts with no indication of abuse or neglect; and chronic problems involving property, unemployment, inadequate housing, or poor money management. Many of these reports result in the family receiving much-needed services, but many do not. Either way, these additional, inappropriate calls to child abuse hotlines significantly increase the number of unsubstantiated cases, misdirect scarce investigative resources, and are an unjustified violation of parental rights.

The determination that a report is unfounded can be made only after

FOR THE LOVE OF BASEBALL[22]

At age eight, my son tried out for the "Lambert Little League" and proudly became a single A Angel. In 1984, he won a trophy for being the Good Sportsmanship Player of the whole league. Chris won a Certificate of Award from the Laurel Elementary School PTA for the Reflections Contest, when he drew a picture of a baseball diamond with himself at bat titled, "I have a Dream of Being a Baseball Star." This was in the second grade.

On May 6, 1985, Monday afternoon, Christopher was practicing pitching and catching in the front yard of our house with two neighborhood boys. They were using a tennis ball and a pitchback (an aluminum frame with a net designed to pitch the ball back to you.) During the game he missed the ball with his mitt and was struck in the nose, in fact, right between the eyes. It left a red mark on his nose and the side of one eye. It didn't hurt much and there was no bleeding so instead of being a sissy in front of his friends, he did not come into the house crying that he was hurt. I was not aware of any injury.

The next day Christopher was forty minutes late coming home from school. I sent my sister to look for him and thinking the baby (Jenny, age 16 months) might enjoy the ride, she took her along. They went up to the school looking for Chris. There she was met by police officials and Christopher, who was scared to death and crying. In front of Chris, the policemen removed my baby from her aunt's arms and told her that they were taking my children for child abuse and we could not see them.

My sister came back home in a state of total hysteria. She stood in the middle of the living room crying and screaming. It took several minutes to find out what was wrong. She kept saying "They took our kids! Oh God, Oh God! Why did they take our kids?"

The police took my children to La Mirada Community Hospital to be examined for possible child abuse. (The hospital has since

an unavoidably traumatic investigation that is, inherently, a breach of parental and family privacy. To determine whether a particular child is in danger, caseworkers must inquire into the most intimate personal and family matters. Often, it is necessary to question friends, relatives, sent me a bill for $373.00.) The hospital report on Chris said, "a small bruise on bridge of nose, redness around one eye and a couple of small scratches on face" (due to baby Jennifer). They recommended no treatment. They x-rayed all of both children's bodies and neither had ever broken a bone in their lives (Thank God). They found no signs of abuse of any kind on Jennifer.

The DPSS [Department of Public Social Services] then had Chris placed in a foster home which already had two children sleeping on the floor and whose playground was the local high school where the children played unsupervised after school hours.

Jennifer was placed in MacLaren Hall where she sustained numerous bruises on her face, ear, arms and legs. Only Jenny can't talk to tell me how it happened.

Christopher told the teacher, school nurse, and school principal about the baseball accident, he told the police and DPSS workers, he told anyone and everyone and they still took my babies away. They wouldn't believe him or even telephone me.

After three days of being unable to eat or sleep, we had a dependency hearing, where the judge ordered my children detained until the trial on July 22, 1985.

On Friday I was finally allowed to visit Jenny in MacLaren Hall, I found her sick, dirty, and covered with bruises. The only answer they could give me was that "maybe another child got to her." By Monday I was hospitalized for stress and severe dehydration.

The following Wednesday we finally went before a judge who released the children to me until trial.

I have pawned my jewelry and I am in the process of selling my car and furniture. I have called every attorney I can find. My job put me on a personal leave of absence so that they would not have to pay my salary until I have solved my personal problems. I'm broke! Now I have two very frightened kids at home besides myself. Am I guilty? I did buy him his first baseball!

and neighbors, as well as schoolteachers, day care personnel, physicians, clergymen, and others who know the family.

Richard Wexler, a journalist in Rochester, New York, wrote about what happened to Kathy and Alan Heath (not their real names):

Three times in as many years, someone—they suspect an "unstable" neighbor—has called in anonymous accusations of child abuse against them. All three times, those reports were determined to be "unfounded," but only after painful investigations by workers. . . . The first time the family was accused, Mrs. Heath says, the worker "spent almost two hours in my house going over the allegations over and over again. . . . She went through everything from a strap to an iron, to everything that could cause bruises, asking me if I did those things. [After she left] I sat on the floor and cried my eyes out. I couldn't believe that anybody could do that to me." Two more such investigations followed.

The Heaths say that even after they were "proven innocent" three times, the county did nothing to help them restore their reputation among friends and neighbors who had been told, as potential "witnesses," that the Heaths were suspected of child abuse."[23]

Laws against child abuse are an implicit recognition that family privacy must give way to the need to protect helpless children. But in seeking to protect children, it is all too easy to ignore the legitimate rights of parents. Each year, about 700,000 families are put through investigations of unfounded reports. This is a massive and unjustified violation of parental rights.

In response, a national group of parents and professionals has been formed to represent those who have been falsely accused of abusing their children. Calling itself VOCAL, for Victims of Child Abuse Laws, the group publishes a national newsletter and has about 5,000 members in over 100 chapters. Every state except Rhode Island has at least one; California has 10. Canada has 9 chapters. In Minnesota, members of VOCAL collected 2,000 signatures on a petition asking the governor to remove Scott County prosecutor Kathleen Morris from office because of her alleged misconduct in bringing charges, subsequently dismissed, against 24 adults in Jordan, Minnesota. In Arizona, VOCAL members were able temporarily to sidetrack a $5.4 million budgetary supplement that would have added 77 investigators to local child protective agencies.

Few unfounded reports are made maliciously. Studies of sexual abuse reports, for example, suggest that, at most, 4–10 percent of these reports are knowingly false.[24] Many involve situations in which the person reporting, in a well-intentioned effort to protect a child, overreacts to a vague and often misleading possibility that the child may be maltreated. Others involve situations of poor child care that, although of legitimate concern, simply do not amount to child abuse or neglect. In fact, a substantial proportion of unfounded cases are referred to other agencies to provide needed services for the families.

Moreover, an unfounded report does not necessarily mean that the child was not actually abused or neglected. Evidence of child maltreatment is hard to obtain and may not be uncovered when agencies lack the time and resources to complete a thorough investigation or when inaccurate information is given to the investigator. Other cases are labeled unfounded when no services are available to help the family. Some cases must be closed because the child or family cannot be located.

A certain proportion of unfounded reports, therefore, is an inherent—and legitimate—aspect of reporting *suspected* child abuse or neglect and is necessary to ensure the adequate protection of children. Hundreds of thousands of strangers report their suspicions; they cannot all be right. But current rates of unfounded reports go beyond anything that is reasonably needed. Worse, they endanger children who are really abused.

INAPPROPRIATE REPORTING
ENDANGERS ABUSED CHILDREN

The flood of unfounded reports is overwhelming the limited resources of child protective agencies. For fear of missing even one abused child, workers perform extensive investigations of vague and apparently unsupported reports. Even when a home visit in response to an anonymous report turns up no evidence of maltreatment, workers usually interview neighbors, schoolteachers, and day care personnel to make sure that the child is not abused. And, as illustrated by what happened to the Heaths, even repeated anonymous and unfounded reports do not prevent a further investigation. All this takes time.

As a result, children who are in real danger are getting lost in the press of inappropriate cases. Forced to allocate a substantial portion of their limited resources to unfounded reports, child protective agencies are less able to respond promptly and effectively when children are in serious danger. Some reports are left uninvestigated for a week and even two weeks after they are received. Investigations often miss key facts, as workers rush to clear cases, and dangerous home situations receive inadequate supervision, as workers ignore pending cases to investigate the new reports that arrive daily on their desks. Decision making also suffers. With so many cases of insubstantial or unproved risk to children, caseworkers are desensitized to the obvious warning signals of immediate and serious danger.

These nationwide conditions help explain why 25–50 percent of the deaths from child abuse involve children who were previously known to the authorities.[25] Tens of thousands of other children suffer serious injuries short of death while under the supervision of child protective agencies.

In one Iowa case, for example, the noncustodial father reported to the local department of social services that his 34-month-old daughter had bruises on her buttocks; he also told the agency that he believed that the bruises were caused by the mother's live-in boyfriend. The agency investigated and substantiated the abuse. (The boyfriend was not interviewed, however.) At an agency staff meeting the next day (two days after the initial report), it was decided *not* to remove the child from the mother's custody, and, instead, to make follow-up visits, coupled with day care, counseling, and other appropriate services. *But no follow-up visit was made.* Eight days later, the child was hospitalized in a comatose state, with bruises, both old and new, over most of her body. The child died after three days of unsuccessful treatment. The boyfriend was convicted of second-degree murder. The father's lawsuit against the agency for its negligent handling of his report was settled for $82,500.[26]

Ironically, by weakening the system's ability to respond, unfounded reports actually discourage appropriate ones. The sad fact is that many responsible individuals are not reporting endangered children because they believe that the system's response will be so weak that reporting will do no good or may even make things worse. In 1984, a study of the impediments to reporting, conducted by Jose Alfaro, who was then coordinator of the New York City Mayor's Task Force on Child Abuse and Neglect, concluded: "Professionals who emphasize their professional judgment, have experienced problems in dealing with the child protective agency, and are more likely to doubt the efficacy of protective service intervention are more likely not to report in some situations, especially when they believe they can do a better job helping the family."[27]

All communities have had their share of news stories about children who have been "allowed" to die. Newspapers, television, and radio all focus on the sensational details of unproved charges and follow up with editorials about helpless children and the need for more reporting. The *New Republic's* "TRB" complained: "A lot of the graphic horror stories in the press are little more than child porn, published or broadcast because editors and producers want to titillate. And when they're not being salacious, the media [are] being mawkish, which sells almost as well."[28]

The result? More media spots calling on people to report suspected abuse; another brochure or conference for professionals describing their legal responsibility to report; and, perhaps, a small increase in agency staffing. But the main result of these periodic flurries of activity is an increased number of unfounded reports.

Professionals and private citizens need to do a much better job of identifying and reporting suspected cases of child abuse, while also guarding against inappropriate reporting. Recognizing appropriately reportable situations is difficult, but the current high rates of simultaneously under- and overreporting are unfair to the children and parents involved and threaten to undo much of the progress that has been made in building child protective programs. A proper balance must be struck.

If child protective agencies are to function effectively, they must be relieved of the heavy burden of unfounded reports. To call for more careful reporting of child abuse is not to be coldly indifferent to the plight of endangered children. Rather, it is to be realistic about the limits to our ability to operate child protective systems.

The
Legal
Framework

3

Reporting Obligations

Since 1964, all states have enacted laws that require the reporting of suspected child abuse and neglect. Unfortunately, these laws are often vague and can be understood only within the context of court decisions and agency practices. This chapter describes who is required to report, who is permitted to report, and the conditions to be reported.

WHO MUST REPORT

Reporting laws were originally directed solely at physicians, who were required to report "serious physical injuries" or "nonaccidental injuries." Physicians were considered the professionals most likely to see abused children and were presumed to be the most qualified to diagnose the signs and symptoms of child abuse and neglect.

Over the years, however, reporting laws have been progressively expanded, to increase the likelihood that maltreated children will be identified. Reporting mandates were first broadened to include most other medical professionals (such as nurses). Then, many nonmedical professionals were added because they are also in regular contact with children and, hence, in a position to identify child abuse and neglect, often before the children need medical care for serious injuries.

Most professionals who serve children are required to report. As Chart 3–1 indicates, in *every* state, those who are required to report now include physicians, nurses, emergency room personnel, coroners and medical examiners, dentists, mental health professionals (sometimes specified as "psychologists" or "therapists"), social workers, teachers and other school officials, day care or child care workers, and law enforcement personnel. And, each year, additional types of professionals are added.

23

Chart 3–1 **Persons Required to Report**

In All States

Physicians

Nurses

Emergency room personnel

Coroners and medical examiners

Dentists

Mental health professionals (sometimes specified as "psychologists" or "therapists")

Social workers

Teachers and other school officials

Day care or child care workers

Law enforcement personnel

In Some States

Pharmacists

Foster parents

Clergy

Attorneys

Day care licensing inspectors

Film or photo processors (largely to detect cases of sexual exploitation)

Substance abuse counselors

Counselors and staff at children's camps

Family mediators

Staff and volunteers in child abuse information and referral programs

"Religious healers" (usually Christian Science practitioners)

NOTE: In about twenty states, everyone must report.

Reporting mandates change frequently, so it is not possible to present definitive information about reporting mandates in each state. Readers who wish such information should review a current copy of their state's law or consult with the appropriate child protective agency in their state. (See Appendix B.)

Unfortunately, some state laws are not as clear as they could be in establishing these reporting mandates, and you may have difficulty determining whether you are included among the mandated reporters. For example, teachers in California who read their state's reporting law may conclude that they are not required to report because they are not a "child care custodian, medical practitioner, nonmedical practitioner, or employee of a child protective agency."[1] However, a later section of the same statute defines a "child care custodian" to include, among others, teachers.[2]

Other states have enacted broadly generalized mandates that create what can only be called a guessing game about who is mandated to report. A few jurisdictions require reports from any person "who, in the course of his employment, occupation, or practice of his profession comes in contact with children."[3] Does this include school bus drivers? What about lunchroom personnel? Other states use such vague phrases as any person "having responsibility for the care or treatment of children"[4] or any person "called upon to render aid or medical assistance."[5] Does the former include baby-sitters? And does the latter include a neighbor to whom a child goes for help?

Whatever the legal ambiguity of such reporting mandates, of course, you have a moral duty to report endangered children. And, since all states provide legal protections for any person who reports, you should do so. But the uncertainty of reporting mandates is significant because the mandates trigger potential civil and criminal liability for the failure to report.

State laws often contain a phrase that limits the requirements of professionals to report only situations "known to them in their professional or official capacity." (A common alternate phrase is "before them in their professional or official capacity.")[6] This phrase recognizes the personal and social pressures that make a broader mandate unenforceable. Thus, for example, physicians are *not required* to report when they suspect that a neighbor's child, who is not a patient, is abused or neglected.

The phrase "before them in their professional or official capacity" has another purpose. When reporting mandates are not limited to children who are actually "before" the professional, a report may be required whenever anyone, even a stranger, claims that a child has been maltreated. This is too broad a reporting mandate, and, hence, the limitation. However, there are times when such information is reliable, for example, when a professional, usually a therapist, learns of possible child abuse or neglect from a parent. The problem is to recognize the difference legislatively. New York's law does so by requiring professionals to report when "a parent or the person legally responsible for the child comes before them in their professional or official capacity and states from personal knowledge facts, conditions or circumstances which, if correct, would render the child an abused or maltreated child."[7]

In neither situation is a report prohibited. Professionals who suspect child abuse can always make a voluntary report like anyone else—and they should.

Everyone must report in some states. About twenty states require a report from "any person" who has reason to believe that a child is a victim of child abuse or neglect. There may be danger, however, in such generalized reporting mandates. One must question the wisdom of what amounts to an unenforceable and, therefore, empty statutory mandate. As Paulsen warned: "Everybody's duty may become nobody's duty."[8]

The preferable approach is to require reports only from members of specific, identifiable professions or groups who will be responsive to such targeting. All other persons should be *allowed* to report, as discussed next.

ANYONE MAY REPORT

Anyone may report a suspected case of child abuse or neglect. Friends, neighbors, and relatives, because they are regularly in the family's home, frequently observe acts of maltreatment; about half of all reports are made by them. (See Illustration 3–1.) A common report from neighbors, for example, is that they have seen (or heard) a parent pick up a young infant and, in a fit of rage, throw it against a wall. Neighbors also frequently report children who are repeatedly locked out of the house or left alone for long periods of time. They sometimes describe how they regularly take such children into their own homes and feed them.

When reporting laws were first enacted in the mid-sixties, many child protective agencies gave second-class status to "nonmandated reports" from persons who were not required to report. Sometimes, these reports were not accepted for investigation; when they were accepted, they were often given the lowest investigative priority—regardless of the apparent danger to the child.

All states now route nonmandated reports through the same process as mandated reports. Moreover, to combat the tendency to accord low priority to nonmandated reports, about twenty states have a specific statutory provision requiring, and almost all the rest have a provision permitting, "anyone" to report. These laws usually give the voluntary reporter immunity from liability for a good-faith report and abrogate any privileged communication that might otherwise apply, as described in Chapter 5.

Child protective agencies, nevertheless, are correct to handle these

Illustration 3–1 **Who Reports**

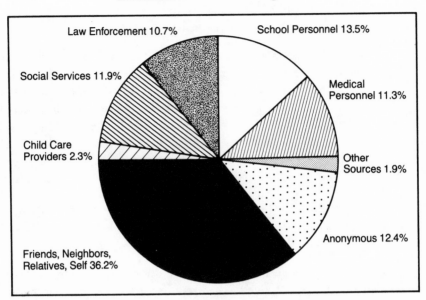

SOURCE: *Derived from Highlights of Official Child Neglect and Abuse Reporting 1984.* American Humane Association, Denver, 1986, p. 12.

nonmandated reports with special care. Some reports are made by disgruntled spouses or relatives who are seeking to gain custody of the children. Nationwide, only about 35 percent of voluntary reports are substantiated by a subsequent investigation. In comparison, almost 45 percent of mandated reports are substantiated.[9] Thus, although voluntary reports are accepted and investigated, child protective agencies must watch for inappropriate or biased reports.

Anonymous reports are accepted in all states. Nationwide, about 12 percent of all reports are made anonymously. Child protective agencies recognize that some callers may not wish to give their names, even after being assured that the parent probably will not learn who made the report. For example, the person reporting may be a teacher or a neighbor who fears a violent parental response to the report. Hence, although some states have laws that require reports to contain the identity of the person reporting, no state refuses to accept anonymous reports. (Some state laws specifically allow reporters to withhold their names.)[10]

Court decisions also support the validity of anonymous reports. For example, in a criminal prosecution, the Wisconsin Supreme Court approved a warrantless search of the defendant's home because an anonymous report gave reasonable cause to believe that there was "an immediate need to render aid or assistance to the children due to actual or threatened physical injury." The facts of the case, as described by the court, illustrate how specific an anonymous report can be:

> On Friday . . . a social worker . . . received an anonymous telephone call around suppertime. The caller indicated that the children may have been battered and were in need of medical attention. The caller identified two children by their last names (and at least one, if not both of the children, by the first name), and indicated that they lived with Boggess, the defendant. Through this information, the caller indicated that the children had different last names than Boggess. The caller also indicated that one of the children, L.S., was limping, and that because of bruises the caller witnessed on L.S., L.S. may have further damage done to his body and should be checked by a doctor. The caller additionally stated that he knew the Boggesses fairly well and that Mr. Boggess had a bad temper. [11]

Nevertheless, agencies do not encourage anonymous reports because of the obvious dangers of investigating reports for whom no one is willing to take responsibility. (Only about 25 percent of all anonymous reports were substantiated in 1978, as compared to 35 percent of the voluntary reports from other nonprofessional sources.)[12] Moreover, not knowing the reporter's identity can hamper the subsequent investigation; it denies the child protective worker someone to interview about the details of the allegations, or from whom to gain other investigative leads. Hence, child protective workers always seek to convince callers to give their names, although they have no choice but to accept anonymous reports *if* they are otherwise valid. (The grounds for rejecting reports are described in Chapter 17.)

THE FORMS OF MALTREATMENT

All forms of child maltreatment must be reported. The federal Child Abuse Prevention and Treatment Act of 1974 (hereafter called the federal child abuse act) requires states to provide for the reporting of all forms of maltreatment in order to receive special grants.[13] Under the act:

> "child abuse and neglect" means the physical or mental injury, sexual abuse or exploitation, negligent treatment, or maltreatment of a child . . . under circumstances which indicate that the child's health or welfare is harmed or threatened thereby.[14]

This definition makes reportable *any parental act or omission that harms a child—or threatens to do so*. As a result, just about every state now requires the reporting of all forms of physical, sexual, and emotional maltreatment.

Marginally inappropriate or inadequate child care, however, is not child abuse or child neglect. Although pushing, shoving, and even slapping an older child may reflect poor judgment, for example, they do not necessarily signal future maltreatment and, so, do not justify coercive state intervention. Almost all parents have physically or verbally lashed out at their children during times of unusual stress; all parents have at least some moments when they neglect to meet the needs of their children. In fact, according to nationwide data, fewer than one in five minor assaults or other examples of poor child rearing will ever grow into anything resembling child abuse or child neglect.[15] Unfortunately, there is no way of knowing which will become more serious with the degree of assurance needed to justify a report.

For this reason, the federal child abuse act limits reportable situations to those in which "the child's health or welfare is harmed or threatened thereby." The injury must be sufficiently *serious* so that there is a danger to the child's "health or welfare."[16] This limitation is meant to protect the rights of parents to exercise their best judgment about how to raise children and to protect regional, religious, cultural, and ethnic differences in such beliefs. It means, for example, that parents who allow their children to watch hours of television are not considered neglectful, even though many of us think that the children would be "better off" doing something else. Similarly, minor scratches that do not suggest more serious danger are not a reason to report.[17]

The need to be careful about reporting such situations was brought home to me by a call from a local radio commentator. She asked what she could do to help her housekeeper of ten years who had just been reported for child abuse. She said that the report was "crazy." The housekeeper had been summoned to her twelve-year-old son's school because he had been misbehaving. She was required to take her son home. As she was leaving the school yard with her son, she whacked him across the rear with her hand. The principal saw this and made a report of suspected abuse on the basis of that one whack—nothing more.

Heartfelt concern for children leads many people to believe that all forms of inadequate or poor child-rearing situations—whether they are seriously harmful—should be reported to the authorities. This is a mistake. Despite its benevolent purpose, a child protective investigation can be a major trauma to the family, leaving psychological scars on the children

Chart 3–2 **Reportable Child Abuse and Neglect**

Physical abuse: physical assaults (such as striking, kicking, biting, throwing, burning, or poisoning) that caused, or could have caused, serious physical injury to the child

Sexual abuse: vaginal, anal, or oral intercourse; vaginal or anal penetrations; and other forms of inappropriate touching or exhibitionism for sexual gratification

Sexual exploitation: use of a child in prostitution, pornography, or other sexually exploitative activities

Physical deprivaton: failure to provide basic necessities (such as food, clothing, hygiene, and shelter) that caused, or over time would cause, serious physical injury, sickness, or disability

Medical neglect: failure to provide the medical, dental, or psychiatric care needed to prevent or treat serious physical or psychological injuries or illnesses

Physical endangerment: reckless behavior toward a child (such as leaving a young child alone or placing a child in a hazardous environment) that caused or could have caused serious physical injury

Abandonment: leaving a child alone or in the care of another under circumstances that suggest an intentional abdication of parental responsibility

Emotional abuse: physical or emotional assaults (such as torture and close confinement) that caused or could have caused serious psychological injury

Emotional neglect (or "developmental deprivation"): failure to provide the emotional nurturing and physical and cognitive stimulation needed to prevent serious developmental deficits

Failure to treat a child's psychological problems: indifference to a child's severe emotional or behavioral problems or parental rejections of appropriate offers of help

Improper ethical guidance: grossly inappropriate parental conduct or lifestyles that pose a specific threat to a child's ethical development or behavior

Educational neglect: chronic failure to send a child to school.

and parents. In the absence of the parent's past "seriously harmful" behavior (or "severe mental disability," as described in Chapter 12), a report should not be made. This does not mean that situations of less damaging child care do not merit social action. Many would benefit from specific social and community services. But these services should be offered for the parent's voluntary acceptance or refusal. Chart 3–2 lists the seriously harmful parental behaviors that should be reported.

The maltreatment of any child under age eighteen must be reported. Like the federal child abuse act, most states chose this age cutoff because

persons over age eighteen are presumed to be capable of protecting themselves from parental maltreatment (ordinarily, by leaving home). Only
Wyoming established a higher cutoff of nineteen years.[18]

In three or four states, the age cut off is raised or eliminated for
older children with special needs that extend the period of their vulnerability. Legislation examples include "mentally retarded persons," "incompe-
tent or disabled children," "handicapped children" under age twenty-
one, and children up to age twenty who have been adjudicated as being
in need of supervision.[19] Once again, you should consult your state's
law and policies to determine the precise reporting requirements.

ENDANGERED CHILDREN

Deciding to report is relatively easy when the child already has suffered
serious physical or mental injury. If the parents cannot explain what
happened and there is reason to believe they are responsible, a report
should be made.

"Threatened harm" must be reported. Society does not wait until a
child is seriously injured before taking protective action, however. The
law requires reports and authorizes agency and court intervention to
prevent *future harm.* Although statutory provisions vary, they commonly
require action if a child "lacks proper parental care," is "without proper
guardianship," has parents who are "unfit to properly care" for him or
her properly, or is in an "environment injurious to his welfare." Such
provisions authorize intervention before the child has been seriously
injured, and even before he has been abused or neglected. Hence, actual
injury is not a prerequisite to a report; children should be reported to
the authorities if they are in danger of serious injury.

Threatened harm is the most pervasive reason for child protective
action. In most cases of child neglect and, to a somewhat lesser degree,
in most cases of child abuse, intervention occurs before serious injury is
inflicted.[20] Unfortunately, "threatened harm" is also the most subjective
basis for reporting and causes the greatest misunderstanding about what
should and should not be reported.

*The parents' past "seriously harmful" conduct should be reported, regard-
less of whether the child was actually harmed.* A report of threatened
harm should be made if the parent's past behavior or current mental
condition caused; could have caused; or, over time, will be capable of
causing *serious* harm to the child. This concept is incorporated into
the examples of "seriously harmful behavior" listed in Chart 3–2.

By having done something whose reasonably foreseeable consequence *could have been* the child's serious injury, parents demonstrate that they are a continuing threat to the child. It is reasonable to assume that unless there is a change in circumstances, what the parents did in the past, they will do again in the future. The mere fact that the child did not or has not yet suffered serious injury does not reduce the need for protective action. As Alfred Kadushin, professor of social work at the University of Wisconsin, asked: "Do we sit by impassively if a parent shoots a child but misses?"[21] Of course not.

Similarly, a report of threatened harm should be made if the parent is presently engaged in a course of conduct whose reasonably foreseeable consequence *will be* serious injury to the child if the behavior continues for a sufficient length of time. Some examples include: a parent who provides a nutritionally inadequate diet for the child that, over time, will cause serious health problems; a parent who inflicts repeated, but otherwise minor, assaults on the child that, over time, will make him or her into an easily frustrated, violence-prone individual; or a parent who provides grossly inadequate emotional support and cognitive stimulation that, over time, will lead to severe developmental disabilities. Although such children have not yet suffered serious injury, that they will is only a matter of time.

PAST MALTREATMENT

A report of child abuse or neglect is based on the reasonable presumption that the conditions that led to the earlier maltreatment remain in effect. It is possible, however, that circumstances have changed and that this presumption should not be applied (or, in technical legal terms, is "rebutted"). For example, the precipitating cause of the parent's behavior may have disappeared or been removed, the parent may have developed the ability to care adequately for the child (either by himself or herself or through treatment), or the provision of voluntary services may reduce the likelihood of a reoccurrence sufficiently to obviate the need for coercive intervention. These are crucial issues in determining whether intervention should actually occur. But they are not issues in the decision to report. Parents who, in the recent past, engaged in behavior that was capable of seriously injuring the child should be reported. The child protective agency has the responsibility of determining whether the parent's emotional condition has improved or whether the factors that led to the parent's past behavior have been nullified.

Nevertheless, the past maltreatment must be relatively recent. Ordinarily, a report should not be based on behavior from many years in the past, unless there is reason to believe that the child or another child may still be at risk. Cases of suspected sexual abuse are an example.

You may see evidence of the further maltreatment of a child who has already been reported. Some states and communities require a fresh report of the subsequent maltreatment. Regardless of the formal policy, though, you should make sure that the worker assigned to the case knows about it.

PARENTAL RESPONSIBILITY

A few experts recommend that all apparently injured children should be reported without any determination of possible parental responsibility. They argue that compelling potential reporters to name the person responsible for the maltreatment may discourage reporting because (1) it is often impossible or too early for a potential reporter to make such a determination, (2) the potential reporter may fear retaliation for blaming a parent, and (3) an "accusatory" report is inconsistent with the rehabilitative and nonpunitive philosophy of child protective agencies.[22]

This approach has been rejected as unworkable and unfair to parents. More than half the states have laws that expressly require "accusatory" reports. In the others, when the statute is silent about whether there must be some connection between the child's condition and the parent's behavior, the practice of agencies is to seek such information before commencing an investigation. The alternative, of course, would be to require the investigation of the millions of innocent injuries that children receive each year. Besides the crushing burden this would place on child protective agencies, it would be an uncalled-for invasion of family privacy. If there is no reason to suspect that the parents are responsible for the child's condition, surely an intrusive investigation cannot be justified.

The maltreatment of a child by any parent, guardian, or custodian should be reported. Parental maltreatment of children, of course, is the primary focus of child protective efforts. However, children are often maltreated while in the care of other adults. The law in most states takes this into account by defining a "parent" to include "the child's custodian, guardian, or any other person responsible for the child's care at the relevant time."[23] A few states go further, defining a "parent" to include "any person continually or at regular intervals found in the same household as the child."[24] (These provisions are primarily intended to cover paramours but have been interpreted to include boyfriends and girlfriends, baby-sitters, siblings, and others.)[25] For reasons of convenience and to avoid clumsy and overlong sentences, this book tends to use the word "parent" to encompass this broader concept of the persons who fall under reporting laws because of the maltreatment they inflict on the children in their charge.

A report should be made even when only one parent seems to be involved in the maltreatment. The nonabusing parent sometimes plays a crucial role in the dynamic that leads to the child's maltreatment by the spouse and others (especially in cases of sexual abuse.)[26] At other times, the parent knows about a child's maltreatment but does nothing to stop it because of fear, negligence, incompetence, or indifference. One mother knew that her husband of approximately six months was a convicted sex offender, and even though she was warned not to leave the children alone with him, she did so. She observed vaginal irritation on her daughter but never asked the child whether she had been sexually abused.[27]

A nonabusing parent has an affirmative duty to protect a child from a spouse's maltreatment. If there is no other way to protect the child, the nonabusing parent *must* call the police or a child protective agency. In a New York case, the mother testified that she tried to dissuade her husband from continuing the verbal abuse of their son, Shane. But the judge concluded that this behavior was not enough and that she should have called the authorities: "The fact remains that she failed to protect her son from an ongoing, serious abuse. She hardly discharged her parental duty to Shane by, in effect, keeping peace at his expense. When her husband persisted in his abuse of the child, she had an obligation to act meaningfully to protect the boy."[28] By failing to report her husband's behavior, the judge ruled, she "allowed" her son to be abused.

Sometimes, however, it is unclear whether the nonabusing parent knew (or should have known) about the maltreatment. Hence, the law purposely does not make the potential reporter responsible for deciding whether both parents are involved. Even if it appears that only one parent was involved, a report should be made. It is then up to the child protective agency to determine who is responsible.

In such cases, though, you should report *only* the parent who seems to be involved in the maltreatment. A Long Island (New York) case is a telling example of the need for care in reporting nonabusing parents: A child protective worker filed a court petition alleging sexual abuse against both the mother and father even though it was the mother who had first told the police that her husband sexually abused the child. There seems to have been no reason to suspect that the mother had in any way been abusive or neglectful, and the county attorney withdrew the petition against her before the trial. A federal court allowed the mother to sue for malicious prosecution, on the ground that the worker and the agency initiated the court action "knowing full well that ultimately [the] said petition must be dismissed."[29]

The parents' failure to protect a child from maltreatment by others should be reported. Sadly, some parents do not protect their children from maltreatment by nonfamily members or even strangers. In one case, for example, the father "allowed his daughters to sleep in the same room as the cousin who had previously victimized them."[30] You must report a parent who knows (or should know) about a child's maltreatment and does nothing to stop it.

Do not report, however, when *neither* parent knows about the maltreatment and the lack of knowledge is not caused by negligence or inadequate concern for the child's welfare. (This can sometimes happen in cases of sexual abuse, when there are no physical signs of maltreatment.) In our society, parents have the primary responsibility for protecting their children. We rely on them to take appropriate action when it is a nonparent who abuses their children. Using a child protective agency in such situations, which the great majority of parents can and will handle, unnecessarily dilutes the agency's resources and the meaning of the child protection law—to the detriment of children who need real and sustained outside help. Only when parents fail in their duty should the agency step in.

Parents who are unaware of what happened (or is happening) to their child should be told immediately, so they can call the police or other appropriate agencies. A report should be made only if they fail to act. In fact, making a report against parents who have not been given the opportunity to take protective action or who did so may lead to a charge of wrongful reporting.

DAY CARE AND INSTITUTIONAL ABUSE

Although easily exaggerated—and sensationalized—the maltreatment of children in residential institutions and day care centers is a serious problem. One conservative estimate is that "residential complaint rates may be twice as large as intrafamilial rates."[31]

In *Doe v. New York City Department of Social Services*, for example, a jury awarded $225,000 to a foster child, Anna Doe, because the agency failed to respond to the maltreatment she suffered during her 13-year placement. According to the federal court:

Anna and her foster sisters testified that starting when she was about ten years of age, she was regularly and frequently beaten and sexually abused by [her foster father.]. She testified that he beat her with his hands and belt all over her body, threw her down the stairs, and on one occasion lacerated her with a hunting knife, that he confined her to her room for days at a time, and ultimately forced her to have intercourse and oral sexual relations with him.[32]

The abuse or neglect of a child in a residential or day care facility should be reported. As a result of cases like Anna Doe's, child abuse reporting laws now require the reporting of suspected abuse and neglect in out-of-home settings. Almost all states now require reports of the maltreatment of children in foster care and residential institutions, and a growing number are requiring reports of maltreatment in day care settings.

Requiring reports of out-of-home maltreatment is based on two considerations. First, children are more vulnerable to maltreatment in day care centers, foster homes, shelters, and other residential facilities because parents may be unaware of what is happening; for children in residential settings, the parents may be out of touch, uncaring, or deceased. Only an independent agency may be able to take effective action. Second, when a child is in the care of a public or private agency, with or without the parent's consent, that agency is as responsible for the child's welfare as any natural parent would be.

The investigation of reports of suspected out-of-home maltreatment raises special problems. No agency should be allowed to investigate itself. An outside, disinterested agency must perform the investigation and it must have sufficient authority to take meaningful corrective action.[33] Otherwise, the chances of an inadequate response are too great. Thus, federal regulations stipulate that no agency may police itself in the investigation of reports of institutional maltreatment.

4

Liability for Failing to Report

The best way to encourage fuller reporting of the suspected maltreatment of children is through increased public and professional understanding. Nevertheless, reporting laws need enforceable provisions for those who refuse to accept their moral obligation to protect endangered children.

CRIMINAL PENALTIES FOR FAILING TO REPORT

Almost all states have a specific law that makes the failure to report suspected child abuse and neglect a crime. Even in those that do not, it may be a crime under general criminal laws.[1] The criminal penalty is usually of misdemeanor level, with the potential fine ranging from $100 to $1,000, imprisonment ranging from five days to one year in jail, or both.

Criminal penalties not only put some "teeth" into reporting laws, they also help mandated reporters to explain to both children and parents why a report must be made; and they make it easier for staff members to persuade their superiors of the necessity of a report. Nurses frequently relate how the mention of potential liability for the failure to report convinces reluctant hospital administrators to act.

Criminal prosecutions for not reporting have, until recently, been rare for three main reasons: (1) problems of proof, (2) the feeling that criminal sanctions are inappropriate because there is no criminal culpability and because an otherwise law-abiding citizen should not be prosecuted, and (3) the fact that the would-be reporter's cooperation is often necessary to prove the case against the parents. A criminal prosecution is also unlikely if the child did not suffer serious injury as a result of the failure to report.

Significantly, though, the number of criminal prosecutions seems to be increasing. In recent years, there have been prosecutions against physicians,[2] psychiatrists,[3] psychologists,[4] teachers (in one case, a nun),[5] social workers,[6] spouses,[7] and friends of the family.[8]

The failure to report suspected institutional maltreatment also has resulted in criminal prosecutions. The head of the institution, for example, can be criminally liable for the failure to respond to information suggesting that a staff member maltreated a child. In one Denver case, a school principal was fined $200 (the maximum penalty) for failing to report the claims of two sets of parents that a teacher was sexually assaulting their third-grade daughters.[9]

The existence of criminal liability depends on whether the failure to report was intentional.[10] In most states, the test is whether the failure was "knowing" or "willful." In these states, a successful prosecution requires proof—beyond a reasonable doubt—that the person was legally required to report, had knowledge of this legal mandate, had a *conscious suspicion* that the child was abused or neglected, and still did nothing.

Thus, a criminal prosecution is possible whenever a mandated reporter fails to report observations of the parents' abusive or neglectful behavior, a child's complaints of being abused or neglected, a parent's description of abusive or neglectful conduct, or the statement of a reputable individual that a child is abused and neglected. Failing to report such direct evidence is the same as saying, "So what? It is none of my business."

Some states do not limit liability to "knowing" or "willful" failures to report. Instead, they establish an "objective" standard, so criminal culpability can be established by proof that the defendant was "*consciously aware of facts . . .* which would cause a reasonable person to know or suspect that a child was being subjected to abuse or neglect."[11]

In these states, a criminal prosecution may be based on circumstantial evidence, such as the child's "suspicious" or "apparently inflicted" injuries. A Los Angeles physician, for example—who apparently knew that a 3-year-old child had been previously removed from her mother's custody—was prosecuted for not reporting *repeated* evidence of severe abuse. According to court documents, the physician did not report evidence of abuse that included "old burns on the chest and left leg, and the absence of the nasal . . . septum." His defense was that he wanted to "give the mother a chance" to avoid further contact with social service workers and that he had attempted to treat the child in his office and at her home. "Thirteen days after [he] began treating her, she died of a massive chest infection resulting from the pneumonia."[12] The physician entered a no-contest plea to involuntary manslaughter.[13]

Because of the stringent legal requirements involved in criminal cases, many prosecutions result in dismissals before trial, acquittals after trial, or reversals on appeal. Nevertheless, the message of these prosecutions is clear: Potential criminal liability for failing to report is a realistic possibility and must be kept in mind when working with children or parents.

CIVIL LIABILITY FOR FAILING TO REPORT

People who are required to report also face civil damage actions, which have proved an equally effective means to encourage better reporting. "In one Michigan district, school administrators responded immediately when faced with a civil action alleging liability for failure to properly report an incident of abuse and distributed pamphlets on child abuse reporting to all faculty members within the district."[14]

A *specific statute may establish civil liability for the failure to report.* Whether a failure to report falls under one of these civil liability statutes depends on the precise wording of the reporting law: The defendant must be legally required to report, and the situation must involve one of the forms of maltreatment for which a report is required.

For example, if the reporting law covers suspected instances of institutional maltreatment (and most do), agency workers, supervisors, and the agency itself may be sued for failing to report the maltreatment of a child in their care. This is what happened in *Borgerson v. Minnesota*, where the state and county licensing officials, the group home, and staff members of the group home were alleged to have failed to report (and respond to) information that juveniles in a locked residential facility were physically abused, given tranquilizing drugs improperly, and placed in isolation without proper safeguards being taken.[15]

Most of these laws impose civil liability only when there is a "knowing" or "willful" failure to report. The "knowing" or "willful" standard for liability is narrower than the ordinary tort standard of "negligence" and avoids penalizing would-be reporters for honest mistakes in interpreting the difficult and ambiguous facts surrounding most cases of child maltreatment.[16] In a civil action, the willful misconduct standard means that the would-be reporter had a *conscious suspicion* (or belief) that the child was abused or neglected, knew that a report was required, and still did nothing.[17]

As in criminal prosecutions, a successful civil suit is most likely when a mandated reporter fails to report direct evidence of child maltreatment. Sometimes the intentional nature of the failure to report seems relatively clear. In Pontiac, Michigan, for instance, a former high school student sued the school's principal, social worker, and the school district, claiming that for an entire year she had sought their advice on how to handle sexual abuse at home but that they did not use the information she provided to make a report.[18]

More often, though, such direct evidence is not available. This does not mean that a lawsuit cannot succeed. Again, as in a criminal prosecution, the defendant's state of mind may be proved "by circumstantial evidence and the inferences which the trier of fact may draw therefrom," as the California Supreme Court explained in one case.[19] For example, the plaintiff can introduce evidence of the child's condition, its diagnostic significance, and any other surrounding circumstances that would lead the court to infer that the defendant actually suspected (or believed) that the child was maltreated.

Many jurisdictions require that a report be made "immediately." Others specify twenty-four hours, forty-eight hours, and so forth. In jurisdictions that require "immediate" reports, the courts would probably hold that there could be a "reasonable" delay while the diagnosis is confirmed and other necessary administrative procedures are followed. Conversely, when a specific time frame is set forth, a court may hold a defendant responsible for damages that occurred *before* the specified time expired if it concluded that an ordinarily prudent person would have acted more quickly. Any delay beyond the specified time would cause presumptive liability, subject to the defendant's ability to raise a valid defense.

The failure to report may be "negligence per se." Under the common law, the violation of a statutory duty, in this instance, the required reporting of suspected abuse and neglect, may be "negligence per se." No legislation that specifically creates civil liability is needed; the failure to comply with a statutory mandate "in itself" establishes the negligence.[20]

Although there are only a handful of reported cases on the subject, none denies the cause of action, and the facility with which such claims are settled (even in states without specific legislation) reflects the strong consensus among practicing lawyers and insurance companies that such liability exists.[21]

Thus, in 1970, a lawsuit was filed in California against the police, two hospitals, and individual physicians who *repeatedly* failed to report a child with severe injuries that were indicative of abuse. When the child was five months old, his seventeen-year-old mother had taken him to the hospital with a long skull fracture. The mother's explanation was that the child had "fallen off a bed." The child was treated and released three days later. The hospital record indicated that the examining physician noted contusions and many old bruises on the child's body and blood blisters on his penis, that he had questioned the mother about these injuries and did not believe her answers, that he therefore had suspected child abuse, but that he had not made a report.[22]

Eight days later, the child was readmitted with marked swelling and discoloration on the left arm from his elbow to his fingertips. The mother signed the child out and took him to another hospital where there was concern "regarding possible child abuse," but the child was "discharged in the hope that it was not so." No report was made by either hospital.

Within weeks, the child was returned to the first hospital, this time with burned fingers, puncture wounds and strangulation marks on his neck, and welts on his back. The child was not breathing at the time of admission. Before respiration was restored, the child had suffered extensive brain damage from the lack of oxygen in his blood. (At the time of the trial, when the child was three years old, his IQ was twenty-four and his physical development was extremely retarded.) The mother's boyfriend was convicted of child abuse; no charges were filed against the mother.

The infant's father, separated from the mother, sued, claiming that the hospitals' failure to report was the proximate cause of the infant's permanent brain damage. The case was settled for $600,000. The lawsuit and the size of the settlement received wide publicity, especially within the medical community.[23]

A second California case, *Landeros v. Flood*,[24] was not settled. In a widely followed decision, the state's Supreme Court held that there could be liability for failing to diagnose and report a case of the battered child syndrome. The lawsuit alleged that an 11-month-old girl had been brought to the hospital with a spiral fracture to one leg that could only have been caused by twisting the leg until it cracked.

The child's mother had no explanation for this injury. The girl also had bruises over her entire body and a linear fracture of the skull, which was in the process of healing. Without taking full body skeletal x-rays, the hospital released the child to her mother and the mother's common-law husband. The hospital made no report of suspected child abuse, as is required by California law. Within 11 weeks, the child was brought to a second hospital, having now sustained traumatic blows to her right eye and back, severe bites on her face, and second and third degree burns on her left hand. At this time, the battered child syndrome was immediately diagnosed and reported to the appropriate agencies.[25]

The California Supreme Court held that the hospital and the physician could be liable for damages if the physician had been professionally negligent or had violated the state reporting law by a knowing failure to report his suspicions that the child's injuries were the result of abuse.

Whether the doctrine of negligence per se creates liability in a particular case depends on whether the defendant is among those required to report and whether the situation involves a reportable condition. So, in states in which the criminal-penalty provision of the reporting law requires a "knowing" or "willful" failure to report, liability under the negligence per se doctrine requires an *intentional* failure to report. Even in states in which the reporting law or criminal penalty clause applies an objective standard of liability (that is, reasonable cause to suspect or believe), courts would probably require evidence of an intentional violation of the statute, as the California Supreme Court did in *Landeros*.[26]

The same limits—that the person is required to report and that the situation must be a reportable condition—do not apply to potential liability under the common-law doctrines of professional malpractice and failure to warn, both of which are discussed next. These doctrines are broader than the doctrine of negligence per se for another reason. Under them, liability is created by conduct that is simply *negligent*. Intentional or willful behavior is not required.

The negligent failure to report may be professional malpractice. In the *Landeros* case, the California Supreme Court held that liability would be established upon proof that "a reasonably prudent physician examining the [child] in 1971 would have been led to suspect she was a victim of the battered child syndrome from the particular injuries and circumstances presented to him, would have confirmed that diagnosis by ordering x-rays of her entire skeleton, and would have promptly reported his findings to appropriate authorities to prevent a recurrence of the injuries."[27]

Although widely applied in other jurisdictions,[28] the *Landeros* case is sometimes narrowly interpreted as making the failure to report a form of professional malpractice only for physicians. But there is nothing in the court's opinion or in general legal doctrines that necessitates this conclusion. In fact, the basic rule applies to all professions.[29]

At one time, it may have been correct to think that only physicians could be expected to possess the knowledge and ability necessary to identify maltreated children. Twenty years of professional training and public awareness campaigns, however, have significantly upgraded the diagnostic skills of many other professional groups. At the same time, there has been a parallel increase in societal expectations about the ability of various types of professionals to identify maltreated children, as reflected in the expansion of mandatory reporting laws to cover most child-serving professionals. Thus, it is likely that teachers, child care workers, social workers, and law enforcement personnel, as well as nurses, dentists, and mental health professionals, who are mandated reporters in most states, may be held liable for their negligent failure to identify and report maltreated children.

The standard of professional negligence, of course, varies from profession to profession. The failure to report direct evidence of maltreatment, such as the Pontiac student's description of being sexually abused, would be strong evidence of negligence for almost any mandated professional. But the standard is considerably less uniform for circumstantial evidence, where a would-be reporter is required to weigh often conflicting, incomplete, and subtle indications of maltreatment.

To assess the diagnostic capabilities of a particular profession, great weight is given to the practice standards established by the profession itself. For example, the National Association of Social Workers' *Standards for Social Work Practice in Child Protection* require all social workers "to have basic knowledge of the indicators of child abuse and neglect" and "to obtain knowledge of the state's child abuse and neglect laws and procedures."[30] Most other child-serving professions have similar standards of practice that create the potential for liability.

Liability based on professional malpractice requires a professional relationship between the person who should have reported and the child. Often, though, the relationship is between the professional and the parent (or some other third party). For example, the professional may be a social worker who is treating the parent for emotional difficulties.[31] If the parent tells the social worker about a child's maltreatment (either by that parent, the other parent, or someone else), under the formal doctrine of professional negligence, there can be no liability because the child is not the social worker's client. Similarly, many reporting laws require a report from professionals only when the child comes "before them in their professional or official capacity." Such reporting laws, like the doctrine of professional malpractice, do not create potential liability when a professional learns, second hand, of danger to a child who is not a client. There may, though, be another basis of liability.

The failure to report may be a violation of a duty to warn of danger to a third party. Since 1976, psychiatrists, psychologists, probation officers, and social workers have been found liable for the failure to warn *third parties* of a clearly recognized danger posed by a client.

The most widely known of these cases, again from California, is *Tarasoff v. Regents of University of California*.[32] "In that case a University of

California student, who was a psychiatric outpatient at a University clinic, followed through on his threat, previously expressed to his therapist, to kill a specific victim. The Supreme Court of California, in a suit by the victim's parents against the University and its therapists, ruled that a psychotherapist owes a duty of reasonable care to third persons who may be intended victims of the therapist's patient."[33] In the court's words:

> When a therapist determines, or pursuant to the standards of his profession should determine, that his patient presents a serious danger of violence to another, he incurs an obligation to use reasonable care to protect the intended victim against such danger. The discharge of this duty may require the therapist . . . to warn the intended victim or others likely to apprise the victim of the danger, to notify the police, or to take whatever other steps are reasonably necessary under the circumstances.[34]

The *Tarasoff* doctrine, although much criticized by mental health professionals,[35] seems to have been adopted by almost all the courts that have considered the question. Furthermore, there is general agreement that not only psychiatrists, but psychologists, social workers, and "psychotherapists" generally have a duty to warn a third party of danger.[36]

The analogy between this situation and that of a therapist who learns of a clear danger to a child while treating a parent or other family member is self-evident. The failure to take protective action (here a report to the authorities, rather than a warning to the victim) is as likely to result in future harm and, thus, creates possible liability.

Liability can be extensive and long-lived. Whatever theory of liability is applied, when the person who allegedly failed to report was employed by an agency or organization, the agency or organization may also be sued and invariably is.[37] This vicarious liability also applies to the acts or omissions of volunteers.

Conversely, since most reporting laws do not lift the obligations of staff members to report when they notify their superior of suspected child maltreatment, staff members may still be liable for the damages caused by the failure to report if they knew or should have known that no report was made. Staff members who are falsely told that a report was made will have a defense against liability unless they knew or should have known that this was untrue.

Most nonlawyers know that there is a statute of limitations on the bringing of lawsuits. Generally, an action must be filed within three to five years of when the harm was done. In all but a few states, however, the statute of limitations usually does not take effect against minor plaintiffs until they reach age eighteen.[38] Thus, the failure to report the suspected maltreatment of an infant may result in a lawsuit up to twenty-one years later. Of course, an action may be initiated on behalf of a child while he or she is still a minor if it is brought by a legal representative or a duly appointed guardian.

The amount of liability that someone who fails to report faces is limited to compensation for the actual harm or injury to the child proximately caused by the failure to report.[39] (There is no liability if there is no further maltreatment.) Potential reporters are not held responsible for maltreatment that occurred before they knew or should have known about the child's situation. The only harms or injuries that are considered are those that occurred *after* the report should have been made. Punitive damages may be imposed if the failure to report was intentional or evidenced reckless disregard of the child's welfare.

As presently imposed, *criminal and civil penalties encourage inappropriate reporting.* Current liability statutes penalize the negligent failure to report while granting immunity for incorrect, but good-faith reports (described in the next chapter). This combination of provisions encourages the overreporting of questionable situations. Fearful of being sued for not reporting, some professionals play it safe and report whenever they think there is the slightest chance that they will subsequently be sued for not doing so. No person should be subject to criminal and civil liability for making a good-faith determination that a child is not maltreated. To reduce the incentive for inappropriate reporting, six states already limit civil liability to the "knowing" or "willful" failure to report. All states should do so, and potential reporters should be made aware of the difference, which is not now the case.

5

Protections for
Those Who Report

In the past, the fear of being unjustly sued for libel, slander, defamation, invasion of privacy, or breach of confidentiality deterred many people from reporting suspected child abuse. This fear existed even though general legal doctrines seem to protect anyone who made a good-faith report. To allay these concerns, all states have enacted laws that explicitly protect those who report.

LEGAL IMMUNITY

All states grant immunity from civil and criminal liability to persons who report. Except in two or three states, immunity applies only to reports that are made in *good faith*.[1] There is no protection for reports that are made maliciously, because of prejudice or personal bias, or because of reckless or grossly negligent decision making. To reassure potential reporters even more, about half the states have laws that establish a *presumption* of good faith.[2]

For fear that abusing or neglecting parents will report themselves and thereby obtain immunity, a handful of states limit the granting of immunity to persons "other than the alleged violator."[3] Such provisions, however, are usually not necessary because most laws grant immunity only for the consequences of the report, not for conduct that underlies the report.

In recognition of the other responsibilities assigned to persons who report, most states specifically extend the grant of immunity to participation in judicial proceedings. About half the states extend immunity to the performance of other acts authorized by law, such as taking photographs and X rays, participating in the removal of a child from parental custody, and cooperating with the child protective agency's investigation.[4]

Immunity provisions do not prevent the initiation of lawsuits that claim damages for wrongful reporting. A lawsuit can always be filed. But immunity provisions do make it difficult, if not impossible, for such suits to succeed—as long as the report was made in good faith. In fact, a complaint that fails to offer sufficient allegations of bad faith will be dismissed before trial.[5]

Most cases that allege the reporter's lack of good faith fail because of the difficulties involved in trying to prove malicious motivation or intent. Rarely is there direct evidence of bad faith. That is what made a 1980 Virginia case and what it had to say about circumstantial evidence of bad faith potentially so important. The defendant, a Virginia physician, was sued for maliciously reporting a child who had numerous bruised knots on his body. (The parents had brought their infant son to the physician for possible blood problems.) Later, it was established that the bruising resulted from the child's hemophilia. The physician moved to dismiss the suit on the ground that he acted in good faith and, thus, was immune from liability.[6]

The court refused to dismiss the lawsuit, ruling that the *allegations* of "grossly negligent" diagnosis were sufficient to allow the case to be considered by a jury. On two occasions, the physician apparently berated the parents, which helped resolve the case in the parents' favor. (The parents had also sought damages for the physician's remarks to them, which, they claimed, caused "mental and physical stress, humiliation, and embarrassment.") In this context, the court stated:

> It might not be unusual if a doctor discussed child abuse with parents in an attempt to promote the best interests of the child. It is quite another matter if a doctor berates, belittles, and verbally condemns parents in an unnecessarily excessive manner, especially if the physician's accusations are made in the absence of exercise of common diagnostic analysis.[7]

After the judge's ruling, the case was settled for $5,000.

This case, even though it went against the physician, should be reassuring to individuals who are considering whether to report. The immunity provisions of reporting laws protect persons who report in good faith, unless they have been reckless in deciding to report or abusive in dealing with the parents.

Although suits for bad-faith reporting are rare and likely to be dismissed, legal fees to defend them can be high, easily running into thousands of dollars. In an apparently unique provision, California reimburses the attorneys' fees of mandated reporters who win suits that are filed against them.[8] All states should consider such legislation.

ABROGATION OF PROFESSIONAL CONFIDENTIALITY

Child abuse and child neglect usually occur behind closed doors, without witnesses. In determining whether a child has been maltreated, a child protection agency must necessarily rely on medical evidence and on the statements of the parents. Children—and their parents—often tell helping professionals what caused the children's injuries. Unless this information can be shared with the child protective agency, there may be no legal way to protect a child from future injury.

However, physicians and many other professionals who are most likely to see abused and neglected children are subject to statutory privileges that make their conversations with patients or clients confidential. Ordinarily, professionals who are subject to such privileges are prohibited from divulging anything told to them within the scope of the privilege, unless the protected person gives permission or the communication involves information about a crime that will be committed in the future.[9] A professional who violates such privileges may be sued by the protected person. Thus, unless the privilege is lifted, many abused children could not be reported.

Professional confidentiality is not a bar to reporting. A legal mandate to report presumably overrides any other law that created a privileged communication, especially if the reporting law was enacted after the law that created the privilege.[10] Nevertheless, to reassure potential reporters about relating information gained as a result of their confidential relationship with clients, most state reporting laws contain specific clauses that abrogate statutorily created privileges. Some statutes abrogate only the privileges governing professionals who are required to report; others abrogate all privileges, even if the professionals involved are not required to report. (In addition, almost every jurisdiction has a specific provision that abrogates all or some privileges for the purpose of participating in judicial proceedings related to abuse or neglect.)[11]

The absence of a statutory abrogation does *not* mean that information cannot be shared. Statutory abrogations of confidentiality are needed only if other state laws or court decisions establish a specific privilege. Although all states make physician/patient communications confidential, social workers, psychologists, and priests, for example, are often not covered. Also, many state laws create a generalized exception to confiden-

tiality rules when a crime has been or will be committed. (In all states,
most forms of child abuse and child neglect, besides being the subject
of civil court jurisdiction, are also crimes.)

Federal laws also make some conversations and records confidential
for schools,[12] drug treatment programs,[13] and alcohol treatment
programs.[14] For each, exceptions have been made for reporting suspected
child maltreatment. However, the rules concerning the release of information under these statutes are complex and vary from community to
community.[15] If you desire further information on this subject, contact
your local child protective agency or the U.S. National Center on Child
Abuse and Neglect.

Families who are already in treatment must be reported. When parents
are already in treatment, some mental health and social service professionals think that making a report violates their ethical obligations toward
parents. This is natural. Throughout their professional training and ca-
reers, great emphasis was placed on guarding the privacy of their clients.
These professionals also fear that reporting the parents to a child protective
agency and testifying against them in court may only reinforce the insecu-
rity and hostility many abusive and neglectful parents feel and may
disrupt the treatment already in progress.

Three or four states give mandated professionals limited discretion
not to report, but only under extremely restricted circumstances.[16] Such
provisions are both healthy and dangerous. Although they graft appropriate
flexibility onto absolute legal strictures, they also weaken the imperative
to report without providing a way to monitor their implementation.
Most professionals do not have the same capabilities as child protective
agencies. Without examining a child to see the severity of his or her
injuries and without visiting the child's home to assess the conditions
there, they cannot accurately determine the degree of risk to the child.
Furthermore, even the most skilled professionals may not be able to
call upon concrete services, such as day care and homemaker care;
may not be able to make regular home visits; and may not view the
protection of the child as their primary responsibility.

A better approach is to formalize a procedure through which the
local child protective agency can review a situation after a report is
made to decide whether a full child protective investigation is necessary.[17]
Although no state seems to have formally adopted this commonsense
solution to a real problem, it seems to be the general practice in a
number of communities.

Thus, except in a few states, mandated professionals have no discretion
about breaking confidentiality and reporting the suspected maltreatment

of a child. The failure to report may expose the child to serious injury and may expose the professional to civil or criminal penalties.

The existence of this absolute requirement to report, though, does not mean that reporting professionals should ignore the trusting relationship they may have developed with the parents. Unless it appears that doing so will endanger the child, they should prepare the parents for the consequences of the report. The necessity of the report and the nature of the investigation that will follow should be described honestly and supportively. If appropriate, the parents should be encouraged to report themselves to the child protective agency, as described in Chapter 18. If you have any question about how to proceed, you can consult with your local child protective agency.

ADVERSE EMPLOYMENT ACTIONS

Employees of public and private agencies are sometimes discharged or otherwise administratively punished for failing to report the suspected maltreatment of a child. If the employee had sufficient information to make a report and knew of the obligation to report, such penalties may be justified. Adverse employment actions may also be appropriate if the employee reported maliciously or recklessly. But, too often, it appears that employees are punished for making proper reports.

All states, of course, have laws that provide immunity from liability for reporting in good faith, even if the report is determined to be unfounded. But some parents seek retaliation against the person who made the report by complaining to the agency, which sometimes wrongly gives in to parental pressure.

A Minnesota case suggests how an agency can do so: A social worker in a private clinic was told by a father that he had hit his child with a belt. The worker informed the father that she would have to file a report of suspected child abuse. The father happened to be the vice president of a company that had a $1 million contract with the clinic to provide counseling for the company's employees, and the father was in charge of writing the contract. According to the worker, the father convinced the clinic director to tell the worker not to file a report. The worker insisted on filing the report and was fired.[18] The resultant publicity led to the passage of an employee antiretaliation law.

Even when the agency eventually supports an employee who reported, the procedure it follows in responding to the parent's complaint can send the wrong message. One parent filed a formal complaint with the state licensing agency, claiming that a visiting nurse had wrongfully reported. Although the parent made no substantial allegations of the nurse's bad faith, the agency took eight months to dismiss the complaint. Those months of uncertainty and stress—and the cost of defending the claim—were not lost on other professionals who were licensed to practice in the state.

By far the greatest danger of wrongful retaliation arises when employees report the maltreatment of children by their own agencies.[19] One social worker's description of what happened to her when she tried to protect a child in her care speaks for itself:

> I was fired from my position as the only social worker at [a center for the treatment of cerebral palsy] because I was advocating for a child who attended the center. The child, an eleven year old who was ambulatory, was tied into a wheelchair from 9 to 3 each day for the past three years in order to prevent his acting out self abusive behavior. A helmet was placed on his head and tied to the back of the wheelchair and his upper arms were tied behind him. No motion was possible. In addition, he was heavily sedated. On the basis of my previous, extensive work with handicapped children, examination of the reports in the child's file and discussions with my colleagues at the agency, I believed that the child had, in addition, been misdiagnosed as severely retarded and was in the wrong program at the Center. After trying, without success, for four months to convince the Center administration, the psychologist and the doctors to untie the boy, to reevaluate him and to plan a proper educational program for him, I contacted the Chairman of the Board of Trustees of our agency and asked him to intervene. Three weeks after contacting him, the child's situation was unchanged and I then notified [the state agency that had placed the child and the state agency responsible for investigating reports of child abuse].[20]

The social worker accepted a $5,000 payment in settlement of her lawsuit after she realized that the legal costs of pursuing her claim might be higher than any additional payment she might receive. She also wanted to put a very unpleasant incident behind her.

The basic employment law of many states should protect employees who report in good faith[21] and some states have passed specific antiretaliation legislation that does so.[22] But both types of legislation suffer from one major limitation: To be protected, the employee must establish a connection between the report and the adverse employment action. This can be difficult. Often, there is a history of poor relations and conflict between the employee and the agency's administrators, and the adverse action is claimed to be based on this history. Or, the action is attributed to the legitimate administrative or budgetary needs of the agency. The connection, thus, comes down to a question of proof, which the employee frequently cannot produce. This is why Minnesota's employee-protection statute creates a "rebuttable presumption that any adverse action within 90 days of a report is retaliatory."[23]

REPORTING IN CONFIDENCE

You may have a good reason for not wanting parents to know that you have reported them to the authorities. You may feel embarrassed about intruding on private family matters or you may be concerned that a report will disrupt a personal or professional relationship. For example, the disclosure of a spouse's or grandparent's report (or cooperation with the subsequent investigation) may cause an angry break in family relations. And some parents may react violently on learning of the report. Thus, professionals, as well as friends and neighbors, may fear for their safety if the parent discovers that they are the source of the report.

Child protective agencies often promise confidentiality to those who report. And most will not tell the parents who made the report. If the parents gain access to their records, most agencies will delete the name of the person or persons who reported the abuse or cooperated with the investigation.[24]

However, no agency can honestly promise absolute confidentiality. If the case goes to court, your testimony may be essential to proving it. (If you testify, the parents will learn your identity, of course.) In addition, if the parents can convince the agency (or a court) that there is reason to believe that the report was made in bad faith, your name will be released so the parents can pursue their legal remedies for a wrongful report. (These realities, especially if they are candidly explained to a potential reporter, often prompt an anonymous report.) Furthermore, parents frequently can guess who made the report. You may be one of the few people who knows about the situation that was reported.

Therefore, if you are thinking about making a report, you should assume that the parents may discover your identity. But this should not discourage you from reporting. If you do not step forward to protect the child, who will?

PART

TWO

Deciding
to
Report

6

Sources of Suspicion

Deciding to report would be difficult enough if all the facts about a child's care were known. But children are usually maltreated in the privacy of the home. Unless the child is old enough (and not too frightened) to speak out or unless a family member steps forward, it is frequently impossible to know what really happened. Thus, the decision often must be based on incomplete and potentially misleading information. That is why reporting is based on the "reasonable cause to suspect" child maltreatment. This chapter describes the sources of that suspicion.

REASONABLE SUSPICIONS

Only "reasonable suspicion" is needed for a report. Because of the difficulty in obtaining information about a child's maltreatment, the law does not require potential reporters to be sure that a child is being abused or neglected or to have absolute proof of maltreatment. In all states, reports are to be made when there is "reasonable cause to suspect" or "reasonable cause to believe" that a child is abused or neglected.[1]

Reporting reasonable suspicions relieves you of the need to make a final or definitive diagnosis of maltreatment, which usually requires a home visit, interviews with parents, and further investigation. Most potential reporters are not in a position to conduct such an extensive inquiry and waiting for unequivocal proof may place the child at great risk. After a report is made, the child protective agency is responsible for determining the child's true situation and, if protective intervention is needed, for taking appropriate action.

A reportable suspicion must be based on objective evidence. The legal injunction to report suspected maltreatment is not an open-ended invitation to report whenever one has a "gut feeling" that a child may be maltreated. A vague, amorphous, or inarticulatable concern over a child's welfare is not a sufficient reason to report. When considering the possibility of abuse or neglect, you must decide whether there is *sufficient*, objective evidence for suspecting abuse or neglect. Ordinarily, the person who makes the report should have personal knowledge of the evidence on which it is based, but a report may be based on information supplied by an apparently reliable third party.

The sources of suspicion on which to base a report may be either

Direct evidence—firsthand accounts or observations of seriously harmful parental behavior—or

Circumstantial evidence—concrete facts, such as the child's physical condition, which suggest that the child has been abused or neglected.

Both types of evidence are discussed in this chapter.

FIRSTHAND OBSERVATIONS

Anyone who has seen a parent engage in seriously harmful behavior toward a child should make a report. As was explained in Chapter 3, the parent's observed behavior need not have caused serious injury to be considered maltreatment; a report should be made when the reasonably foreseeable consequence of the parent's behavior could have been (or, in the future, will be) the child's serious injury.

The most likely persons to *observe* actual instances of abuse and neglect are friends, neighbors, and relatives who are often in the home. Professionals who happen to be in the home may also see a child being maltreated. Visiting nurses attending to the needs of a child or parent, caseworkers visiting the home for public assistance matters, police officers called to settle a domestic dispute, and firefighters responding to an alarm are but a few of the outsiders who may observe a parent's inability to care for a child or who even may see a parent physically assault a child. Former New York City Family Court Judge Nanette Dembitz described one such case:

One of the most heart-sickening neglect and abuse trials I have ever held concerned . . . Somala S., 7 months. . . . A policeman who was climbing up a fire escape chasing a suspected mugger, by chance heard Somala crying and saw her lying in a room by herself in a dresser drawer. When he took her to Bellevue Hospital, she was in such a state of malnutrition and dehydration that she is permanently blind and braindamaged.[2]

Although most observed acts of maltreatment occur in the home, they can be seen in other settings as well. The parent may so completely lose control that he or she becomes oblivious to the presence of outsiders, or the parent may have an unconscious desire to be discovered; allowing abusive behavior to be observed may be an unconscious call for help.

Such behavior signals serious danger to the child and requires prompt action. In one notorious case from suburban Westchester County, New York, a public assistance worker observed a mother beat her child in the agency's waiting room. (The mother was there to inquire about public assistance, and her child became restless and fidgety while they were waiting.) The worker reported the incident to the agency's child protective unit, only two floors above the waiting room, but because of administrative breakdowns, no action was taken. Two months later, the child was taken to the hospital convulsing and bleeding from the mouth. The child died in the hospital.[3]

Unfortunately, the opportunities for such observations are relatively limited. Abusive parents usually do not assault their children in the presence of outsiders. On the other hand, a visit to the home may reveal young children who are left alone or placed in dangerous or unhealthy situations or other circumstantial evidence of the need to report.

THE CHILD'S STATEMENTS

Children are often the best source of information concerning possible maltreatment. They can give moving—and frequently decisive—evidence about their parents' behavior. Subject to the exceptions discussed later, any child's description of being abused or neglected should be reported.

Older children, especially, often seek help from an adult whom they know and trust. A schoolteacher who seems to be concerned about the child, a social worker who the child gets to know, a volunteer in a runaway shelter in which the child seeks refuge, a friendly neighbor, or any other approachable adult may be told about acts of abuse or neglect in the home. Many cases of sexual abuse, for example, come to light only after the child has told an outsider, usually a teacher, about the situation. You should support and encourage a child who seeks your help.

Even when the child does not initiate the discussion, an adult may want to question the child if there is a possibility that the child is being abused or neglected. For example, a nurse may want to ask how a child received some suspicious or ambiguous injuries, a schoolteacher may want to ask why a child's physical condition or school performance has suddenly deteriorated, or a neighbor may want to ask why a child is not in school. Often, the child will tell the questioner about being maltreated. That happened in a New York case when the school nurse observed scratches and bruises about the face and neck of an eleven-year-old girl and, on further examination, discovered numerous open sores and scabbed surfaces on her buttocks, thighs, and shoulders. When asked about the cause of these injuries, the young girl said that her father repeatedly beat her.[4]

Even very young children should be questioned. Although what they say may not be sufficiently reliable for use in court, their answers may shed light on the situation or provide additional leads for exploration. The only time children should not be questioned is when there is already sufficient evidence to report and it appears that doing so may expose them to further emotional trauma or to a parent's anger or retaliation.

Children are often afraid to tell about being maltreated by their parents. Hence, the interview should be conducted in private and definitely outside the presence of the parents, as illustrated by what happened to Tammy Nelson. The Missouri hotline had received numerous reports that Tammy was "being sold by her mother to an older man for the purpose of having sex, and that Audrey Nelson, the children's mother, forced her children to watch her perform sex acts with various partners and perhaps forced them to participate." Caseworkers investigated these allegations twice over a six-month period. Unfortunately, their investigation "basically consisted of a brief interview of the children, possibly within hearing distance of Audrey. The children, as well as Audrey, denied the allegations of the callers," but they may have done so because they were interviewed in the presence of the abuser. As the federal appeals court noted: "The investigators seem not to have interviewed the children individually or apart from their mother, nor did they interview possible witnesses or request physical examinations for the children."[5]

Arrange the timing and location of the interview to make the child feel as comfortable as the circumstances permit. Whether or not sexual abuse is the issue, it is generally advisable to have someone of the same sex interview older children, or at least be present during the interview.

Try not to frighten or traumatize the child, who may already feel hurt, fearful, or apprehensive. Begin the interview with generalized, nonjudgmental, and open-ended questions. Avoid questions that can

Chart 6–1 **Guidelines for Interviewing Children**[6]

Do:

- Make sure the interviewer is someone the child trusts.
- Conduct the interview in private.
- Sit next to the child, not across a table or desk.
- Ask the child to clarify words/terms that you do not understand.
- Be supportive; the child is likely to be frightened about telling "family secrets."
- Stress that anything that happened was not the child's fault.
- Tell the child if any future action will be required.
- Be truthful; do not make promises that you cannot keep.

Do Not:

- Allow the child to feel "in trouble" or "at fault."
- Criticize the child's choice of words or language.
- Probe or press for answers that the child seems unwilling to give.
- Suggest answers to the child.
- Display shock or disapproval of the parents, the child, or the situation.
- Force the child to remove clothing.
- Conduct the interview with a group of interviewers.
- Leave the child alone with a stranger.

---

be answered by a simple "yes" or "no." Leila Whiting, formerly the director of a child abuse project for the National Association of Social Workers, recommends such questions and comments as these: "Can you tell me what happened?" "I know that when kids get hurt, there is usually something upsetting going on at home," or "I can see that you are upset and I am interested in hearing about it."[7] Permit the child to answer questions in his or her own words. Listen carefully to what the child says; express concern, not shock or disbelief. Try to get a clear idea of what is troubling the youngster, but do not press for every detail. (Chart 6–1 contains some useful guidelines for interviewing children.)

"Anatomically explicit" dolls, which used to be called "anatomically correct" until people took a good look at the relative proportions of their various parts, are too misleading to be used for diagnostic purposes. They should be used only as a treatment tool and then only by trained professionals after a diagnosis of sexual abuse has been made.

Report any child's description of being abused or neglected unless there is a specific reason for disbelieving it. A child's otherwise credible statements should not be disregarded simply because of the child's age. "When a child readily indicates that a particular adult hurt him, it is almost always true," according to Dr. Barton Schmitt.[8] Making the report does not mean that you are vouching for the accuracy of the child's statements, merely that the statements are of sufficient credibility to justify an investigation.

There is always the danger that a child's description of being maltreated is untrue. If there is no independent corroboration of the child's statements, this possibility should be kept in mind before you make a report, especially if the child retracts the statement. Since these issues are most serious in cases of possible sexual abuse when there may be no physical evidence, they are discussed in Chapter 8.

Conversely, the child may deny being maltreated. Once again, the child's statements must be assessed within the context of the overall situation. For example, a child's description of an accident or a fight with a playmate that is consistent with the injuries sustained may be a strong reason for deciding not to report. But a child's explanation that is inconsistent with the injuries sustained may be additional evidence of abuse. Although some further probing may be appropriate, the child should not be pressed too hard. The child is unlikely to change his or her story, and further questioning may put the child at risk. (The child may tell his or her parents about the questioning, which could trigger another abusive episode.) Unless someone else can provide a satisfactory explanation, a report should be made.

Whether or not it is retracted, the child's description of being abused or neglected may be admissible in a subsequent court action. It certainly will help guide the child protective agency's investigation. Therefore, the child's statement and description of the conditions under which it was given should be written down and kept on file. (If a tape recorder is available, use it unless doing so will disturb the child.) Because the reliability of the child's statement may subsequently be challenged, any evidence that tends to confirm it should also be carefully recorded.

If the interview reveals sufficient information on which to make a report, you should tell older children what you will do on their behalf and what will happen to them. The best guide to what younger children should be told is the specific questions they ask. It is important to reassure children of all ages that they are not to blame for their parents' maltreatment or for the actions taken by the authorities against their parents.

THE CHILD'S CONDITION

The child's body, tragically, often provides the most telling evidence of physical abuse. For children who are too young or too frightened to tell what happened to them, unsatisfactorily explained injuries (or other physical or emotional conditions) may be the only way to discover that they have been maltreated and the only way to prove it, should court action be necessary. That these injuries are circumstantial evidence does not make them a less important basis for a report. In fact, given the problems of bias, poor perception, and faulty memory that can distort the observations of eyewitnesses, circumstantial evidence may be more trustworthy than direct evidence.

First applied in a 1965 case from Brooklyn, New York, the legal doctrine of *res ipsa loquitur* (a latin phrase meaning "the thing speaks for itself") permits an inference of abuse or neglect to be drawn from the child's age and injuries, since "in the ordinary course of things [that] does not happen if the parent who has the responsibility and control of an infant is protective and non-abusive." Although there apparently was no direct evidence to connect the one-month-old child's injuries to the parents, the judge held that "without satisfactory explanation I would be constrained to make a finding of fact of neglect on the part of a parent or parents."[9] This approach has been endorsed by many other courts and has been statutorily codified in many states. Illinois law, for example, provides that

> proof of injuries sustained by a child or of the condition of a child of such a nature as would ordinarily not be sustained or exist except by reason of the acts or omissions of the parent or other person responsible for the care of such child shall be *prima facie* evidence of child abuse or neglect, as the case may be.[10]

Although the use of circumstantial evidence is most commonly associated with the battered child syndrome, it is not limited to situations of suspected physical abuse. It applies with equal validity to any physical or emotional condition of the child that is "of such a nature as would ordinarily not be sustained or exist except by reason of the acts or omissions of the parent." As Chart 7–2 indicates, many injuries are determined to be inflicted because of a combination of their nature and location (for example, bruises on the buttocks and lower back or on the genitals and inner thighs, slap marks on the cheeks, pinch marks on the ear lobes, and choke marks on the neck).

The parent is held responsible for the child's condition on the assumption that the child was in the parent's custody at the relevant time.[11] However, you need not prove that the child was in the parents' immediate custody at the precise time of the injury. Most injuries cannot be dated with that degree of precision, and specific proof of the parents' hourly comings and goings is generally not available. (See Chart 13–3.) Hence, it is only necessary that the injuries were sustained or the condition arose during a general period when the child was in the parents' custody. If the parents cannot convince you that the child was actually in someone else's custody at the time in question, make a report.

If only one parent had custody of the child at the relevant time, a report should be made against only that parent. In many cases, however, you may not know (or are unable to prove) which parent abused the child, but not knowing should not prevent you from reporting. If both parents had general custody of the child during the relevant time, the injuries amount to circumstantial evidence against each of them.[12] (This often leads one parent to describe how the other inflicted the child's injuries.) Similarly, when the parents are divorced or separated and they have joint custody or one parent has custody and the other visitation, a report based on the circumstantial evidence of the injuries should be made, so that the child protective agency can determine who is responsible.

For most potential reporters, the opportunity to observe a child's body is limited to those portions that are not covered by clothing. Signs of obvious neglect—a severely dirty or smelly body or grossly inadequate clothes, for example—will be apparent. But the signs of abuse—bruises and other marks—may be hidden. This is one reason why, even on the hottest days, some abusive parents dress their children in long-sleeve shirts and long pants.

Sufficiently serious injuries on the exposed portions of the child's body should, of course, be reported if they are not satisfactorily explained. Less serious injuries, though, should not be reported without more evidence that suggests maltreatment. Thus, you may want to ask the child whether there are additional injuries on other parts of his or her body and, depending on the circumstances, you may want to examine the child's body.

Physical examinations should be conducted in a way that minimizes the inherent emotional trauma to the child. They should be performed in private (with only necessary persons present) and with great concern for the child's sensibilities. The extent of the examination depends on your relationship to the child, the child's age, whether you are the same sex as the child, and the opportunity for privacy. As a general rule, except for very young children, intimate examinations should be performed by medical personnel.

THE PARENTS' STATEMENTS

The parents are the most important potential source of additional information, of course. Most parental statements are made in response to questions about a child's condition or behavior. The circumstances under which parents should be interviewed and how the interview should be conducted are discussed in Chapter 13.

In addition, many parents, deeply fearful of harming their children, turn for help to others—to friends, to relatives, to clergy, and to helping professionals—when they feel things slipping beyond their control. As efforts to encourage parental self-help increase, more parents can be expected to seek counseling and assistance from others.

A parent's description of abusive or neglectful behavior, unless long past, should be reported. Although doing so "may smack uncomfortably of betrayal of a confidence when the parent has confessed his fault only because he was desperately seeking help for the child or psychotherapy for himself,"[13] the primary issue is the protection of an endangered child. If the person to whom the parent confides is covered by a reporting mandate, as are most helping professionals, there really is no choice: Failure to report opens the professional to criminal prosecution and a civil lawsuit.

It is not necessary that the parent actually admit to having abused a child for a report to be made. First, a parent's statements may be a ground for a report because they provide circumstantial proof of abuse. Farfetched explanations of suspicious injuries, explanations that are at variance with clinical findings, and other inappropriate behavior can establish reasonable cause to suspect that a child was maltreated.

Second, certain parental statements, behavior, and general demeanor may suggest that a parent is suffering from *severe* mental disabilities that, as described in Chapter 12, make future abuse or neglect likely. They, too, should be reported. Parental threats to kill or otherwise harm a child are the most extreme example of such evidence.

Accounts of the maltreatment of a child from one parent or other family members should be reported. Since the maltreatment of most children occurs at home, eyewitnesses are usually family members. They are an important source of reports, although the statements of disgruntled spouses or other relatives with a possible interest in gaining (or shifting) custody of the child must be weighed with great care. As New York Judge Nanette Dembitz explained: "One parent may accuse the other to deflect blame from himself; or the accusation of child abuse may be used vindictively in a deteriorated relationship, like the sometimes exaggerated or false complaints by one parent against the other in a child-custody case."[14]

PRIOR REPORTS

Theoretically, any person who is required to report would find information about prior reports of suspected maltreatment helpful in reaching a decision. But child abuse records contain information about the most private aspects of personal and family life. Whether or not the information is true, its improper disclosure can violate the sensibilities of all those involved and can be deeply stigmatizing. If such a large number of strangers have access to records, guarding against unauthorized disclosure of information is all but impossible. More important, such enormous and widespread access to personal and family data unreasonably compromises the privacy of the children and families involved. Some professionals also see a danger that many of those who receive such information may not know how to evaluate it intelligently; a potential reporter's decision, for example, may be inordinately influenced by the presence or absence of a prior record.

All states, therefore, have laws that make child protective information and records confidential. Most of these laws make unauthorized disclosure a crime; some also impose civil liability for unauthorized disclosures.

Confidentiality, however, is not absolute. The information in records is available to those who make critical child protective decisions. Hence, most states have established limited exceptions to the confidentiality for child protective workers, law enforcement officials, physicians, foster care or treatment agencies, parents or guardians, courts, grand juries, relevant state officials, and researchers.[15]

Ironically, agencies seem to use confidentiality as much to hide their own malfunctioning as to protect the privacy of individuals. Clients and advocacy groups are frequently denied access to case records on the false ground of confidentiality—even when the records are sought for a valid purpose. In one case, a court order was needed for clients to gain access to records that, they claimed, would prove a pattern of religious and racial discrimination by foster care agencies.[16] Similarly, an Arizona foster care agency sought to deny a mother access to the names of the other children placed in a foster home. The foster father had murdered her daughter and injured her son. Because this information would help the mother find out whether the father had previously abused other children placed in his care, the appellate court ordered the agency to provide it.[17]

Confidentiality is also used against workers who seek to expose the weaknesses of their agencies. In 1981, administrative disciplinary proceedings were initiated against Irwin Levin, a New York City caseworker who released case records to the press. He claimed that he wanted to prove that many child abuse deaths "stemmed from . . . staff incompetence and irresponsibility in handling clients."[18] Unfortunately, in doing so, he apparently released information that identified clients. The agency first sought to fire Levin. In a compromise agreement, Levin agreed to a demotion and reduction in salary. It took *three years*, a harshly critical report from the agency's inspector general, and personal intervention by the mayor, before Levin was vindicated and reinstated with back pay.

OTHER SOURCES

The foregoing are the primary sources of information concerning the possible maltreatment of a child. Other sources, though not in themselves grounds for a report, can assist in the assessment of ambiguous situations. These supplemental sources, which include previous questionable injuries to the child, the family's prior history, home conditions, and the behavior of the child or parents, are discussed as they arise in the next six chapters.

7

Physical Abuse

R eporting physical abuse is easy when there is obvious evidence that the parents inflicted serious physical injury on a child. But it is often hard to decide what to do when the actual injury is not "serious," especially if the parents claim that they were exercising their right to reasonable corporal punishment or when there is no direct evidence to connect the parents to the child's condition, so that a report must be based on circumstantial evidence.

Children who have already been seriously injured are in clear danger of further maltreatment, as are their siblings. However—and this is the key to understanding when to report—the parents' conduct need not have already seriously injured the child for it to be considered "abusive" or "neglectful" and for it to be the grounds for a report. As was explained in Chapter 3, a report should be made if the parent did something that was *capable of causing serious injury.*

"REASONABLE" CORPORAL PUNISHMENT

All states recognize the right of parents to discipline their children as long as the punishment is "reasonable" or not "excessive."[1] As former New York Family Court Judge Nanette Dembitz explained: "Physical discipline is considered part of the parents' right and duty to nurture his child."[2] Such beliefs run deep in our culture; the Bible admonishes: "He that spareth the rod hateth his son, but he that loveth him chasteneth him betimes."[3]

"Reasonable" corporal punishment should not be reported. Even though a growing number of people believe that all forms of corporal punishment, no matter how moderate, are emotionally harmful to children and should be considered maltreatment, parents have a legal right to use reasonable force in disciplining their children. Only a parent who has overstepped this legal right should be considered abusive.

To put it bluntly, parents are allowed to spank their children's bottom with their hands. In most jurisdictions, a hairbrush and even a belt (not the end with the buckle) can be used as long as no serious welts or cuts result.

The punishment must be "reasonable," however. By definition, a parent who intentionally engages in "seriously harmful behavior" is not being "reasonable." A child's misbehavior, no matter how egregious, *never justifies conduct whose reasonably foreseeable consequence was or could have been the child's serious physical injury.* This includes any punishment that results in a broken bone, eye damage, severe welts, bleeding, or any other injury that requires medical treatment.

Corporal punishment of infants is a special concern. Parents may not slap infants on the face (their skulls and brain tissue are not strong enough to sustain the blow) and doing so reflects a seriously distorted sense that the child is willfully misbehaving. In fact, a forceful assault to the head of a child of any age is so dangerous that it is usually considered "unreasonable." So is punching, in general, pulling out hair, burning the child, throwing a child, and assaulting the child's genitals.

Religious beliefs and cultural practices do not justify or excuse severe corporal punishment. As one New York case explained, the criminal law defense of reasonable corporal punishment is "in no way intended to permit the cruel beating of children, nor were the freedoms guaranteed to us by the First Amendment intended to embrace such behavior in the name of religion."[4]

On the other hand, the parent's intent can be crucial. An injury caused by a true accident, that is, a one-time injury that was an *unforeseeable* consequence of otherwise reasonable corporal punishment, is not maltreatment. Likewise, the injury may have been the result of a true accident, caused, perhaps, by horsing around. Of course, you may not be able to gauge the parent's true intent and if you have any real question, you should make a report. It will be up to the child protective agency to determine what happened.

Physical punishments that do not create a danger of serious physical injury are nevertheless reportable if they amount to emotional abuse. For example, in one widely cited case, a Syracuse, New York, judge held that twenty-six marks on the back of a seven-year-old boy with emotional difficulties, marks that were visible three days after the beating was administered, were evidence of immoderate and unreasonable corporal punishment. The court also held that "punishment administered to an 11-year-old boy who is undergoing [emotional] therapy; . . . . punish-

---

Chart 7–1 **Is the Punishment Reasonable?**

Punishment whose reasonably foreseeable consequence was or could have been the child's serious physical injury is "unreasonable" and should be reported. In less severe cases, the following factors are used to decide whether corporal punishment was "reasonable":

- Was the purpose of the punishment to preserve discipline or to train or educate the child? Or was the punishment primarily for the parent's gratification or the result of the parent's uncontrolled rage?
- Did the child have the capacity to understand or appreciate the corrective purpose of the discipline? (Very young children and mentally disabled children cannot.)
- Was the punishment appropriate to the child's misbehavior? (However, no matter how serious a child's misbehavior, extremely hurtful or injurious punishment is never justified.)
- Was a less severe but equally effective punishment available?
- Was the punishment unnecessarily degrading, brutal, or beastly in character or protracted beyond the child's power to endure?
- If physical force was used, was it recklessly applied? (Force directed toward a safe part of the body, such as the buttocks, ordinarily is much more reasonable than is force directed toward vulnerable organs, such as the head or genitals.)

---

ment which requires him to hold his ankles and keep his knees straight for variable lengths of time; punishment which causes him to scream [and to vomit], is a punishment beyond the child's endurance and a punishment beyond his capacity to understand as correction . . . [and] a degrading punishment as well."[5]

To assess such cases, you should consider a number of factors, including the child's age and physical and mental condition, the child's misconduct on the particular occasion and in the past, the parents' purpose, the kind and frequency of punishment inflicted, the degree of harm done to the child, and the type and location of the injuries.[6] Chart 7–1 transforms these factors into questions to guide your decision making. There are many borderline cases in which people will disagree about whether a particular punishment crossed the line between reasonable discipline and maltreatment, but in most cases, the application of the factors presented in Chart 7–1 will help you decide. (The degree to which emotional punishment is permitted is discussed in Chapter 11.)

"SUSPICIOUS" INJURIES

"Suspicious" injuries suggesting physical abuse should be reported. Injuries that "speak for themselves" are one of the most important means of detecting child abuse. If the parents cannot satisfactorily explain what happened, you should make a report.

Almost any traumatic injury could be the result of a parental assault, but most are not. Childhood is a time of bumping, banging, and falling down. At some time or other, most children get cut or bruised. Indeed, physical injuries, some minor and some not so minor, are signs of the physical activity, the carefree exuberance, and the rapid growth and associated awkwardness that mark a normal childhood. Thus, most traumatic injuries cannot be the basis of a report—unless the statements of the parents, the child, or other witnesses indicate that the child was assaulted.

Some traumatic injuries, though, have telltale characteristics that distinguish them from the expected injuries of childhood and that strongly suggest physical abuse. These injuries are so distinctively associated with physical assaults that they are, by themselves, independent evidence of child abuse. If not satisfactorily explained by the parents (as described in Chapter 13), these apparently inflicted injuries, called "suspicious" injuries, should be reported to the authorities. No further evidence of parental culpability is needed.

This concept of "suspicious" injuries (what the medical profession calls "pathognomonic" injuries) is at the core of the battered child syndrome. First coined in 1962 by Dr. C. Henry Kempe and his associates, the battered child syndrome is now an accepted medical diagnosis in cases in which a child (generally under age three) exhibits "evidence of fracture of any bone, subdural hematoma, failure to thrive, soft tissue swelling or skin bruising, in any child who dies suddenly, or where the degree and type of injury is at variance with the history given regarding the occurrence of the trauma."[7] Many statutes[8] and court decisions[9] expressly approve the use of the battered child syndrome to establish parental culpability, even in *criminal prosecutions.*[10] The diagnostic significance of suspicious injuries is so widely accepted that no specific legislation is needed for the syndrome to be used in deciding to report child abuse.

The battered child syndrome, however, is merely one example of the types of circumstantial evidence that raise a reasonable suspicion of abuse. You should make a report whenever the child has even one suspicious injury, that is, an injury that, to quote a common statutory provision, "would ordinarily not be sustained or exist except by reason of the acts or omissions of the parent."[11] It is not necessary for there to be a pattern of injuries or for the child to be diagnosed as being a battered child—with one major proviso.

Most minor childhood injuries, even if apparently inflicted, should not be reported. To be deemed suspicious, an apparently inflicted injury must suggest sufficiently harmful parental behavior to amount to child abuse.[12] Laws requiring reports of child abuse are limited to situations of serious danger to children, as described in Chapter 3. This does not mean that only "serious" or life-threatening injuries are suspicious. But for a minor injury to be deemed suspicious and, therefore, to be the basis of a report, it must suggest either (1) "unreasonable" corporal punishment or (2) an assault that caused or was capable of causing serious injury (what this book calls "seriously harmful" parental behavior).

A number of factors, either individually or in combination, lead to the conclusion that an injury is suspicious:

- *The child's level of development.* It takes a certain level of physical development to injure oneself. For example, it is next to impossible for a pretoddler to fracture a femur (upper thigh). In fact, given the limited ability of infants to move about and to harm themselves, *any* traumatic injury and any poisoning of pretoddlers is considered suspicious.

- *The shape of the injury.* Many assaults are inflicted by identifiable objects. The child's body often shows the outline of a belt buckle, human teeth, a hand, a coat hanger, or a hot iron. Similarly, the shape of some immersion burns suggest intentional dunking.

- *The location of the injury.* When children fall or bang into things, they tend to injure their chins, foreheads, hands, elbows, knees, and shins. The same is not true for injuries to the thighs, upper arms, genital and rectal areas, buttocks, and the back of the legs or torso. Only rarely are such injuries caused by anything other than a physical assault. Similarly, "45 percent of inflicted burns involve the perineum or buttocks—sites which are most always chosen as punishment for enuresis [bed-wetting] or toilet-training resistance."[13]

- *The degree of force needed to produce the injury.* Children do not injure easily. It takes substantial force to cause a bruise that remains visible for more than a few hours. Even more force is needed to break a young bone or to cause serious abdominal injuries.

- *The type of injury.* It is almost impossible for some injuries to be self-inflicted. Epiphyseal-metaphyseal (corner or joint) fractures, for example, are caused by the violent shaking of a child or by the violent pulling, jerking, or twisting of one of the long bones. The origin of choke marks on the child's neck is equally clear.

- *The number of old and new injuries.* Although physical abuse can be a one-time, isolated event, it is often a steadily escalating pattern of physically assaultive behavior.[14] Multiple injuries on various parts of the body that are unlikely to be hurt in a fall and that are in various stages of healing are not signs of an accident-prone child. They are signs of child abuse. However, the absence of prior injuries should not be taken as conclusive evidence that the child is not abused. The injuries may have healed, leaving no trace, or they may be undiscovered. The absence of prior injuries is but one factor to be weighed in deciding whether a child's present injuries are suspicious.

Chart 7–2 lists some of the most frequently observed suspicious injuries. The traumatic injuries described in the chart are considered "suspicious" because they are almost always caused by physical assaults against the child that amounted to unreasonable corporal punishment or that caused (or were capable of causing) serious injury. Unexplained, they are sufficient grounds for a report (unless informed, expert opinion has determined that a differential diagnosis, also described in the chart, establishes an alternate cause for them). The chart, as well as the foregoing discussion, is necessarily an abbreviation of a substantial body of literature. Readers (especially medical professionals) who wish more detailed information about suspicious injuries should refer to the many fine treatments of the subject.[15]

Identifying—and obtaining—an object or implement that matches the size and shape of the child's injuries can fortify the determination that they are suspicious. Such "real" evidence can also be decisive in a possible court hearing. And, as described in Chapter 6, the child's statements, even when not a clear description of abuse, can also help assess ambiguous injuries.

Lay persons can identify many suspicious injuries. Some injuries, such as marks from a belt buckle, are obviously inflicted; that they would not ordinarily have been sustained but for the acts or omissions

(continued on page 81)

Chart 7–2 **Frequently Observed "Suspicious" Injuries**

The following are examples of traumatic injuries that are not ordinarily sustained by children except by reason of unreasonable corporal punishment or other acts of child abuse. (Some require medical diagnosis, but most do not.) Unless satisfactorily explained, they are, in themselves, sufficient reason to report if the child was in the parent's general custody during the relevant time.

Injuries to Pretoddlers
- Any traumatic injury, from a bruise to a broken bone.

Bruises, Welts, Lacerations, and Scars That Last at Least Forty-eight Hours
- Distinctively shaped injuries, suggesting the object used to inflict them, such as a belt buckle; a looped wire or cord; a coat hanger; scissors; a spatula or other cooking utensil; or a whip, rope or strap.
- Pressure bruises on the neck that resemble finger tips, whole fingers, and entire hands, suggesting that the child was choked, and similar bruises on the torso, shoulders, or around the elbows or knees, suggesting that an intense grip was used to throw or shake the child (often associated with subdural hematoma and retinal damage).
- Human bite marks (identified as paired crescent-shaped bruises, often showing individual tooth marks, and distinguished from marks from animal bites, which have a deeper, narrower, often incisive character).
- Extensive pinch marks (identified as small, crescent-shaped bruises facing each other).
- Circumferential tie marks around the ankles, wrists, or waist, suggesting that the child was bound by a rope, cord, or dog leash.
- Tattoos or other forms of mutilation.
- Puncture wounds that resemble the end of a fork, comb, or other distinctive object.
- Injuries to areas that are unlikely to be traumatized in a fall, such as the thighs, upper arms, genital and rectal areas, buttocks, and the back of the legs or torso.
- Clustered injuries, suggesting repeated traumas to a selected site (often the buttocks).
- Injuries on several different body planes, suggesting that the child was hit from several different directions.
- Multiple, apparently inflicted injuries in different stages of healing, suggesting repeated beatings (for bruises, identified by the different coloring of each bruise or group of bruises).

Chart 7–2 **Frequently Observed "Suspicious" Injuries (*continued*)**

EXCLUDED: Minor injuries caused by reasonable corporal punishment and more serious injuries that are the unintended—and unforeseeable—consequence of otherwise reasonable corporal punishment.

Differential Diagnosis

- Birthmarks, particularly "Mongolian spots," should not be mistaken for bruises. Mongolian spots are present at birth and generally last until the child is two or three years old. These spots are grayish blue, do not change color with time, and are commonly located on the buttocks and back. The incidence of discoloration varies among racial groups, with rates as high as 90 percent for some racial minorities.
- Erythema—abnormal redness of the skin caused by capillary congestion (or inflammation).
- Petechiae (pinpoint hemorrhages) or purpuric spots (which are larger) on the skin or mucous membranes caused by infectious diseases, such as typhus or typhoid.
- Bleeding disorders, such as hemophilia and von Willebrand's disease, which may make the child susceptible to easy bruising.

Burns

- Distinctively shaped dry or "contact" burns, suggesting the object used to inflict them, such as a heated wire, an iron, a space heater or radiator, or a hot plate.
- Flame burns, especially on the ends of fingers or toes, suggesting that a match or candle was held to them.
- Small, circular lesions, especially on the palms, soles, abdomen, neck, buttocks, or genitals, suggesting that the child was burned with a cigarette, cigar, match tip, or incense punk.
- Splash burns on the child's back, suggesting that, rather than an accidental spill, the burns were caused by someone throwing the hot liquid as the child sought to escape.
- Immersion burns that are glovelike on the hands; socklike on the feet; and doughnut shaped around the buttocks, perineum, or genital, suggesting that part of the body was intentionally dipped—and perhaps held—in hot water. Inflicted burns are distinguished from accidental burns from hot bath water by (1) the severity of the burn, suggesting that the child was held in the water, and (2) a distinct boundary line between burned and unburned areas and the absence of splash marks, suggesting that the child was tightly gripped and carefully lowered into the hot liquid.

(*continued on next page*)

Chart 7-2 **Frequently Observed "Suspicious" Injuries (*continued*)**

NOTE: Second-degree immersion burns can be produced by hot tap water in fewer than 5 seconds.

- Multiple burns, in different stages of healing, suggesting repeated burnings (indicated by new burns, blisters, ulcers, and old pigmented scars).

Differential Diagnosis

- For small, circular burns—bullous impetigo, which is characterized by lesions of various sizes; that occur in groups; that have pussy crust; and that increase in number while the child is in the hospital; in rare cases, the lesions may be mosquito bites the child has scratched.
- For burns from hot water—scalded-skin syndrome or toxic epidermal necrosis, caused by staphylococcus aureus and characterized by generalized red and tender skin and unexplained blebs at such scattered sites that it would be nearly impossible to have inflicted them with hot water; they continue to appear after hospitalization.

Mouth and Facial Injuries

- Marks, bruises, or lacerations at the corners of the mouth, suggesting that the child has been gagged.
- Torn or lacerated frenula (the membrane connecting the gum and lips), suggesting a severe pulling or twisting of the lips or forced feeding.
- Swollen lips, extensively broken or chipped teeth, and lacerated or bruised gums or frenula, suggesting repeated blows to the mouth or forced feeding.
- Ulcers or caustic burns in the mouth, suggesting that the child was fed lye, cleaning fluid, or other caustic substances.
- Two black eyes without accompanying injury to the nose (virtually impossible to sustain in a fall or other accident unless there is an injury to another part of the head, which may or may not appear to be inflicted).
- Retinal hemorrhages and detachments, when accompanied by other evidence of severe shaking (such as subdural hematomas; pressure bruises or grab marks on the torso, shoulder, or around the legs or upper arms; or both).

Head Injuries

- Bald patches on the scalp apparently caused by severe hair pulling, often accompanied by surface bleeding or subsurface hemorrhaging or swelling.
- Skull fractures apparently caused by a blow rather than a fall (a blow is suggested by a coup injury, that is, an injury on the same side of the brain as the head trauma, indicating a stationary head; a fall is suggested by a contracoup injury, that is, an injury on the opposite side of the brain

Chart 7–2 **Frequently Observed "Suspicious" Injuries (*continued*)**

as the head trauma, indicating a moving head). However, children often fall when they are hit, so a skull fracture that is suggestive of a fall does not rule out child abuse.

- Skull fractures with a shattered eggshell pattern, suggesting that the child's head struck a hard surface with an extremely forceful impact, for example, if the child was thrown to the floor or against a wall.
- Subdural hematomas (bleeding between the brain and the skull), whether or not accompanied by visible trauma to the head, suggesting that the child was struck on the head or severely shaken.

Bone Injuries

- Spiral, transverse, or other injuries to arm and leg bones that suggest twisting or pulling, and that younger children are unlikely to inflict on themselves. However, on older children, spiral injuries to the arms and legs are not, in themselves, suggestive of abuse. (Other evidence, though, may lead to the conclusion that they are inflicted injuries on which a report of abuse may be based.)
- Metaphyseal or corner fractures of long bones (a kind of splintering at the end of the bone), epiphyseal separations (a separation of the growth center at the end of the bone from the rest of the shaft), and periosteal elevations (a detachment of the periosteum from the shaft of the bone, with associated hemorrhaging), suggesting that the child was violently shaken or that the long bones were pulled, jerked, or twisted.
- Rib fractures, especially if accompanied by pressure bruises (shaped like fingers or hands) on the rib cage, suggesting that the child was squeezed so hard that the ribs broke.
- Multiple fractures, in different stages of healing, suggesting repeated assaults (identified by a complete bone survey).

CAVEAT: Certain diseases in which the bones become fragile can cause otherwise suspicious fractures.

Abdominal Injuries

- Any traumatic injury to internal organs, such as the spleen, liver, or intestines (whether or not accompanied by external signs of trauma), suggesting that the child was kicked, punched, or poked with extreme force.

NOTE: Nonmedical personnel should suspect traumatic abdominal injuries when they note swelling, tenderness, or black and blue marks on the abdomen or constant vomiting with no apparent reason. Abdominal injuries are often life-threatening. Even apparently minor black and blue marks on the abdomen,

(continued on next page)

Chart 7–2 **Frequently Observed "Suspicious" Injuries (*continued*)**

which could be caused by harsh finger poking, may signal severe injuries.
Immediate medical attention should be sought.

Starvation

- Severe malnutrition or dehydration, while usually signs of neglect, sometimes suggest the intentional withholding of food and water.

Ingested Substances

- Any poisoning, although usually the result of negligence or a true accident,
  may be intentional, especially if the child is less than one year.
- Any ingestion of sedatives, tranquilizers, narcotics, or other drugs, especially
  if the child is young and has a sleep problem that bothers the parents
  (suggesting that the drugs were used to quiet a restless or crying baby).
- The ingestion of excessive amounts of salt or diuretics that, by raising the
  level of salt in the blood, may cause seizures and brain damage.

NOTE: Unintentional poisoning should be reported if there is reason to suspect
that the parents were careless or negligent in keeping the substance out of the
child's reach.

Repeated Injuries

- A history of repeated, traumatic injuries (a fracture today, a burn the month
  before, a laceration before that, and so forth), suggesting an ongoing pattern
  of physical abuse.

CAVEAT: The absence of prior injuries or the failure to discover them is not
conclusive evidence that the child is not abused.

Untreated Injuries

- Severe injuries that are untreated or signs of delays in seeking treatment,
  such as infected burns, suggesting that the parents are indifferent to or do
  not want others to know about the child's condition.

Death

- Any death from traumatic injuries or poisoning.
- Any other unexplained death, whether there are visible signs of trauma or
  other wrongdoing.

CAVEAT: Before you report an unexplained death of a child under one year,
you must consider the diagnosis of sudden infant death syndrome.

NOTE: The reporting of suspicious child fatalities is important because there
may be other children at home, the parents may have another child sometime
in the future, and a criminal prosecution may be appropriate.

Illustration 7–1 **Apparently Inflicted Surface Injuries**

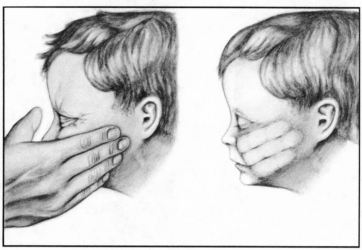

Characteristic bruise resulting from forceful slap

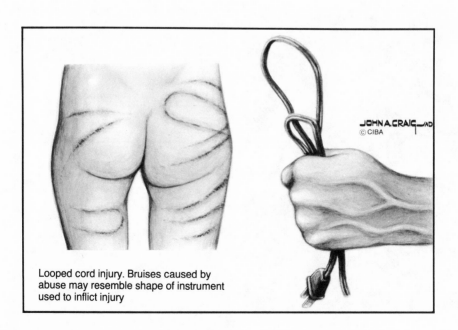

Looped cord injury. Bruises caused by abuse may resemble shape of instrument used to inflict injury

Illustration 7–2 Apparently Inflicted Twisting Bone Fractures

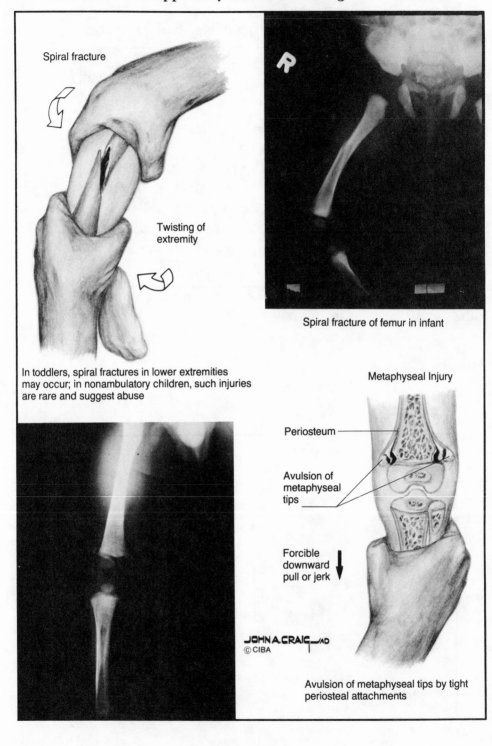

Spiral fracture

Twisting of extremity

In toddlers, spiral fractures in lower extremities may occur; in nonambulatory children, such injuries are rare and suggest abuse

Spiral fracture of femur in infant

Metaphyseal Injury

Periosteum

Avulsion of metaphyseal tips

Forcible downward pull or jerk

JOHN A. CRAIG—AD
© CIBA

Avulsion of metaphyseal tips by tight periosteal attachments

Illustration 7–3 **Apparently Inflicted Restraint Injuries**

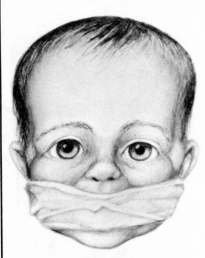

Child may be gagged as punishment
or to stop persistent crying

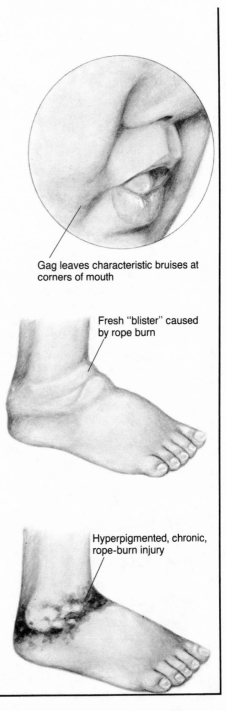

Gag leaves characteristic bruises at
corners of mouth

Fresh "blister" caused
by rope burn

JOHN A. CRAIG_AD
© CIBA

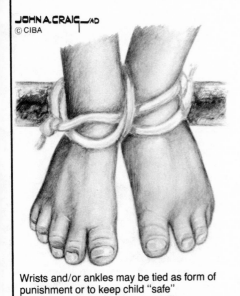

Wrists and/or ankles may be tied as form of
punishment or to keep child "safe"

Hyperpigmented, chronic,
rope-burn injury

Illustration 7–4 **Apparently Inflicted Burn Injuries**

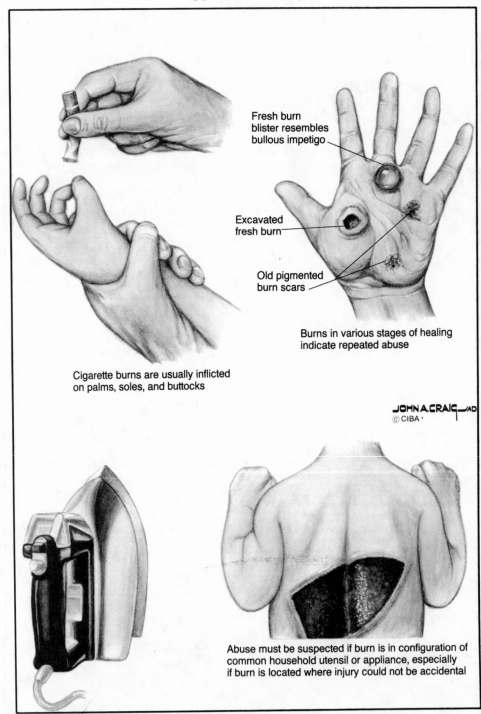

Fresh burn blister resembles bullous impetigo

Excavated fresh burn

Old pigmented burn scars

Burns in various stages of healing indicate repeated abuse

Cigarette burns are usually inflicted on palms, soles, and buttocks

JOHN A. CRAIG AD
© CIBA

Abuse must be suspected if burn is in configuration of common household utensil or appliance, especially if burn is located where injury could not be accidental

Illustration 7–5 **Apparently Inflicted Immersion Burns**

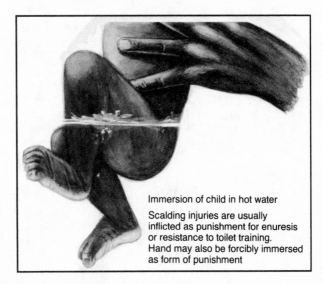

Immersion of child in hot water

Scalding injuries are usually
inflicted as punishment for enuresis
or resistance to toilet training.
Hand may also be forcibly immersed
as form of punishment

Scalding injury to feet, perineum,
and buttocks; burns correspond to
child's posture on "dunking"

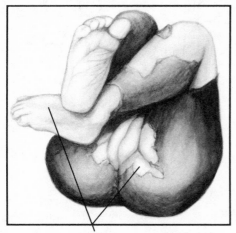

Fresh second- and third-degree
burns on feet and perineum

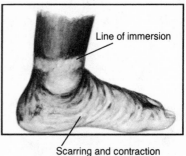

Line of immersion

Scarring and contraction
of healed burn

of the parents is a matter of "common knowledge."[16] The inflicted origin
of other injuries, though, can be established only by an expert's diagnosis
(usually made by a physician or specially qualified nurse, social worker,
or investigator.)[17] That is why Chart 7–2 uses so many technical, medical
terms.

Experts often hesitate to report because they cannot determine *to a*

Illustration 7–6 **Location of Injuries**

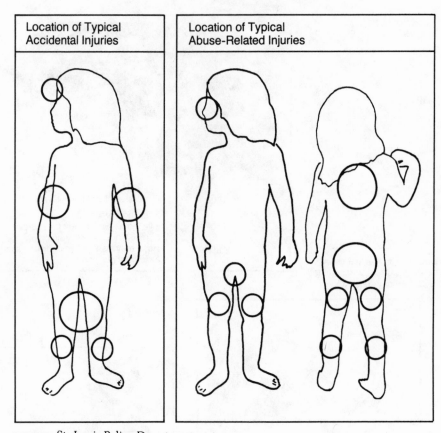

Location of Typical Accidental Injuries	Location of Typical Abuse-Related Injuries

SOURCE: St. Louis Police Department.

certainty that the child was abused. But certainty is not necessary. A report is required if there is a reason to *suspect* that the injury was inflicted. You need not exclude other possibilities; that will be the job of the child protective agency.

THE CHILD'S BEHAVIOR

The appearance and actions of many abused children differ little from those of other children. Some children, though, react to physical abuse by suppressing or exaggerating certain aspects of their personality. This adaptive behavior may begin as early as infancy and may continue long into adulthood. Thus, as evidence that the child's injuries were inflicted, one judge cited the fact that, each time she was returned to the custody of her parents, the child developed nervous behavior, including "a pattern of abnormal nervous behavior involving nose picking, apprehension, and withdrawal, as evidenced by jerking of the head and shoulders and staring into space."[18] (The child also evidenced further unexplained injuries each time she was returned.)

"Behavioral indicators" of child abuse, therefore, have a valid place in decision making. Particularly when there is an otherwise unexplained change in behavior, these indicators provide important clues for potential reporters to pursue and crucial corroborative evidence of maltreatment.

Unfortunately, behavioral indicators tend to be misused. Unusual behavior is being reported, *on its own*, without physical or any other evidence and without statements of the child or others. Hotlines are accepting reports that "Mary is shy in class" or that "Mary is overly friendly."

This is a mistake. The lists of behavioral indicators now being circulated, standing on their own and without an accompanying full history of past and present behaviors, should not be the basis of a report. There are too many other explanations for such behavior. It is essential that this point be made. Otherwise, every shy or overfriendly child in the country will be reported.

Therefore, although not independent grounds for a report of abuse, the *extremes* of child behavior listed on Chart 7–3 can assist you in assessing ambiguous injuries and parents' explanations that are of borderline plausibility. In weighing the significance of the behaviors described in the chart, you should consider whether the behavior is extreme when viewed within the context of how other children of the same age and social situation normally behave. You should, of course, be careful to consider other explanations for the child's behavior.

Chart 7-3 **Children's Behaviors Used to Assess Ambiguous Situations**[19]

Many abused children look and act like any other children. Some, however, react to physical abuse by suppressing or exaggerating certain aspects of their own personality. This adaptive behavior may begin as early as infancy, and it may continue long into adulthood. Hence, although not independent grounds for a report of abuse, the following *extremes* of child behavior can assist in the assessment of ambiguous injuries and parental explanations of borderline plausibility.

- *Extremely fearful behavior.* Some abused children may feel in constant danger of being attacked. They may regularly and overtly display fear of their parents, for example, by pulling away in fright or by being overly compliant with their parents' wishes. Others may display fear indirectly. They may not want to go home, for example, and yet, when the parent arrives, they may instantaneously agree to leave.

  Some abused children are unusually wary of physical contact, shrinking from the touch or approach of any adult. They also may seem unduly apprehensive when other children cry, as if expecting that the child will be hit for bothering nearby adults.

- *Extremely aggressive, demanding, or rageful behavior.* Such provocative behavior may be the child's attempt to gain attention. Some abused children are so emotionally starved for adult attention that they will provoke it by any means possible, even if the attention results in punishment and physical assault. In addition, children who frequently pick fights with their playmates or disrupt other children may be imitating the behavior of their parents. Such displaced retaliation against peers may seem like a safe way to vent their anger.

- *Overly compliant or passive behavior.* Some abused children have learned that any attention from the parent may lead to a violent assault. To avoid such hurtful confrontations, these children suppress the normal childhood drives of curiosity, anger, playfulness, self-assertion, and the need to say no. They withdraw into the background as much as possible. When asked to do something, they quickly respond. These children sometimes submit to painful medical procedures without complaining or crying, suggesting that they have learned to tolerate pain or suffering.

- *Extremely dependent behavior.* Some abusive parents meet their own emotional need to feel in control by keeping their children dependent on them.

Chart 7-3 **Children's Behaviors Used to Assess Ambiguous Situations** (*continued*)

They will punish any signs of independence in the child. Hence, an abused child may evidence unusual clinging, babyish behavior long after a child in a more healthy family situation would be relatively self-reliant.

- *Role-reversal behavior.* Some abusive parents cannot meet their own emotional needs and so turn to their children for nurturance and support. In response, their children may have learned to comfort and care for them as a defense against being attacked by their frustrated or unhappy parents. These children are unusually sensitive to changes in their parents' mood, even anticipating them. In times of stress, they often will be seen hugging, stroking, and kissing their parents.

- *Indiscriminately friendly behavior.* Some abused children are so insatiably hungry for affection that they are inappropriately friendly with strangers and playmates. However, they may be unable to relate normally to either children or adults.

- *Extreme lags in development.* When children must use the energy normally directed toward growth and development to protect themselves from abusive parents, they often fall significantly behind in toilet training, motor skills, language development, and social skills. Their attention may seem to wander and they may easily become self-absorbed. Developmental lags also may be the result of emotional deprivation or organic brain damage caused by physical assaults or nutritional neglect. Conversely, children with serious physical handicaps or other disabilities are sometimes at a higher risk of being abused because they are so difficult and frustrating to care for.

- *Signs of physical neglect.* Many, but by no means all, abused children are also physically neglected by their parents. Besides suspicious injuries, these children may evidence the signs of physical nelgect; they may appear hungry or malnourished, tired or listless, dirty and unbathed, and they may have apparently unattended physical, medical, or dental problems.

CAVEAT: In weighing the significance of the behaviors described here, you should consider whether the behavior is extreme when viewed within the context of how other children of the same age and social situation normally behave. In addition, you should consider explanations for the child's behavior other than abuse.

8

Sexual Abuse

For too long, revulsion toward acts of sexual abuse prevented adults from seeing what was happening to tens of thousands of innocent children. When children came forward seeking protection, too often they were not believed; many were punished for saying such terrible things about their parents (or other adults). With greater awareness, the number of substantiated cases of sexual abuse rose tenfold, from about 13,000 in 1975 to over 130,000 in 1986.[1]

No child is too young to be sexually abused. Physical signs of sexual abuse are found even in infants. Hence, indications of sexual abuse should not be ignored or discounted simply because the child seems too young to be the object of someone's sexual desires.

Reporting suspected sexual abuse, however, raises special problems because it often must be based on ambiguous medical findings or the uncorroborated statements of very young children or of potentially biased parties (such as an estranged spouse). The severe stigma of such charges, even if later determined to be unfounded, requires added care in deciding whether to report.

BEING EXPLICIT

Most people feel uncomfortable discussing specific acts of sexual abuse. But in deciding whether to report—and in preserving evidence—it is important to be precise about what happened to the child. (See Chart 8–1.)

At its extreme, "sexual abuse" includes sexual intercourse and "deviate sexual intercourse."[2] Sexual intercourse may occur without orgasm and without complete penetration of the penis into the vagina. "Deviate sexual intercourse" includes "sodomy," or anal or oral intercourse, fellatio, cunnilingus, and anilingus. As a matter of law, most states define it as any "contact between the penis and the anus, the mouth and penis, or the mouth and the vulva."[3]

86

Chart 8–1 **Acts of Sexual Abuse**[4]

"Sexual intercourse" means

(a) any penetration, however slight, of the vagina or anal opening of one person by the penis of another person, whether or not there is the emission of semen;

(b) any sexual contact between the genitals or anal opening of one person and the mouth or tongue of another person;

(c) any intrusion by one person into the genitals or anal opening of another person, including the use of any object for this purpose, EXCEPT that, it shall not include acts intended for a valid medical purpose.

"Sexual contact" means the intentional touching of the genitals or intimate parts (including the breasts, genital area, groin, inner thighs, and buttocks) or the clothing covering them, of either the child or the perpetrator, EXCEPT that, it shall not include:

(a) acts which may reasonably be construed to be normal caretaker responsibilities, interactions with, or affection for a child; or

(b) acts intended for a valid medical purpose.

"Exhibitionism" means:

(a) the masturbation of the perpetrator's genitals in the presence of a child;

(b) the intentional exposure of the perpetrator's genitals in the presence of a child, if such exposure is for the purpose of sexual arousal or gratification, aggression, degradation, or other similar purpose;

(c) any other sexual act, intentionally perpetrated in the presence of a child, for the purpose of sexual arousal or gratification, aggression, degradation, or other similar purpose.

"Sexual exploitation" means allowing, encouraging or forcing a child to:

(a) solicit for or engage in prostitution;

(b) engage in the filming, photographing, videotaping, posing, modeling, or performing before a live audience, where such acts involve exhibition of the child's genitals or any sexual act with the child as defined above.

These acts, however, may be only the last step in a steadily worsening situation. For this reason and because of their inherent harmfulness, exhibitionism and improper sexual touching or contacts are also considered sexual abuse. They include the digital manipulation, rubbing, or penetration of the young person's genitals or intimate parts, including the fondling of the buttocks or of a female's breast.[5] (The touching of intimate parts need not be direct; it may be done through the clothing that covers them.)

Parents and other caretakers, however, often touch the private parts of children, especially younger ones, for entirely innocent reasons—to change a diaper, for example, or to give an affectionate pat on the behind. To exclude these normal parental touchings, child abuse statutes mandate reports only when the touching is for the purpose of sexual arousal or gratification (of either the adult or the child).[6]

Any parent who permits a child to be sexually exploited should be reported. Sexual exploitation is another form of reportable sexual abuse. All fifty states have special statutory provisions that prohibit the use of minors in sexually explicit performances, films, photographs, or other visual materials. California's statute is typical; it defines sexual exploitation to include

> posing or modeling alone or with others for purposes of preparing a film, photograph, negative, slide, or live performance involving sexual conduct by a minor under the age of 17 years alone or with other persons or animals, for commercial purposes, is guilty of a felony.[7]

As the foregoing suggests, the sexual conduct being protrayed need not be "legally" obscene, as courts define the term.[8]

Because these are generally criminal statutes, most, like California's, specify that the purpose of the exploitation must be commercial, but some states do not.[9] For reporting purposes, however, it does not matter whether the exploitation is commercial. You should report noncommercial exploitation as well, because it falls under the more general definition of seriously harmful behavior toward children.

To aid in the discovery of these cases, some states require reports from commercial film and photographic processors when they have reasonable cause to believe that materials submitted to them depict a minor engaged in "an act of sexual conduct."[10] But, once again, any person is legally permitted to report any form of maltreatment, including sexual exploitation.

DO CHILDREN LIE?

Most cases of sexual abuse come to light only because the child, a sibling, another family member, or a parent seeks outside help. That is how Dawn B was protected:

[Dawn B] came to [her teacher] and said "she was having problems at home. Her father was touching her and making her do things." About three weeks later, she came to the teacher again crying that the "same things are going on." The school counselor then called the child's mother and filed the child abuse complaint.[11]

Other cases are uncovered when a trusted outsider who, concerned about a child's apparent unhappiness or discomfort, tries to find out what is bothering the child.

The child's statements may be the only evidence of suspected sexual abuse, so if there is to be a report, it must be based *solely* on them. Such statements are so important that, to facilitate their use in court, states have relaxed the rules of evidence concerning corroboration, hearsay, and the testimony of very young children.[12] In one court case, the son was able to testify that he watched his father sodomize his sister.[13]

The child's statements can be used to establish any form of maltreatment, but in cases of sexual abuse, in which there are often no witnesses and only ambiguous physical indicators, the child's statements may be the only real evidence. In such cases, the central question becomes, Are the child's statements reliable?

Some experts assert that "children never lie." But contrary to such rhetoric, there is always the danger that a child's description of being maltreated is untrue. Like some adults, some children lie, exaggerate, or fantasize.

You are not expected to determine the truth of a child's statements. That is the job of the child protective agency. As a general rule, all doubts should be resolved in favor of making a report. *A child who describes being sexually abused should be reported unless there is clear reason to disbelieve the statement.*

When should you question a child's statements? Basically, there are two situations, the major difference between them being the child's age. For young children, the key issue is whether a distorted version of the incident may have been fixed in the child's mind by others who questioned the child about the possibility of abuse. Has an interested party (such as a parent in a custody dispute) or a careless interviewer (who used leading or suggestive techniques) implanted a distorted or untrue idea in the child's mind?

A real problem is created when children are interrogated with leading questions. For example, in one case, a three-year-old told an adult that some candy had fallen into her underpants. By the time a child protective worker interviewed the child, the candy in the underpants had become a candle in the vagina. It took many months to establish that her initial statement had been accurate and that the story about the candle had been the result of a sequence of misinterpretations by adults that had eventually become fixed in the child's mind.

For older children, who may know the implications of what they are saying, the primary issue is the question of motive: Is there some reason why the child, usually an adolescent, may want to be out of the home? Some older children try to escape what is, for them, an unhappy home situation by claiming to be maltreated. Thus, you may try to find out whether there has been a history of conflict between the parents and the child. A teacher or guidance counselor, for example, could review school records to see whether there are "psychological reports, behavior incidents, disciplinary reports which bear on credibility such as theft, lying, false accusations, etc., a psychiatric diagnosis with reference to fantasies, delusions, and the like."[14]

Sometimes, the child waits a long time—perhaps even years—before revealing the sexual abuse. Merely because the child has not sought help before is no reason to assume that he or she is lying. Fear, ignorance, or other factors are valid reasons for delay. Dr. Vincent Fontana described one case of

> financially comfortable parents living in a pleasant, clean house in a friendly neighborhood who are without friends. They have four teenagers who have never had visitors. One day, the oldest girl, age seventeen, went to the police and told them that she is the mother of a baby living at home and that her own father is the father of the baby; that he had been having sexual relations with her for more than four years and was now doing the same with her younger sisters. The mother, when questioned, admitted knowing about the situation for years; but had not reported it to the authorities for fear of losing her husband.[15]

You should explore the reasons for a long delay. You may ask, for example, "Why didn't you tell your mother?" But be prepared for agonizing responses like, "He threatened to kill me" or "I didn't tell my mother until I learned my father was also abusing my other three sisters."[16]

The child's retractions of an earlier statement does not necessarily mean that no report should be made. Children sometimes retract their previous description of being maltreated, whether given spontaneously or in response to questioning. There are good reasons to question the validity of such retractions, however. Some retractions result from parental coaching or threats. For example, one court described how, on "at least four instances . . . caseworkers observed bruises or welts on the child's ankles, hands and on other parts of her body. Upon questioning, the now seven-year-old child either attributed the injuries to her mother, remained silent, or remarked that 'mommy says not to tell.' "[17] Thus, it is important to know whether the parents have had access to the child.

Other children retract previous statements when, after having been placed in foster care, they decide that they want to return home to their families, friends, and accustomed environment. A manual for child protective workers explains that "a child who has fabricated sexual abuse allegations in order to punish or get even with the caretaker may be less likely to retract her statements than the child who is upset with negative repercussions of her acknowledgment and who reverses her position in an attempt to return life to normal."[18]

Some experts take this clinical wisdom to illogical lengths. They claim that a child's retractions or denials are actually a sign that the child was abused. They may describe a "Sexual Abuse Accommodation Syndrome,"[19] in which the child "accommodates" to the abuse by denying it. Unfortunately, this theory does not leave room for bona fide recantations, and thus is dangerously deficient.

Therefore, a retraction places a large question mark over the child's original statement, but the latter should not be automatically discounted. Both must then be carefully evaluated before you come to a conclusion.

Even if you decide that the retracted statement was untrue, you should see whether the family needs help from a social service or mental health agency. The fact that a child has made an untrue allegation of sexual abuse is a sign of emotional problems in the child or family dysfunction that merits further exploration.

PHYSICAL INDICATORS

In some cases, the child is too young or is unwilling to describe what happened, and no one else steps forward to do so. There may be physical indicators of sexual abuse, though.

Bodily injuries or other physical findings that suggest sexual abuse should be reported. Even ambiguous physical indicators of sexual abuse are important because they can corroborate a child's statement. Without them, the issue comes down to who you believe: the alleged perpetrator or the alleged victim? However, as will be seen, the absence of physical evidence does not disprove the child's statements (as it sometimes does in cases of physical abuse).

Chart 8–2 **Physical Indicators of Sexual Abuse**

The following physical conditions may, in themselves, be a sufficient reason to make a report. Some of the traumatic injuries listed here are the results of violent, painful, and unpleasant sexual contacts that are unlikely to be voluntary—whatever the child's age. If these injuries are not satisfactorily explained, a report should be made.

Other injuries in the list, however, are simply signs of sexual activity, which may or may not be related to sexual abuse, or of illness or poor hygiene. Therefore, these signs of sexual activity should not be automatically equated with proof that the child was sexually abused. Whether they should be the basis of a report depends on the child's apparent maturity and social situation, as well as the statements of the child, the parents, and others who are familiar with the situation.

- Underclothing that is torn, blood stained, or shows signs of semen
- The presence of semen in oral, anal, or vaginal areas
- The presence of foreign objects in rectal or vaginal cavities
- Vaginas that are torn, lacerated, infected, or bloody (as well as broken hymens)
- Penises or scrotums that are swollen, inflamed, infected, or show signs of internal bleeding
- Bite marks on or around the genitals
- Anal areas that are swollen, torn, lacerated, or infected or that have lax muscle tone suggestive of internal stretching
- Scarred or mutilated sexual organs or other parts of the body
- Venereal diseases in oral, anal, and urogenital areas (especially in prepubescent children)
- Unusual vaginal or urethral irritations or discharges unless they are the apparent result of excessive rubbing (during cleaning) or self-stimulation
- Repeated cystitis, especially in prepubescent girls
- Pregnancy, especially in young adolescent girls

A child who was violently forced into sexual activity may have visible signs of the assault, such as suspicious injuries or torn or bloody clothing (with perhaps evidence of semen) (see Chart 8–2). One appellate court described how "the unexplained evidence of vaginal and rectal penetration and the marks and contusions on the children's bodies overwhelmingly support a finding that they [were maltreated]. Several caseworkers, a doctor and a nurse observed bruises on the children's torsos and faces."[20]

Barring some credible explanation from the parents, such as a confirmed assault by a third person, these injuries are strong evidence of sexual abuse.

The great majority of sexual abuse cases, however, do not involve violent or forced physical assaults:

> Patterns of family incest usually take place over a long period of time, from six months to several years. Incestuous practices are not usually related to a single event, but follow a continuum of increased sexual involvement beginning with parental fondling and leading to overt sexual stimulation. . . . Characteristically, the participation of children in incest is willful, resulting from learned behavior that is motivated by eagerness for acceptance and compliance with parental authority, rather than being a product of violence.[21]

In these nonviolent cases of sexual abuse, physical evidence is often ambiguous or nonexistent. This is especially true in cases of alleged fondling, oral sex, and minimal penetration, where the evidence, if there is any, is usually limited to *signs of sexual activity*, such as minor injuries, bruises, or redness to sexual organs (caused by forced penetration or rough handling), also listed in Chart 8–2. Physicians are becoming increasingly adept at finding such evidence, which can form the basis of a court adjudication, as well as of a report.[22]

Unfortunately, these physical indicators are often assigned more diagnostic significance than is justified. Some of the traumatic injuries listed in Chart 8–2 are the results of violent, painful, and unpleasant sexual contacts that are unlikely to be voluntary, whatever the child's age. If they are not satisfactorily explained, a report should be made. Other injuries in the list, however, are simply signs of sexual activity, which may or may not be related to sexual abuse. And some may be signs of illness or poor hygiene.

For older children, signs of sexual activity cannot be automatically interpreted as signs of sexual abuse. These signs may merely be the result of sexual activity with peers. Whether or not we like it, children today become sexually active much earlier than in past generations. The need for clear guidelines notwithstanding, there is no specific cutoff between the age when one or the other is the case. Children under age 13 are unlikely to be involved in intimate sexual activities with their peers, but even with young adolescents, mores are changing.

In young children, though, signs of sexual activity should be reported. Young children ordinarily do not engage in the types of activities that

FAMILY DYNAMICS OF CHILD SEXUAL ABUSE[23]

Because all families are different, it is unwise to adopt too many generalizations about the dynamics that surround intrafamily child sexual abuse. Nonetheless, the following characterizes some of the most common issues and dynamics associated with incestuous families.

- *Secrecy*. Child sexual abuse is usually able to exist and continue in homes only where it is kept a secret between the victim and the abuser or where its occurrence is denied by others. Although some sexual abuse occurs in conjunction with physical abuse, the use of force to maintain the secret is rare because it isn't necessary. Aside from being naive, compliant to an adult authority, and susceptible to bribes and promises of rewards (especially the intangible rewards of special attention and affection), victims are often threatened with dire consequences to themselves, the abuser or the rest of the family should they disclose the abuse. Incestuous families often contain secrets of many kinds, as well as a general lack of communication among family members. In families when more than one child is being sexually abused, it is not uncommon for none of the siblings to know about the others.

- *Denial*. The extent of awareness that sexual abuse is occurring varies among families and is sometimes related to the duration of the abuse. Some mothers deny or ignore their conscious awareness that their child is being abused by their partner; for some, it is an unconscious awareness which they cannot allow themselves to see; while other mothers are truly unaware of the abuse until the moment of disclosure. Conscious denial is often related to a parent's fear of family disintegration, legal consequences or the reaction of the other spouse. Unconscious

would cause such injuries. Thus, without a satisfactory explanation, a report should be made. But here, too, there can be ambiguity. For example, a frequently noted suspicious symptom, unusual vaginal or urethral irritations or discharges, can have an alternate medical explanation or can be the result of excessive rubbing (during cleaning), poor denial is often a result of the "blinders" erected by a mother who is unconsciously seeking to protect herself from facing her own childhood victimization. The reasons for denial are not as important as the emphasis on helping the non-abusive parent to support the victim once the abuse is disclosed.

• *Power.* Often there exists a striking imbalance of power within incestuous families. The father may maintain a strict authoritarian role which, in effect, subjugates all other members of the family. He may tend to regard his sexual involvement with his child as part of his prerogative. In other cases of father-daughter abuse, the mother may appear to hold all of the power in the family. In such instances, child sexual abuse may serve as an unconscious form of retaliation.

• *Isolation.* Individual and family isolation, both physical and emotional, often characterizes incestuous families. Parents may have few social or familial ties to others outside the nuclear family and are resistant to reaching out for help with their problems. Victims and their siblings get the message that problems stay at home, and usually become quite isolated from their peers in their attempts to maintain the family secrets.

• *Role reversal.* Poor communication, underlying hostility, and a strained or non-existent sexual relationship between the parents often contribute to the breakdown of the relationship between the adults in the home. The mother, often in a very depressed state, may increasingly abdicate her role of wife and mother, while a daughter (often the oldest) begins to take on more and more adult responsibilities in the family. This type of classic role reversal situation appears to contribute to some fathers' abilities to regard their daughters as adults and to rationalize their acceptability as sexual partners.

hygiene, or self-stimulation. And it is often impossible to tell which it is.

For this reason, Chart 8–2 calls these injuries "indicators" rather than evidence of sexual abuse. Ambiguous or borderline situations must be judged on a case-by-case basis, taking into account the statements of the child and parents, as well as the child's apparent maturity and social environment. In addition, certain behaviors of the child, discussed next, although not an independent basis for a report, can be helpful in assessing these borderline situations.

Opportunities to observe these physical indicators of sexual abuse are quite limited, of course, because clothes usually cover them. About the only time they are detected is during a medical or physical examination. Such physical examinations should be conducted only by physicians who are experienced in such cases and who are aware of the child's sensitivities and the emotionally harmful effects of past maltreatment. Sexually abused children may already have been traumatized by adults who have "played around" with their private parts; they should not be further traumatized by a cold, forced, or otherwise threatening examination. (The examination should include medical and social histories from both the child and the parents.)[24]

BEHAVIORAL INDICATORS

To assess both ambiguous physical indicators and the child's otherwise uncorroborated statements, an increasing number of therapists are using the presence of certain behaviors in children as diagnostic tools to bolster the conclusion that abuse occurred. (Their absence, though, does not prove that the child was not abused.) (*See* Chart 8–3.)

Using these behavioral indicators is a tricky business, however, because they have too many alternative explanations that are not related to sexual abuse. A sudden decline in a child's performance at school, for example, may be a result of the stress of a divorce rather than of a parent's sexual abuse. Hence, *behavioral indicators are not, in themselves, sufficient grounds for a report.* They should not be used, even by the most impressive expert, unless the child describes having been abused or the existence of suspicious injuries is established. Even then, alternate explanations for the child's behavior must be considered.

This does not mean that you should do nothing when you see such troubled behavior. The children's behaviors listed in Chart 8–3 are an indication that the possibility of sexual abuse—or other emotional problems—should be explored. To medical personnel, for example, they suggest the need for a full physical examination of the child. To *any* caring individual, they suggest the need for further inquiries about the child's situation. For example, a teacher who observes a child's unwilling-

Chart 8–3 **Children's Behaviors Used to Assess Physical Signs of Sexual Activity**

The following behaviors are *not* sufficient reason, in themselves, for a report. There are too many other explanations for them that have nothing to do with sexual abuse. They are properly used only to help assess the significance of signs of sexual activity found on the child's body. (They also signal the need to consider the possibility of sexual abuse when responding to the child's apparent emotional problems.)

- Difficulty in walking or sitting.
- Unwillingness to disrobe in the presence of others, as when changing for a gym class.
- Excessive fear of being approached or touched by persons of the opposite sex.
- Fear of going home.
- Running away from home.
- Adolescent prostitution.
- Sexual behaviors or references that are bizarre or unusual for the child's age.
- Sexual knowledge that is too sophisticated for the child's age.
- Seductiveness that is not age appropriate.
- Behavior that is withdrawn, infantile, or filled with fantasy (the child may even appear to be retarded).
- Attempted suicide.
- Dramatic changes in behavior or school performance.
- Unusual accumulations of money or candy.
- Indirect allusions: A sexually abused child may seek out a special friend or a teacher to confide in. These confidences may be vague and indirect, such as "I'm afraid to go home tonight," "I'd like to come and live with you," or "I want to live in a foster home."

ness to change for a gym class (or a sudden deterioration in a child's schoolwork) should keep the possibility of sexual abuse in mind while seeking to help the child. Discreet—and open-ended—questions (such as "How are things going?" and "Is there anything happening that you want to tell me about?") permit children to share their problems with a teacher or other reassuring adult. The gym class situation, by the way, is one of the most common ways in which sexual abuse is discovered. (Interviewing children is discussed in Chapter 6.)

Sometimes the parent's behavior will confirm the sexual abuse. I once represented a 13-year-old boy who claimed that he was having sexual intercourse with his mother. The male investigator was not sure whether to believe the boy until he made a home visit: The mother spent the entire one-hour interview dressed only in a bra and panties.

9

Physical Neglect

Although child abuse gets more attention in the media, the neglect of children is much more common and can be just as harmful. More children die of physical neglect than from abuse. But less than 4 percent of all neglect cases result in the child's serious injury,[1] and in these less serious cases, you must often distinguish between child neglect and living conditions that are a function of the family's poverty.

THE POVERTY CONNECTION

Most cases of physical neglect involve poor and minority families. Compared to the general population, families who are reported for maltreatment, nationwide, are four times more likely to be on public assistance and almost twice as likely to be black. About 30 percent of abused children live in single-parent households and are on public assistance; the comparable figure for neglected children is about 45 percent.[2]

Given these realities, many commentators blame poverty for the parents' behavior. Certainly, "poverty exposes parents to the increased likelihood of additional stresses that may have deleterious effects upon their capacities to care adequately for their children."[3] Lest all poor families be stigmatized, though, it is important to remember that most poor families do not abuse or neglect their children. In any one year, fewer than one in five families on welfare are reported for suspected abuse or neglect,[4] and an even smaller percentage of such reports are substantiated.

Poor children should be assured of their basic needs, including adequate food, clothing, shelter, and medical care. But when the problem is the parent's low income, the answer must come from income support programs (such as public assistance, food stamps, Medicaid, and child support). Child protective agencies have not been established as society's response to poverty, and for them to assume this role weakens their ability to respond to serious cases of actual abuse and neglect.

Chart 9–1 **Situations of Poor Child Rearing to Which Reporters Frequently Overreact**

Case finding and reporting of neglect (especially physical neglect) has become overzealous in some communities. To be poor, out of work, living in marginal housing, and also accused of child neglect for conditions over which the person has no control is unjust. The following conditions are prone to overreporting.

- *Clothing neglect:* Examples are wearing torn pants, wearing cast-off clothing, or not having a raincoat or gloves.
- *Nutritional neglect:* Examples are eating unbalanced meals, eating too many "junk foods," or cultural food preferences. Even skipping breakfast can be normal if it's the child's choice. We must remember that approximately one third of adults prefer not to eat breakfast.
- *Hygiene neglect:* Examples are coming to school with a dirty face, dirty hair, or dirty clothing. If the child is not malodorous and the problem is periodic, it is probably of minimal importance.
- *Home environment neglect:* Mildly unsanitary homes are quite common. We should not be over critical of housekeeping below standards, such as poorly washed dishes or a house that is covered with dog hair and needs vacuuming.
- *Cultural deprivation or intellectual stimulation neglect:* This term is often directed at families whose children allegedly are not talked to enough or presented with sufficient creative toys. All too often this term is applied to children with developmental delays due to normal variations or prematurity.
- *Safety neglect:* Many normal accidents are called safety neglect to the detriment of the parents, for example, blaming the parents for burns that occur on space heaters despite numerous precautions the parents have taken. On a practical level, some unsafe environments cannot be changed.
- *Minor acute illness neglect:* Insect bites, lice, scabies, and impetigo occur in children from all socioeconomic groups. Often parents are blamed for diaper rashes and cradle cap. Parents may be criticized because they have not given their child antipyretics before bringing them to the physician for a fever. Parents may be blamed for not coming to the clinic soon enough for an ear infection that they did not know existed.

SOURCE: B. Schmitt, "Child Neglect" in N. Ellerstein, ed., *Child Abuse and Neglect: A Medical Reference*, Churchill Livingstone, New York, 1981, pp. 304–5.

Almost all states, therefore, have provisions that are designed to delineate differences between welfare and child protective functions. In the District of Columbia, for example, the law expressly excludes from the definition of child neglect "deprivation . . . due to the lack of financial means."[5] Other states prohibit a finding of abuse or neglect unless the parents are "financially able" to care for their children or were "offered financial or other reasonable means to do so."[6] Chart 9–1 lists the situations of poor child rearing to which reporters frequently overrract.

Nevertheless, children who are actually neglected need protection. The neglect of children is not excused simply because the parents are poor. Instead, laws establish "a minimum baseline of proper care for children that all parents, regardless of lifestyle or social or economic position, must meet."[7] Thus, in assessing such cases, you should ask yourself two questions:

1. Does the care of the child fall below commonly accepted community standards? To justify a report, the deviation must be clear and should not be the product of reasonable differences in culture or lifestyle. For example, children must be fed nutritionally adequate meals. Soda and potato chips do not constitute an adequate diet.
2. Has the child's physical or mental condition been impaired or is it in danger of being impaired? Again, using nutrition as an example, if the child seems hungry and emaciated, a report should be made.

PHYSICAL DEPRIVATION

It is easy to say that neglect is the failure to provide adequate care. But what is "adequate"? All would probably agree that not feeding a child for days at a time; sending a child out in freezing temperatures with nothing on but underwear; or allowing dirt, urine, and feces to accumulate on a child's body until it stinks are examples of reportable conditions. But these are obviously extreme cases. How does one decide whether to report less severe cases?

Signs of severe physical deprivation that suggest general child neglect should be reported. Usually, the child's body will be the best indication of seriously inadequate care. Chart 9–2 lists the signs of severe physical deprivation that require a report.

Severe dirt and disorder in the home that suggests the general neglect of the child should be reported. Especially dirty and disorderly home conditions may be "the immediately observable symptoms" of the parent's

Chart 9–2 **Signs of Physical Deprivation**

The following conditions are merely circumstantial evidence of physical neglect. No report should be made if they can be satisfactorily explained.

- Children who suffer severe and unexplained developmental lags. At the extreme, these children evidence the "failure-to-thrive syndrome," that is, they fall below the fifth percentile of weight, height, and motor development for children of their age. A diagnosis of neglect is confirmed if the child's condition improves during hospitalization or after being placed in foster care.
- Children who are chronically hungry. These children may come to school hungry and with no provision made for lunch; they may be seen begging, rummaging, or stealing for food.
- Children who evidence malnutrition. These children may have distended abdomens, brittle and broken fingernails, and pale or sunken skin. They are usually underweight but they may be grossly overweight because their diet may provide sufficient calories but be severely deficient nutritionally.
- Children who are chronically tired or listless. These children may be seen falling asleep in class, in therapy groups, or in play groups; they also may have poor concentration.
- Children who repeatedly have apparently unattended physical problems and medical problems, such as untreated or infected wounds.
- Children whose dental problems are severe and apparently untreated.
- Children who are chronically dirty and unbathed. These children may smell of urine or other foul odors, have severe and recurrent diaper rashes or other skin disorders associated with poor hygiene, or ringworm or body vermin.
- Children who are repeatedly dressed inadequately for harsh, winter weather. These children may not have shoes or coats to protect them from the cold and may suffer recurrent illnesses that are associated with excessive exposure, such as pneumonia and frostbite.
- Children (especially younger children) who are chronically late for day care or school or are chronically absent.
- Children who state that there is no one at home to care for them. These children may come to school early and stay late, and their parents may seem seriously addicted to alcohol or drugs.

As this list indicates, many signs of severe physical deprivation should be *chronic* before being reported. To be considered chronic, they should be observed over a period of time or there should be reason to suspect that they are long-standing problems.

Chart 9–3 **Reportable Dirt and Disorder in the Home**

The following examples of *severe* dirt and disorder in the home are suggestive of the general neglect of a child. To justify a report, they should represent a substantial deviation from general neighborhood norms:

- Human or animal excrement on the floors or walls
- Urine-soaked mattresses or furniture
- Toilets being used but not in working order
- The lack of washing facilities
- Garbage left inside the house to rot
- Encrusted or multilayered dirt throughout the house
- Eating utensils that have obviously been reused over and over again without washing
- Extreme infestation by rodents or vermin
- Obviously insufficient quantites of nutritious food in the house (for example, cupboards and refrigerators that are barren of food)
- Rotting, molding, insect-infested, or otherwise contaminated food
- Refrigerator not working or missing
- Stove not working or missing
- The lack of water, electricity, or gas
- General and severe household disrepair (such as broken windows, unhinged doors, or holes in the walls)
- Inadequate sleeping arrangements (for instance, no bed or mattress and blankets for each family member, whether or not the bed or mattress is shared)
- Extreme overcrowding not imposed by the size of family, the amount of the public assistance grant, or housing conditions in the community

---

inability to meet the child's basic physical and emotional needs.[8] Because it is often hard for an outsider to assess the actual quality of care a child is receiving, a report should be made even when a child does not seem to be harmed, as long as the conditions are as bad as those described in Chart 9–3. (Such conditions can actually be dangerous, as described in the next chapter.)

The dirt and disorder must be "severe." That means it must be substantially worse than most other home conditions in the general neighborhood. The violation of middle-class norms of housekeeping should not be confused with child neglect. Such things as broken or dusty furniture, overcrowding, and general "messiness" are not reasons to report (although they may be a reason to encourage the parents to seek assistance from other community and social services).

Reporting based on dirt and disorder in the home must be approached with great caution, lest the poor living conditions imposed on families by poverty and discrimination lead to an inappropriate report. Those that are caused by the parents' inability to afford or find better housing should not be reported. Instead, the parents should be offered help in finding better housing. The parents' unresponsiveness to reasonable offers of help is a clear reason to report.

MEDICAL NEGLECT

Medical neglect is the parents' failure to provide the medical, dental, or psychiatric[9] care needed to prevent or treat serious physical or psychological injuries or illnesses. It includes the failure to provide, consent to, or follow through with

- preventive care, such as immunizations
- diagnostic care, such as medical examinations and hospitalizations
- remedial care, such as surgery or regular medication, or
- prosthetic care, such as eye glasses or an artificial limb.

Apparently untreated injuries, illnesses, or impairments that suggest medical neglect should be reported. Medical neglect is most commonly detected by physicians and nurses when parents refuse to consent to or follow through with needed treatment and by schools when parents fail to have their children immunized according to state law. Many other persons, though, may observe apparently untreated children. For example, a social worker may discover a seriously ill child while making a welfare-related home visit. A day care center may be worried about a hearing-impaired child whose parents refuse to obtain a hearing aid, even after being told repeatedly that the child's poor hearing is an obstacle to learning.

Sometimes parents delay getting needed medical care for their children. For example, one court described a 2½ year old with "a swelling upon the upper part of the forehead, blood on his head, deep scratches and bruises on the nose and face," whose "the mother did not act promptly when she first discovered the baby was injured. . . . Some twelve hours later, a delay that could have been fatal, she rushed the baby to a hospital, presumably, having suffered pangs of remorse."[10] Such cases should be reported immediately.

The parents' failure to provide needed medical care can be caused by ignorance, misunderstanding, or poverty. In such situations, a report is warranted only if, after appropriate counseling and referral, the parents still fail to provide the needed care. Parents are not considered neglectful for the failure to provide medical care unless they are financially able to do so or were offered financial or other reasonable means to do so.

Medical neglect does not include *all* parental failures to obtain or accept recommended treatment. A parent is not required to "beckon the assistance of a physician for every trifling affliction which a child may suffer, for everyday experience teaches that many of a child's ills may be overcome by simple household nursing."[11]

A report should be made only if the lack of treatment threatens to cause serious harm to the child.[12] Thus, minor scratches or lacerations, though untreated, should not be reported. But a report is warranted if such minor injuries become seriously infected and the infection threatens to spread to other parts of the child's body. Some states define medical neglect to include the failure to provide or to consent to cosmetic surgery that is designed to reduce a child's emotional distress, but most do not.[13]

Neither the personal convictions nor the religious beliefs of parents justify withholding needed medical care for serious conditions. Most cases of medical neglect involve a general pattern of parental unwillingness or inability to care properly for a child. However, a report may also be needed when the parents are, in all other respects, adequate and even "good" parents. Sometimes parents seek qualified medical advice but then deliberately decide to forego some or all the recommended treatment. The decision may be based on an independent appraisal of the need for or utility of the medical treatment. (This commonly occurs in the treatment of what appears to be terminal cancer.)[14] Or, more likely, the decision may be based on religious beliefs about all or certain forms of medical treatment.

Almost all states now have laws that require consideration of a parent's convictions before deciding that a child is being medically neglected. Most are like California's:

Cultural and religious child-rearing practices and beliefs which differ from general community standards shall not in themselves create a need for child welfare services unless the practices present a specific danger to the physical or emotional safety of the child.[15]

Similarly, mandatory immunization laws frequently exempt children whose parents have religious objections. And most states expressly exclude "treatment by spiritual means" from their definitions of neglect.

Thus, reasonable parental refusals to consent to treatment should not be reported. But when the lack of medical care endangers the child's health or well-being, you should not hesitate to report such cases. Child protective agencies and the courts will intervene to protect the child, even if this means overruling deeply held parental beliefs.[16] (To protect parental sensibilities, though, many states have adopted a provision similar to Missouri's, which provides that "any child who does not receive specific medical treatment by reason of the legitimate practice of the religious belief . . . , for that reason alone, shall not be considered to be an abused or neglected child.")[17]

Newborns who are denied nutrition, life-sustaining care, or other medically indicated treatment should be reported. In 1982, most Americans were shocked to learn that an Indiana newborn with Down's syndrome died because his parents refused to allow corrective surgery for his digestive system. Shortly after the parents decided against the surgery, the baby was reported to the local prosecuting attorney who sought, but was denied, a protective order from the Indiana courts. The baby died nine days after birth while an appeal was pending before the U.S. Supreme Court. Because the family's anonymity was preserved, such cases became known as "Baby Doe" situations.

In response to this and similar cases, the federal Child Abuse Act was amended in 1984 to require state child protective systems to receive and investigate reports of infants who are denied nutrition, life-prolonging surgery, or other medically indicated treatment. The only exceptions are if

(A) the infant is chronically and irreversibly comatose;

(B) the provision of such treatment would (i) merely prolong dying; (ii) not be effective in ameliorating or correcting all of the infant's life-threatening conditions; or (iii) otherwise be futile in terms of the survival of the infant; or

(C) the provision of such treatment would be virtually futile in terms of the survival of the infant and the treatment itself under such circumstances would be inhumane.[18]

Medical facilities can decide to provide emergency care to children who appear to need it, as described in Chapter 5. In nonemergency cases, when there is time to obtain a court order, the facility should seek one or, as is more likely, request a child protection agency to do so. Other persons and agencies that are concerned about a child's immediate medical needs should contact a child protective agency or the police as soon as possible.

10

Endangerment
and Abandonment

Providing a safe environment for a child is a major responsibility of parents. Those who are careless or who have difficulty caring for themselves because of mental incapacity or drug abuse often do not. Thus, endangerment is frequently the concrete manifestation of the child's general neglect.

PHYSICAL ENDANGERMENT

Almost all childhood accidents are preventable. That is, they probably would not happen if parents took extraordinary precautions and supervised their children closely and constantly. But to expect such superhuman efforts would be unfair to parents (as well as unrealistic) and it would deny children the needed freedom to explore, on their own, the world around them. Though perhaps "preventable," accidents are a part of growing up, even some serious ones. Nevertheless, parents have a duty to protect children from the foreseeable dangers around them. The chronic or ongoing failure to do so, whether by acts of omission or commission, is called "physical endangerment."

"Accidental" injuries that suggest gross inattention to the child's need for safety should be reported. When the parent's failure to protect the child from foreseeable accidents is part of a general pattern of inattention, the danger of further accidents is great. "An example is the child who has already fallen off a sofa, and in the office setting the mother leaves the same child unguarded on the examining table. Such an action should indicate that this particular child is at risk for additional accidents."[1]

That the parents may not consciously wish the child to be injured does not diminish the child's need for protection. Often, the homes in which these children live are marked by chronic disorganization, recurrent

---

Chart 10–1 "Accidental" Injuries That Should Be Reported

"Accidental" injuries should be reported when

1. Descriptions of the accident provided by the parents, the child, or others suggest that it was caused by gross or continuing inattention to the child's need for safety, for example, that the child is regularly left alone or otherwise placed in a physically dangerous situation.
2. The parents seem indifferent to *repeated* accidents, such as repeated ingestions of poisonous substances or repeated bites from the family dog.
3. A home visit reveals dangerous home conditions.
4. Direct observation of the parent's behavior suggests gross inattentiveness to the child's need for safety.

---

crises, and overall neglect of the child's physical and emotional needs. Chart 10–1 lists the conditions that suggest the need to report a child's accidental injuries. Although only continuing dangers should be reported,[2] you may not know enough about the family to be able to tell whether they are ongoing. If you are not sure, make a report.

Children who are left in physically dangerous situations should be reported. Most reports of "physical endangerment" involve cases in which the child did not actually suffer an injury but could have. Either the child was left in an unreasonably dangerous environment or the child was too young to be left alone. In these circumstances, a report should be made whether or not the child has actually been injured.

There are an unlimited number of ways in which young children can be placed in dangerous situations—both at home and away from the home. For instance, some children are locked in cars while their parents go shopping or attend a movie. This is inherently dangerous behavior, but on a hot day, when the temperature in a closed car quickly rises to over 120 degrees Fahrenheit, it can be fatal. Other children, as young as three or four, are dropped off in parks or allowed to roam their neighborhoods with no supervision. This can be especially dangerous at night or when the child can gain easy access to nearby abandoned buildings, construction sites, railroad tracks, highways, or unprotected waterways or wells. And, of course, there is always the danger that the child will be abducted, raped, or otherwise hurt by strangers.

Whether or not the child is left alone, some environments pose an unreasonable risk of injury. The degree of danger depends on the child's age and maturity, as well as on the actual conditions. Just as children

Chart 10–2 **Dangerous Home Conditions**

- Structurally unsafe housing
- Gas leaks and other fire hazards
- Broken stairs or no railings on stairs
- Easily accessible open windows or upper-story doors leading to unguarded, unsafe, or nonexistent fire escapes
- Poisonous substances, such as cleaning compounds, rat poisons, or medicines, or dangerous objects, including knives or guns, that are within easy reach of children
- The placement of infants on high beds or in cribs without safeguards to prevent the child from falling
- Small, easily swallowed objects that are within easy reach of children
- Vicious or uncontrolled animals
- Broken, jagged, or sharp objects that are lying around the house
- Exposed heating elements or fan blades
- Bare or exposed electrical wires or broken wall outlets
- Furniture or other large objects that may easily fall over and injure a young child
- Heating that is inadequate to raise the inside temperature of the house to over 50 degrees Fahrenheit
- Unsanitary conditions, including festering garbage or human or animal excrement, that are so severe that they create a clear danger of disease
- The presence of assaultive or otherwise dangerous persons who, by their past behavior toward the child or other children, pose a demonstrated threat to the child's physical well-being

need safer environments than do adults, younger children need safer environments than do older ones. A school-age child does not ordinarily climb out open upper-story windows, but parents must assume that a toddler will be tempted to do so.

Although dangerous circumstances usually involve unsafe physical surroundings, it is also neglect to leave children in the care of dangerous persons, as discussed in Chapter 3. Hence, you should report the presence of assaultive or otherwise dangerous persons who, by their past behavior toward the child or other children, pose a demonstrated threat to the child's well-being.

Chart 10–2 lists the most commonly observed dangerous conditions in the home. Many of the dangerous conditions listed in the chart can be the result of a temporary lapse in parental care. A report should be made only if they *appear* to be long-standing or part of an overall pattern of inattention to the child's need for a safe and healthy environment. In one case, for example, six children were found living in a house that had been "without electricity for two months and thus had no working water supply or plumbing. Also, there was no furnace or refrigerator, and only a traveler's chest, which frequently had to be stocked with ice, was available to keep food from spoiling."[3] The father repeatedly used excessive force in disciplining some of the children, and teachers described some of the children as nervous and emotionally disturbed. They were often kept home from school without justification.

You should be careful, however, not to confuse the living conditions imposed on families because of poverty with the parents' neglect of children. Although all parents, no matter how poor, have a duty to protect their children from dangerous environments, physically shabby households should not be equated with dangerous conditions. Moreover, the dangerous conditions must be caused by the parents. Parents are not responsible for a landlord's poor maintenance unless they refuse to move out of an unsafe, run-down, or abandoned building (assuming, of course, that a suitable alternative is available).

Young children who are left alone should be reported. Some children are simply too young to be left alone—no matter how safe the home environment seems. Before age six, most children simply do not develop a sufficient awareness of personal safety. Their natural curiosity, combined with the unavoidable dangers of any home environment, is a sure prescription for an accident. Children aged six to ten can be left alone for progressively longer periods, as they gain maturity.[4]

The appropriateness of leaving a child alone depends not only on the child's age but also on the age of any other children left with the child. A sufficiently older child may provide adequate supervision for a child who is otherwise too young to be left alone. Conversely, a child who is old enough to be left alone may be too young to care for a younger child.[5]

The need for easy decision making notwithstanding, there is no way to specify when children are old enough to be left unattended or for how long. For example, sleeping infants can be left (for a short time) with greater safety than can toddlers who are awake. Furthermore, the parent may have a legitimate reason for leaving the child that justifies the risk taken, at least for a short time.[6] One tragic case illustrates how hard it is to assess such situations:

Chart 10-3 Is the Child Too Young to Be Left Alone?

Consider the following factors in deciding whether a child was too young to be left alone:

- The child's age and maturity.
- The child's health or special need for constant supervision.
- The relative safety or dangerousness of the child's environment.
- The reason for leaving the child.
- The length of time the child is left.
- The responsibilities assigned to the child. For example, was a young child expected to prepare his or her own meals or baby-sit for an even younger child?
- The availability and capability of older siblings to care for the child.
- The availability of the parents, neighbors, or others in case of problems. For example, did the child have a telephone number of someone to call for help?
- Any past history of injuries or accidents when the child was left alone.

Three preschool children suffered smoke inhalation in a fire in their home, and one of the children died. The mother had left the children for 30 minutes to walk her fourth child to school because he had been beaten up on his way to school the previous day. The mother was accused of child neglect. The case was given heavy coverage in the press, and the mother decompensated and required psychiatric care.[7]

The leaving of children alone and unattended, as a ground for reporting child neglect, is frequently criticized as a form of middle-class bias against the poor and various minority groups. Too often, this criticism is justified. Nevertheless, it is also true that leaving children home alone can be dangerous. Hence, each situation must be judged individually, using the factors listed in Chart 10-3.

The child protective agency or the police must decide how best to protect a child who is found in an unreasonably dangerous situation. Such children usually are taken into protective custody and placed in an emergency foster home or shelter. However, this experience can be deeply traumatic to the children, and a growing number of communities provide emergency homemakers or other in-home care that obviate the need to remove the children.

ABANDONMENT

Parents who feel that they cannot care for their children, either temporarily or permanently, should make suitable arrangements with relatives, friends, or social service agencies. Some parents, however, simply desert their children.

Apparently abandoned children should be reported. How do you tell whether parents have abandoned a child? Some parents express their intention to do so. More often, though, the circumstances demonstrate the parents' intent. They leave infants and very young children on doorsteps of churches, hospitals, or neighbors' homes; in the restrooms of gas stations; or at home, in no one's care, after they move away. Some parents leave children in the care of other adults without saying when they will return (or do not return when they said they would) or without saying where they can be reached (or cannot be reached where they said they could). The parents' failure to make financial arrangements for the child during their absence is further evidence of their intent to abandon the child.

There may be a good explanation for the parents' behavior. For example, the parents may have failed to reclaim a child from a baby-sitter because they were in an automobile accident that left them unconscious. Such justifications are rare, however, and seeking them not your concern. Whenever it appears that a child has been deserted, a report should be made so a child protection agency can arrange suitable care for the child. If the parents turn up later, the agency (and, perhaps, the courts) will decide whether the parents were justified in their behavior.

Although there is some disagreement, most child protective agencies do not consider it abandonment when parents expel older children from the home or refuse to allow them to return because of serious misbehavior. An older child (usually a child over age sixteen) should not be considered "abandoned" if the parents' refusal to accept custody is based on their inability to control the child's behavior. Such "locking out" may not be the wisest response to the problems of adolescents and it can have disastrous consequences, as appears to have been the case of John W. Hinckley, President Reagan's assailant. But it is not child abuse. These children and their parents need help and counseling, but not the sort ordinarily available through child protective agencies. It makes no sense to label parents who are already at their wits end as "abusive" or "neglectful" unless the child's misbehavior is directly attributable to specific parental conduct, as is described in the next chapter.

11

Psychological Maltreatment

Parents can cause serious psychological harm to their children even when they provide adequate physical care.[1] State laws tend to describe this concept with subjective and overbroad terms like "emotional harm" or "mental injury." To emphasize the need for highly sophisticated judgments in this area, which are often best made by mental health professionals, this book adopts the recommendation of the Airlie House experts that it be called "psychological maltreatment." The group concluded that this broader phrase better delineates the parental behaviors that can cause serious conduct, cognitive, affective, or other mental disorders in children.[2]

EMOTIONAL MALTREATMENT

All but a few states mandate reports of emotional maltreatment, and the remaining accept them on a voluntary basis. Similarly, all national standard-setting organizations recommend the intervention of a child protective agency when parents emotionally abuse or neglect their children.[3]

Nevertheless, no ground for protective intervention has been more harshly criticized by civil libertarians than emotional maltreatment, largely because legal and agency definitions tend to be vague and overbroad.[4] Many states define emotional maltreatment to include any act that would "impair" the child's mental or emotional health.[5] One state manual defined emotional neglect to include the failure to provide "adequate affection and love." However, it is possible to be more specific about what should and should not be reported.

Emotional abuse is an assault on the child's psyche, just as physical abuse is an assault on the child's body. Its most severe forms are close confinement and torture. These acts are considered forms of emotional abuse because, although they may sometimes result in physical injury, the great danger they pose is to the child's psychological condition.

Common forms of close confinement include tying children to bedposts and other furniture (for hours, days, or weeks); locking children in closets and other dark places (again, for hours, days, or weeks); and keeping older children, especially adolescents, in the house for weeks or months at a time. Common forms of torturous conduct include regularly forcing children to eat unpalatable and loathsome substances, such as black pepper and soap, and forcing children to stand, squat, or walk for hours at a time. And, it should go without saying, all types of sexual abuse or exploitation are also forms of serious psychological abuse. (Forcing older children to wear clothes of the opposite sex is less common but also a cause for concern.)

As in the case of corporal punishment, *disciplining a child through verbal castigation or punishment is permitted only if it is "reasonable."* It is abusive to lock a child in a closet for days at a time, but the withholding of the child's privileges would ordinarily be considered a reasonable exercise of parental discipline. Although such issues are hardly ever discussed in the case law or statutes, South Carolina's Child Protection Act of 1977 codifies the concept of the reasonable withholding of privileges by permitting "(1) restrictions relating to attendance at amusements, concerts, social events or activities, or theaters; (2) restrictions on the amount of exposure to secular activities such as television, extracurricular school activities or community recreational activities; (3) instructions, directions, or mandates relating to public or private elementary or secondary education or attendance at churches or other places of religious worship."[6]

Emotional neglect (what child development specialists would call "developmental deprivation") is a gross failure to provide the emotional nurturing and the physical and cognitive stimulation needed to prevent serious developmental deficits in children. Emotional neglect includes leaving newborns untouched in cribs or cradles except for feeding and changing (the hair on the rear of the infant's head is characteristically worn away from the lack of movement); gross parent/child role reversal; severely inappropriate parental responses to the child's developmental milestones; and all forms of the maternal deprivation syndrome, whether caused by disturbances in attachment or by disturbances in separation-individuation.

The foregoing are all relatively severe forms of emotional maltreatment, for which the effects on the child are clear or easy to predict. But in less severe cases, assessments become more difficult. Even mental health professionals have difficulty predicting, with any degree of certainty, whether a particular parent's behavior will result in severe harm to the child.

Therefore, the Airlie House experts recommended a two-level approach to the reporting of psychological maltreatment. For such extreme acts as close confinement and torture, no demonstrable harm to the child is required. Similarly, some extreme forms of emotional neglect have unambiguous signs, for example, nonorganic failure-to-thrive.[7] Both professionals or lay persons who discover such serious conditions should report them immediately.

Less severe acts, such as inadequate nurturance and habitual scapegoating, belittling, taunting, and rejecting behavior, which result in demonstrable harm to the child, should also be reported. Of course, there should be a link between the parent's behavior and the child's behavioral or emotional problem. (Because it is often difficult to establish such a link, an important factor in assessing the situation can be the parent's failure to seek or accept help for the child's emotional problems, as discussed next.)

If there is no demonstrable harm from these less severe acts, however, only mental health professionals who are qualified to assess their future harmfulness should report them.[8] This decision should be based on a careful consideration of the severity, chronicity, and context of the parents' acts or omissions. Laypersons are simply unable to make such judgments.

FAILURE TO TREAT A CHILD'S PSYCHOLOGICAL PROBLEMS

Direct evidence of a parent's behavior toward a child is the most reliable basis of a report of emotional maltreatment. But, as in cases of physical abuse, it is often unavailable. What about circumstantial evidence of emotional maltreatment?

Emotional maltreatment can take its toll on children. The behavioral and physical disorders that are commonly associated with emotional maltreatment are listed on Chart 11–1. However, even the casual observer will note that each of the conditions listed could have many other causes besides emotional maltreatment. Unlike some physical injuries that are suggestive of maltreatment, emotional injuries are not pathognomonic; they do not "speak" for themselves and, by themselves, cannot be used as a basis of a report. Failure-to-thrive, for example, although often associated with maltreatment, may be caused by organic or environmental

Chart 11–1 **Behavioral and Physical Disorders Associated with Emotional Maltreatment**[9]

- Failure-to-thrive or less extreme (but still severe) deficits in growth or development
- Habit disorders (such as head banging, sucking, biting, rocking)
- Conduct disorders (such as antisocial or destructive behavior)
- Neurotic traits (sleep disorders, speech disorders, and inhibition of play)
- Psychoneurotic reactions (hysteria, obsession, compulsion, phobias, and hypochondria)
- Extremes of behavior (excessive compliance and passivity or overly aggressive and demanding behavior)
- Overly adaptive behavior (inappropriately adult or inappropriately infantile)
- Developmental lags (physical, mental, or emotional)
- Sudden and severe drops in the child's school performance, emotional appearance, or general functioning
- Attempted suicide.

The foregoing conditions can have any one of a number of organic or environmental causes besides emotional maltreatment. Therefore, they are not grounds for a report unless the parents reject appropriate offers of help for the child's problems or voice indifference or seem apathetic to them.

---

factors that are beyond the parents' knowledge or control. As Goldstein, Freud, and Solnit pointed out: "A child can become emotionally disturbed in response to parental attitudes, fateful events, to a combination of these, or entirely because of internal or inborn factors."[10]

Short of placing the child in a controlled environment and waiting to see if there is an improvement, there is no reliable way of distinguishing between those emotional disturbances that are caused by parental maltreatment and those that have other explanations. Hence, it is deeply unfair to suspect that *all* children with emotional problems are maltreated, and it is irresponsible to make a report on this basis alone.

A child's emotional disturbance, though, may set the stage for a report. Attempts to discover what is troubling the child may reveal something about the parents' behavior or ability to meet the child's needs. The child's description of home conditions, for example, may signal the need for a report. Or, the parents' response to the child's problems may indicate the possibility of maltreatment. "The parents of an emotionally disturbed child generally accept the existence of a problem. They are concerned about the child's welfare and are actively seeking help. The parents of an emotionally maltreated child often blame the child for the problem (or ignore its existence), refuse all offers of help, and are unconcerned about the child's welfare."[11]

Parental failures to treat a child's severe psychological problems should be reported. As Leila Whiting, when she was director of a child abuse project for the National Association of Social Workers, explained: "Once a child is hurt, the parent becomes the key factor in deciding whether the situation is reportable; that is, when the emotional disturbance is pointed out to the parent, perhaps repeatedly, and the parent refuses to remedy it despite support, then he or she may be reported as being emotionally abusive."[12] The parents' refusal, of course, could also be considered a form of medical neglect.

A 1983 Pennsylvania case involved such a report from a high school guidance counselor. In dismissing the parents' claim of improper reporting, the court described the care with which the counselor decided to report the parents' failure to treat the psychological problems of their son, Alexander:

> Before Appleby [the guidance counselor] made her referral and recommendation, she conducted approximately eight interviews with Alexander. Appleby involved the parent plaintiffs in one counseling session where she disclosed her findings and conclusions that Alexander needed professional mental health analysis and asked them to obtain that help on their own. On numerous occasions Appleby sought the advice of the school psychologist, McMullen. . . . It is also undisputed that [the mother] initiated a phone conversation with Mrs. Appleby during which at the very least, family problems were discussed. Prior to [making a report], Appleby spoke with Alexander's parents and asked them why they had not contacted Crisis Intervention on their own, an issue which had been discussed at the counseling session when the parents, McMullen and Appleby were present. . . . The fact that Appleby failed, refused or declined to divulge confidential information to the parents at the counseling session which might have been relayed to her by Alexander in confidence [was proper].[13]

This kind of careful decision making reduces legal vulnerability for improper reporting, and, more important, reflects the highest standards of professional behavior.

Even in the absence of direct evidence of the parent's harmful behavior, therefore, a report should be made if (1) the child evidences a severe emotional, behavioral, developmental, or psychological problem *and* (2) the parents reject appropriate offers of help or seem indifferent or apathetic to the child's condition. The child protection agency will then assess the child's total home situation to determine whether protective action is necessary.

IMPROPER ETHICAL GUIDANCE

A child's ethical values and social behavior are influenced by a wide range of personal, familial, and environmental factors, many of which are beyond the control and sometimes the understanding of parents. Nevertheless, parents have the responsibility to impart basic ethical and social values to their children, or at least to attempt to do so.

The failure to impart ethical standards of behavior is often lumped under the term "inadequate supervision," which it is. However, because the phrase brings to mind the inadequate supervision involved in leaving children alone or in dangerous situations, this book adopts the more descriptive (and honest) terminology: "improper ethical guidance."

"Improper ethical guidance" is an amorphous concept that can lead to subjective application. Therefore, it becomes reportable only when *specific* parental behavior seems likely to threaten the child's ethical development and behavior. Chart 11–2 describes the four major grounds for reporting suspected improper ethical guidance.

The strongest reason to report improper ethical guidance is the parents' condonation of or indifference to a child's serious misbehavior. But parents who provide grossly inappropriate models of ethical behavior for their children, the last ground for a report listed in Chart 11–2, should also be reported. Children identify with their parents, seeing them as role models of adult behavior. Thus, the behavior of parents, whether good or bad, tends to be reflected in the children's behavior. Although the degree of incorporation varies widely, it is an inherent part of all parent/child interactions.

In the past, there was a much greater willingness to initiate child protective action on the basis of parental lifestyles. Public agencies sought to enforce high standards of "moral" behavior for parents—or at least for mothers. That is why this form of neglect often was called "moral neglect." Courts frequently took children away from their mothers because of the mothers' sexual misconduct, that is, for having sexual relations with men to whom they were not married.[14] Frequently, the sexual misconduct involved a technically "adulterous" relationship with one man and was raised in the context of a matrimonial custody case.[15]

Changing marital patterns and social mores have made such cases largely a thing of the past—at least in most large urban or suburban

Chart 11–2 **Grounds for Reporting Suspected Improper Ethical Guidance**

- Children who, *with their parents*, engage in criminal behavior (such as stealing, drug use or dealing, prostitution, or child pornography).
- Children who are left by their parents in the custody of "unsavory persons" whom the parents knew or had sufficient reason to know may encourage or force the children to perform illegal or antisocial acts.
- Apparent parental indifference to the whereabouts, associates, and misbehavior of their child. However, great care must be taken to distinguish between indifference caused by the parents' lack of concern and indifference caused by the failure of past efforts to control the child.
- Parents whose lifestyle provides a *grossly* inappropriate model of ethical behavior for their child.

areas. Thus, in writing for the federal government, one respected researcher concluded: "Mothers who are prostitutes do not necessarily neglect their children."[16] According to her, unless the child shows "adverse effects," no report should be made. Many child protective agencies, in urban areas at least, would probably agree.

The modern trend is to initiate child protective action only if the parent's lifestyle provides a grossly inappropriate model of ethical behavior. In almost all communities, a parent's sexual behavior is considered reportable only if it is open and notorious, if the child observes a series of unrelated adults spending the night with his or her parent, if the child witnesses sexual acts, or if the child actually participates in the parent's sexual activities.

Similarly, one or more convictions, by themselves, may not be a reason to report a parent, but a particularly unsavory or criminal lifestyle would be. Thus, one appeals court affirmed a finding of neglect on the basis of the parent's "antisocial" behavior, including "the offenses of harassment, criminal solicitation and public intoxication, as well as such physical abuse of the child as putting beer in his baby bottle."[17]

EDUCATIONAL NEGLECT

Children need an adequate education to succeed in contemporary society. At a minimum, they need to know how to read and write and to perform basic arithmetic, and they need a rudimentary understanding of their community and political environment. Parents have a legal obligation to encourage and facilitate their children's education by requiring them to attend school. Their failure to do so is educational neglect. (This contrasts with truancy, in which the child's nonattendance is beyond the parents' control.)

Even when a child's nonattendance does not seem serious, it can signal the existence of potentially much more dangerous conditions, as illustrated by the case of Tammie and Clint Z, who lived with their father in upstate New York. In one six-month period, Tammie was absent from school thirteen times and Clint was absent twenty-one times. Their grades were "below average" and "unsatisfactory."

The mobile home in which they lived lacked hot water. When the children did go to school, they were often "unkempt and dirty." Over much of that six months, Tammie had a chronic skin rash, which was eventually diagnosed as scabies. Every day after school, the children's father brought them to a restaurant where "they were generally left unsupervised" until almost midnight. On at least one occasion, their father ordered them to wait in a car for as long as three hours while he stayed in the restaurant.[18]

In a small number of cases, parents do not send their children to school because of deeply held convictions about how they want their children to be educated. But the courts have repeatedly held that their right to do so is extremely limited. Religious beliefs, for example, are not an excuse for keeping a child out of school. (The U.S. Supreme Court, though, has recognized the limited constitutional right of Amish parents not to send their children to high school.)[19]

Moreover, except in extraordinary circumstances, parents also do not have the right to keep their children at home when they disagree with the form or content of the instruction given at school,[20] although they do have a constitutional right to send their children to any properly licensed private school of their choice.[21] Most states also allow parents to educate their children at home if strict criteria are met for the content, quality, and quantity of home instruction.[22] (Many states have formal procedures for licensing home instruction.)

School officials are usually the first persons to notice a child's absence from school. However, before they report such children to a child protective agency, most school systems try to work with the parents to resolve any problems that are preventing the children from attending school. These efforts usually are made by the school attendance or truancy unit, the child guidance unit, or the school's social service staff. Many school districts have established policies, sometimes in writing, that define when absences from school should be reported.

In actuality, school districts rarely report cases of educational neglect to child protective agencies unless this form of neglect is part of an overall pattern of parental inattention to the children's needs and the parents seem unamenable to help or reject help. For example, some parents cannot mobilize themselves sufficiently to get their children up, dressed, fed, and on the way to school each morning. Some parents are so indifferent to their children's needs that they make no effort to counteract the normal childhood discouragements, phobias, and other problems of growing up that lead many children to lose the desire to attend school. Other parents exploit their children; they keep them at home to do chores, to care for younger siblings, or to take care of the parents.

Although most reports of educational neglect come from schools, the child's failure to attend school may be noticed by others as well. For example, a neighbor may see a child outside playing when he or she should be in school, or someone visiting the home during school hours may see the child indoors. Such reports may be the only way the situation comes to light, because the school may not even know of the child's existence (the child may never have been enrolled in school, or the family may have recently moved into the school district).

Unexplained and chronic absences from school that suggest educational neglect should be reported. State laws usually define educational neglect in absolute terms, so the failure to send a child to school for even one day is technically defined as neglect. However, no community applies the law that strictly. To be considered child neglect, the child's nonattendance must be chronic. Hence, seeing a child out of school once or twice is not, by itself, sufficient grounds for a report. The child may be ill or just recovering from an illness, or the nonattendance may be caused by a temporary family problem over which the parents will soon gain control.

A report of educational neglect should be made only if the child is frequently seen out of school during school hours or there is some other reason to believe that this is a regular occurrence. For example, a report may be warranted if the child's absence from school is mentioned to the parent and the parent voices indifference or seems apathetic to the child's situation.

12

Parents with Severe
Mental Disabilities

Parents who suffer from *severe* mental disabilities are often unable to care for themselves, let alone their children. Such parents should be reported even though their children may not yet have suffered actual harm or injury. A few state laws specifically require reports of one or more forms of severe mental disability, but even in the absence of such provisions, a report is required under the general legal mandate to report endangered children, described in Chapter 3.

SEVERE AND DEMONSTRABLE DISABILITIES

Extreme cases of parental brutality and neglect make us all eager to protect as many children as possible from *future* maltreatment. This had led some authorities to suggest the reporting of "high-risk" parents, that is, parents with a propensity toward abuse or neglect.[1] But such sophisticated psychological assessments of future parental behavior are beyond even the best clinicians.[2]

Despite years of research, there is no psychological profile that accurately identifies parents who will abuse or neglect their children in the future.[3] As Garbarino and Stocking pointed out: "Indeed, the most detailed and fully developed of these profiles designated some 60 percent of the general population at risk for becoming involved in child abuse."[4] "The ability to separate out a distinct group of parents (or future parents) who will *physically* abuse or seriously neglect one or more of their children will probably never be possible," concluded Dr. Ray Helfer after years of research.[5] Cast in this light, a report cannot be based on a psychological diagnosis that an individual is a high-risk parent who may maltreat a child in the future. A more trustworthy measure is needed.

Parents who suffer from severe impairments of judgment or ability to

123

function should be reported. In the absence of suitable arrangements for their children, state intervention is essential—no matter how caring such parents may seem. A report should be made, even if the child is not yet harmed and even if the parent has never had custody of the child.[6] To wait until the child shows signs of abuse or neglect would unreasonably endanger many children.

This is not the same as saying that such children must be removed from their parents' custody. In many cases, supportive services provided by the child protective agency or another public or private agency may permit disabled parents to care for their children. But that is a question to be resolved by the child protective agency. If you do not report such parents, the helping process cannot begin.

However, there must be a connection between the parent's disability and the likelihood that the child will be abused or neglected. Thus, for example, the parent's disability should be current or at least so recent that its continued presence can be assumed. Long past disabilities should not be the basis of a report.

There are many degrees of parental incapacity, and a prediction of future serious injury to the child—and, therefore, a report—is justified only in cases of *severe* mental disability when danger to the child can be presumed. As one court explained:

> Given her long history of mental illness marked by aggressiveness, poor impulse control, paranoia and persecutory delusions, her recent relapses, the absence of any assurance that relapses will not recur and the obvious fact that infants of this age require a high degree of care and attention lest serious consequences befall them, we consider it immaterial that the psychiatrist did not observe her interacting with her child.[7]

But in less severe cases, where it is possible that the parents are adequately caring for the child, a report should be made only if there is reason to believe that a child is at risk: for example, if a child has a "suspicious" or "ambiguous" injury, if the child shows signs of severe physical deprivation, if the child seems to be suffering from emotional or developmental problems, or if you observe specific instances of the parent's inability to care for the child.

Great care must be taken lest legitimate concern for a child's welfare results in an overreaction to a minor or easily remediable parental problem. Many observers believe, for example, that courts and child protective agencies often take children away from parents when abuse or neglect is unlikely or when a small amount of supportive services would enable the parents to care adequately for the child. For example, one court

Chart 12–1 Severe Mental Disabilities of Parents That Should Be Reported

Even if the parents have not yet abused or neglected a child, the following parental disabilities are a sufficient reason to report—unless there is clear evidence that the parents can adequately care for the child.

Severe Mental Illness: overt psychosis or a major depression that so severely impairs the parent's judgment or ability to function that future abuse or neglect is likely

Severe Mental Retardation: an organic brain dysfunction that so severely impairs the parent's judgment or ability to function that future abuse or neglect is likely

Severe Alcohol or Drug Abuse: regular or continuous drug or alcohol abuse that so severely impairs the parent's judgment or ability to function that future abuse or neglect is likely

Inability to Care for a Newborn: observations by medical personnel of such severe lapses in the parents' judgment or ability to function or care for the infant that future abuse or neglect is likely.

---

described how the mother's various hospitalizations for psychiatric treatment "did not establish neglect or unfitness *per se*," especially since there was "no evidence of maltreatment of the children by the petitioner or that in the past they suffered harm at her hands. Whenever she felt a possible recurrence of her disability, [the] petitioner would voluntarily sign herself into a hospital facility for treatment, apparently after first arranging for the care of the children."[8]

Unfortunately, it is not possible to establish precise criteria for deciding when a report should be made. To underscore the need to assess an individual parent's impairment, this book emphasizes that the parent's mental disability must be *severe and demonstrable*. Chart 12–1 lists the forms of severe mental disabilities that may be the basis of a report.

The danger of overreaction makes it especially important that voluntary resolutions of such situations be attempted. In addition, it is important to avoid labeling as "abusive" or "neglectful" parents who have not yet failed in their obligation to care for a child, especially if they have never done anything "wrong." (For example, if a parent's mental capacity is totally destroyed as a result of an automobile accident and no suitable arrangements have been made for the child, the child needs to be cared for, but, certainly, the parent's conduct has not yet been harmful to the child.) As in all child welfare cases, the parents should be offered assistance in meeting their responsibilities toward their children even if

Chart 12–2 **Frequent Symptoms of Psychosis**

The diagnosis of psychosis should be left to a trained professional. Nevertheless, the following symptoms can be used as a guide in deciding whether parents are likely to abuse or neglect their children.

1. *Social withdrawal.* This may show itself in marked shyness when around people, efforts to avoid social situations, or, in an extreme, staying by oneself all the time, like the mother who refuses to leave her bedroom.

2. *Loss of contact.* We see this, while interviewing, in the woman who seems unaware of what is going on around her, who drifts in and out of focus in her conversation, who seems at times to be staring aimlessly at a point far out in space. There is also the client who dashes around in disorganized fashion while with you. Silence is not the only expression of being out of contact, living in daydreams.

3. *Inappropriateness of mood.* One version of this is called "lability," in which mood veers wildly from sadness to hilarity and back again, as with a perpetual adolescent. Another form is shown by the person who laughs in the midst of discussing something painful, or smiles vacantly in the face of bad news. Perhaps most frequent, however, is the patient whose mood is inappropriate because it never seems to change. It ranges from dull apathy to torpid stolidity. This is also called "flatness of affect."

4. *Bizarre behaviors and grimaces.* Sometimes the client will talk to herself, laugh at nothing at all—unless she is responding to inner voices! Strange movements with arms, legs, facial contortions and the like are worth noting.

the help that is offered is extreme—the placement of the child in foster care. Although the acceptance of such offers of assistance may be far from voluntary, at least it permits the parents to reassert their rights after they recover without facing the obstacle of a previous finding of "neglect." Only if the parents refuse to cooperate or are too ill to make a reasoned decision, should a report be considered.

SEVERE MENTAL ILLNESS

Parents who suffer from a severe mental illness are simply incapable of providing adequate care for their children. For example, one appellate

Chart 12-2 **Frequent Symptoms of Psychosis (*continued*)**

5. *Disturbances in the stream of thought.* It is useful to note whether the client talks gibberish. Coining new words or using malapropisms is sometimes indicative that a person heretofore intact is breaking down. Some persons also show an inability to break off a stream of speech, repeating the same thing over and over like a record that is stuck; related to this may be a need to mimic everything they hear.

6. *Delusional systems.* These are sometimes hard to discern. Some of the distortions of reality are relatively mild. That is, we know that something is wrong, but is it wrong enough to indicate psychosis? A woman absolutely refused to have her son vaccinated so he could enter school. She was convinced that if he were vaccinated he would die. Forty or 50 years ago this belief was not uncommon among fearful mothers. But what does it mean now?

7. *Hallucinations.* Many clients are wise enough to refuse to admit having such symptoms except under highly skillful questioning. Therefore, we often infer the presence of hallucinations from bizarre reactions of the sort mentioned under point 4. The presence of hallucinations is ominous, of course.

8. *Severe Anxiety*—a kind of formless, chronic state of terror. Not all psychotics experience this, but most do. It is not true that psychotics as a rule have no insight and are unaware there is anything wrong with them. A great many can feel themselves losing contact; they regard their own symptoms as strange and frightening. Anxiety is both the cause and the effect of this illness. It shows itself in myriad ways.

SOURCE: N. Polansky, C. De Saix, and S. Sharlin, *Child Neglect: Understanding and Reaching the Parent* (New York: Child Welfare League of America, 1973), pp. 48–49.

---

court described how a mother suffered from "schizophrenia chronic undifferentiated type" so severe that "she is unable now and will likely remain unable in the future to properly care for a child."[9] Another court concluded that a mother with a similar diagnosis posed "a real and serious possibility of leaving an infant unattended."[10]

Parents who suffer from overt psychoses that are so severe that the parents are significantly detached from reality or major depressions that are so severe that the parents cannot cope with the world around them should be reported.[11] Chart 12–2 describes the most frequent symptoms of psychosis.

Parental behavior or statements are the most common indication of severe mental illness. You should report parents of infants or very young children who say that they feel themselves slipping out of control or who say that they fear they may hurt or kill their children.[12] Mental health agencies have been "confronted by cases in which a psychotic mother has threatened to cut off the child's arms and legs [and] cases in which a newborn infant has been sent home with a mother who has discussed her child's 'evil intentions' with the nurse in obstetrics."[13]

A parent's threats to kill a child are often clear evidence of severe mental disturbance. They require an immediate report, even if the child has not yet been injured. A judge in Staten Island, New York, for example, described how a mother told her caseworker that she was "very depressed," "wanted to end it all," and would "take the children with her." She asked: "What do I have to do to get help, something stupid like dangling one of my kids over the ferry?" The judge ruled that "the mere utterance of a threat to kill or seriously injure one's child" establishes the need for protective action.[14]

A distinction must be drawn, however, between a parent's threats to kill or harm a child and a parent's descriptions of anger or loss of control. Apparently serious threats to harm a child must be reported. Expressions of anger toward a child and of fears of losing control, on the other hand, require further assessment. Many parents have "angry thoughts" about their children; some find themselves thinking about beating their children. That the parents have summoned the courage to tell an outsider about such feelings is a reflection of how disturbing these feelings can be. In parents of newborns and infants, such feelings are a signal of serious danger that cannot be ignored. But in parents of older children, the verbalization of these feelings is an all-too-common symptom of problematic parent/child relationships. Although such feelings are destructive and the parents may benefit from treatment, they do not necessarily lead to actual abuse or neglect. Thus, for parents of older children, "angry thoughts" warrant a report only if there are sufficient additional reasons to believe that they signal real danger to the child.

SEVERE MENTAL RETARDATION

Extremely retarded parents should be reported. The parent's mental retardation should, of course, have a clear relationship to the quality of care the parent is able to provide for the child. Polansky, De Saix, and Sharlin found that "the quality of the care given the children does not seem to be grossly affected until the mother's score drops below 70. Inadequate and neglectful care may be expected when the IQ of the mother is below 60."[15] They concluded, therefore, that many parents of borderline retardation (with IQs between 68 and 83) and even many mildly retarded parents (with IQs between 52 and 67) can care adequately for their children.

But beyond these few guidelines, no generalizations are possible; the variables are too great and the ability to measure them with relative precision is too limited. The decision to report a parent's mental retardation must be made on a case-by-case basis.

DRUG AND ALCOHOL ABUSE

Parental abuse of alcohol has always been a threat to children, and heroin and other drugs have been child protective problems since at least the 1960s. But American children now face a problem many times more serious: crack, a derivative of cocaine. As Dr. David Bateman, director of perinatology at New York's Harlem Hospital, explained: "Heroin was a man's drug and we just didn't see as much of it in pregnant women. Many more women are on crack than ever were on heroin."[16]

No one knows how many women now use crack and other drugs, but the number of reported crack-exposed babies has been increasing rapidly. In New York City, for example, the number of such babies just about doubled between 1986 and 1987, increased 85 percent in 1988, and then increased another 14 percent in 1989—to 4,875 drug-related births a year.[17] Even at its peak in the late 1960s and early 1970s in big cities like New York, heroin withdrawal affected only one-tenth as many newborns.[18]

"These mothers don't care about their babies and they don't care about themselves," said Dr. Jing Ja Yoon, chief of neonatology at Bronx Lebanon Hospital. "Crack is destroying people—I've never seen mothers like this before."[19] The Ramsey County Minnesota Department of Human Services, after reviewing 70 cases of "cocaine-attached" households in mid-1988, found that these parents are "extremely volatile with episodes of 'normal' behavior interspersed with episodes of unpredictable, dangerous and even violent behavior."[20]

Cases of drug-crazed battering of children are becoming more common. Some attribute Lisa Steinberg's murder to the effects of cocaine on both Joel Steinberg and Hedda Nussbaum. In another well-publicized New York case, a five-year-old girl was found dead in her parent's apartment with a broken neck; she also had a broken arm, large circular welts on her buttocks, and cuts and bruises on her mouth. Her nine-year-old brother was found the next day huddled in a closet, with both legs fractured, eight other broken bones, and bruises covering his body.[21]

Other babies of drug addicts die of neglect. In one case, a 10 month old died after being left overnight in an overheated room (it reached 110 degrees) while his mother visited her boyfriend.[22] Social workers tell of three year olds who feed themselves from refrigerators and of seven year olds who know how to use illegal drugs after watching their parents use them.[23]

Parental alcohol or drug abuse that is severe enough to make future child abuse or neglect likely should be reported. Many states have laws that make serious drug or alcohol abuse prima facie evidence of child neglect.[24] But, again, such specific laws are not necessary. Severe alcohol or drug abuse can so strikingly impair a parent's judgment and ability to cope that the need to report falls under general statutory provisions concerning the threat of harm.

Most parents deny that they abuse drugs or alcohol, of course. But a surprising number admit to their addiction. For example, some drug-addicted mothers freely describe the size of their habit, the difficulties they have in obtaining a sufficient amount of drugs to satisfy their habit, and their inability to care for their children. (Except in those states in which any level of drug addiction must be reported, the parent's participation in a treatment or counseling program does not establish, *by itself*, that a report should be made. The parent, perhaps with outside help, may be adequately caring for the child.)

Newborns who show signs of fetal exposure to drugs or alcohol should be reported. A mother's dietary or chemical habits during pregnancy can put her unborn child at special risk. A pregnant woman who continues to use crack, cocaine, heroin, methadone, or large quantities of barbiturates or alcohol is likely to give birth to a child with severe health problems.

Untreated neonatal addiction to heroin, for example, can be fatal. The dangers encountered by heroin babies were described in a New York City case:

> [The] baby was born normally without apparent symptoms until 24 hours after birth, [when he] began to exhibit unmistakable narcotic withdrawal symptoms; preconvulsive tremors, hyperactivity, incessant crying, ravenousness alternating with vomiting. . . Sedatives (phenobarbitol), dark and quiet were required for seven days before the child became physically well. Without careful therapy, the child might have suffered convulsions and death.[25]

Fetal exposure to cocaine has equally serious effects and is not as easily remedied. Cocaine constricts the blood vessels in the placenta and the fetus, cutting off the flow of oxygen and nutrients and often causing miscarriages, stillbirths, and premature and low-birth weight babies, often with various physical and neurological malformations. Some crack-exposed babies have deformed hearts, lungs, digestive systems, or limbs; others have what amounts to a disabling stroke while in the womb.[26] Death rates may be twice as high for crack babies as for others.

Most states now accept reports of prenatal drug exposure. Some specifically require them.[27] In other states, courts and agencies hold that "a new-born baby having withdrawal symptoms is prima facie a neglected baby."[28] Because of the need to mobilize child protective efforts, states have begun accepting reports while the mother is still pregnant.

The absence of withdrawal symptoms or side effects, though, is not conclusive evidence that the parent does not use drugs or that the situation should not be reported. Not all babies who are born to even heavy drug users exhibit withdrawal symptoms. (Anywhere from 30 to 50 percent do not.) Although medical studies have yet to develop specific measures of prediction, it appears that the existence and severity of withdrawal symptoms are functions of the type, dosage, and regularity of drug use. All babies born to drug addicts should be reported because, after all, they will be in danger when at home.

INABILITY TO CARE FOR A NEWBORN

Very young children are the most vulnerable to serious injury and death. More than three-quarters of all child abuse fatalities involve children who are less than six years old, and more than half involve children age two or under.[29] So that these most vulnerable children can be protected, they must be identified as soon after birth as possible.

Hospital maternity wards are an excellent setting for observing early parent/child interactions that are suggestive of later abuse or neglect. Dr. Barton Schmitt, director of Colorado General Hospital's Child Protection Team, gave the following thoughtful description of maternal behavior that indicates a "high risk" of future maltreatment:

The following information can be noted in the newborn nursery by the physician or the nurses. First, claiming behavior should be observed before the mother is discharged. It can be normal for a mother to feel that the baby is really not hers for a few hours or days; but, if she does not accept the baby as "hers" as evidenced by naming him, wanting to hold him, and wanting to feed him by the time the baby is three days old, a serious delay in maternal attachment has occurred and requires evaluation. Second, the mother may consider the child a disappointment as evidenced by her disparaging comments that he is "ugly," "diseased," or "defective." This situation is especially dangerous if, in truth, the child does not have any of these disorders. Most mothers consider their normal newborn to be beautiful. Third, the high-risk mother may be revolted by the child's odor, drooling, regurgitation, urine, or stools.[30]

Over the years, numerous efforts have been made to translate this kind of clinical wisdom into questionnaires, checklists, or other screening devices to identify parents who will later abuse or neglect their children. However, these "high-risk" indicators are just that. They indicate only that there is a high *risk* of the future maltreatment of a child, not that maltreatment will actually or even probably happen. They cannot be used as a basis of reporting because, as their authors carefully point out, they incorrectly identify far too many parents as being potentially abusive or neglectful. (They are, nevertheless, valuable screening devices for neonatal counseling and follow-up programs.)[31]

The parent's demonstrated inability to care for a newborn should be reported. Certain specific parental behaviors in the maternity ward do provide a sufficient basis for a report, however. What parents are unable to do in the hospital, where they have help, they are unlikely to be able to do at home—alone. You should report concrete examples of parental inability to care for a newborn, such as those listed in Chart 12–3. Such observations are a sufficient basis for your report, but your decision is made easier, either for or against a report, the more you know about the quality of care provided to other children in the family or of the home conditions in general.

As a general rule, the conditions listed on Chart 12–3 should be reported as soon as they are observed. Those that do not involve parent/child interaction, such as severe mental disabilities and the past maltreatment of other children, should be reported even before the new child's birth. Doing so will give the child protection agency added time to mobilize and develop an appropriate case plan.

On the other hand, many of the situations listed in the chart involve an assessment of the parent's relative inability to care for the child or to function generally in society. In some cases, the hospital staff may conclude that the quality of child care will improve rapidly through short-term parental education or counseling. If the hospital operates or has access to the Visiting Nursing Service or another neonatal follow-

Chart 12–3 **Reportable Maternity Ward Observations**

- A parent's lack of impulse control, as demonstrated by spanking or becoming furious at a newborn.
- A parent's inability, even after instruction, to feed, change, or otherwise care for the infant.
- A parent's refusal to consent to needed medical care for the infant (unless it is heroic treatment for a terminally ill infant).
- A parent's failure to take an infant home when medically ready for discharge. This form of rejecting behavior is so extreme that it is a cause for great concern; it is also a form of abandonment.
- A parent's failure to visit an infant (usually premature) who remains in the hospital for lengthy additional care (another version of abandonment).
- A parent's failure to prepare for the infant's homecoming, such as the failure to prepare a layette. This is an early and objective sign of the parent's future inability to plan for and to meet the child's needs.
- A parent's past maltreatment of other children—especially if the children have been removed from the parent's custody. (Child protective agencies often do not know about the mother's subsequent pregnancy or delivery, and so cannot protect the newborn.)
- A parent's severe alcohol or drug abuse. (The latter often is accompanied by drug withdrawal symptoms in the child.)
- A parent's severe mental retardation or illness.
- The parent's *serious* postpartum depression, manifested by excessive crying, anxiety, and confusion.

The foregoing reportable conditions have been stated in gender-neutral terms because, although such conditions usually are observed in mothers, their presence in fathers is a cause for equal concern.

up program, a decision to report may be deferred while efforts are made to work with the parents. (The major exception to this discretionary delay in reporting involves cases in which the child would be in immediate and severe danger if sent home with the parents.) Parents who refuse to accept such help, later prove uncooperative, or show little ability to care for the child on their own should be reported promptly. Infants are extremely vulnerable and a delay could be fatal.

13

Interviewing Parents

You are under no legal obligation to speak to parents. If sufficient independent grounds for a report exist, you do not have to seek their explanation for the child's condition or statement. However, there are often good reasons for interviewing the parents before a report is made. This chapter describes when and how to do so. Although this chapter is largely directed to professionals, all potential reporters may find it helpful.

SEEKING EXPLANATIONS

It is almost always appropriate to ask both the child and the parents about the origin of the child's injuries, unless doing so will endanger the child (or you). (Interviewing children is discussed in Chapter 6.)

First, you may have a vague feeling that something is wrong at home, but no real evidence on which to base a report. An interview may reveal crucial information about possible maltreatment, often when you notice a child's minor bruises or changes in the behavior that do not justify a report yet worry you. No law requires you to question the parents to see whether a report is needed, but tactfully doing so is entirely appropriate and may save the child from more severe injury.

Second, even when there is evidence to support a report, you may want to know whether the parents can provide a reasonable explanation of the situation. Although you have no duty to exonerate the parents, you can thus protect them—and the children—from a needless and possibly traumatic child protective investigation.

Both parents should be interviewed, if possible. You should seek the parents' explanation for the child's condition; the parents' description of the precautions they took to prevent the injuries (if they claim that the injuries were accidental); and the parent's description of the medical care, if any, that was obtained for the child's injuries. You should also ask whether the child has been injured before. Try to find out as much as possible about any previous injury or injuries. Also ask the parents to describe how they care for the child. Seek as much information as possible about feeding practices, personal hygiene, sleeping arrangements, medical care, supervision and baby-sitting, and the physical conditions of the home. Last, if you work in an agency that can provide ongoing supportive, counseling, or treatment services, you may also seek information about the family's internal dynamics and overall situation.

No one should pretend that asking these kinds of questions is easy. The parents are likely to be hostile or at least suspicious, and you may well feel embarrassed and uncomfortable about inquiring into these kinds of private family matters. Successful interviews require a combination of tact and persistence.

Each parent should be questioned separately. The interview is not an inquisition. Forceful interrogation is inappropriate and does not elicit as much information as subtle probing. Furthermore, "situations that appear to be maltreatment may turn out to be something else. Thus it is well to conduct oneself professionally by adhering to facts, and by avoiding placing blame and making judgments and accusations. . . . It is important not to alienate the family."[1] (This is especially important for professionals who are likely to continue serving the family, perhaps for many years to come.) Properly conducted, the interview can

> establish rapport with the family and set the stage for on-going working relationships between the family and health and social service professionals.
>
> Families frequently "shop around" for a hospital or doctor in cases of child abuse and neglect—in some cases to avoid being identified and in others to find someone who will identify them and therefore help. This initial contact for a hostile family can allay their fears and convince them to stay and get help; or for a family quietly seeking help it can bring them into the system.[2]

The exact tone of the interview will vary, depending on the setting and the kind of relationship between you and the parents. Chart 13–1 provides some guidelines that may help you conduct a smoother and more productive interview.

Although questioning of parents rarely elicits an outright admission of abuse or neglect, it often reveals sufficient information to require a report. For example, the parents' explanations of how a young child received suspicious injuries may be inconsistent with the appearance of the injuries, making it likely that the injuries were inflicted. You should also be alert to any vagueness or inconsistency in accounts, either over time or between the parents.

Chart 13–1 **Guidelines for Interviewing Parents**[3]

- Interview both parents, but do so separately.
- Make the parents feel as comfortable as possible. (Conduct the interview in private.)
- Be professional, direct, and honest.
- Tell the parents that the child's physical condition or behavior is a matter of concern. In most cases, though, it is neither necessary nor appropriate to say that abuse or neglect is suspected.
- At least initially, focus your questions on the child's condition and its possible causes.
- Ask open-ended questions; for example, ask the parents whether they know what happened.
- Do not try to prove abuse or neglect through accusations or demands. It rarely helps to ask: "Did you hit your child?"
- Do not press inconsistencies, but note them carefully.
- With rare exceptions, do not confront the parents with the child's description of being abused or neglected or otherwise betray the child's confidences. (One exception is when the child's statements are such outright fabrications or distortions of reality that the child's need for therapy is indicated and parental cooperation must be obtained.)
- Do not display anger, repugnance, or shock.
- Be attentive to what the parents have to say; pick up the nuances in their statements. For example, if a parent expresses difficulty in caring for the children, you may follow-up with a comment such as, "It must be difficult to keep up with things when you have such active children."
- If appropriate, you should inform the parents that a report of suspected child maltreatment will be made. If you do so, you may also wish to offer them continued support and assistance during the child protective investigation.

Other information can be as important as an actual admission. You should note any statements in which the parents reveal extremely unrealistic or inappropriate expectations about their children. Be especially alert to parents who report severe problems in toilet training when the child has burns or bruises on the buttocks or upper thighs. Also be concerned about parents who angrily describe how an infant deliberately tries to irritate them or whose behavior suggests that they are suffering from severe mental disabilities. Since the parents' statements may be admissible in a subsequent court proceeding, and certainly will be central to the child protective agency's investigation, everything you learn should be written down and placed on file.

UNSATISFACTORY EXPLANATIONS

Under certain limited circumstances, suspicious injuries may have an alternate explanation that obviates the need for a report. The injuries may have been caused by an unusual or freak accident or by a rare bone or blood disease; they may have been the unintended—and unforeseeable—consequence of otherwise reasonable corporal punishment; or someone other than the parents, say a playmate, may have inflicted the injury. Chart 13–2 summarizes the three ways in which parents can satisfactorily explain a child's suspicious injuries.

Obviously, if the parents cannot explain how a young child received a suspicious injury, a report should be made. "A frequent statement is that the parents do not know what has happened but the child was well when he was put to bed last night and when he was awakened, he appeared unable to use his arm or his leg" (because it was broken).[4] Such claims of ignorance are sometimes accompanied by the parents' "guess" that the injuries may be self-inflicted. For suspicious injuries in younger children, such claims should be given little credence. As Dr. Barton Schmitt explained: "Normal parents know to the minute where and when their child was hurt. They also show complete willingness to discuss it in detail."[5]

As children grow older, they spend an increasing amount of time out of the house and outside the immediate supervision of parents. It is less possible, then, for parents to account for suspicious injuries, and it is less reasonable to hold parents responsible when they cannot explain how a child was injured, especially since the child should be old enough to tell what happened. Thus, for older children, you may accept a parent's claim of ignorance. But this should be a deliberate decision—after also questioning the child.

What if the parents give an explanation? Parental explanations should not be rejected out of hand. Most parents do not abuse their children, and most minor injuries are not caused by abuse. You should keep an open mind and listen to what the parents have to say. Of course, this means that you may make a mistake, that parents who are actually abusive may be able to convince you that their child's injuries were accidentally inflicted or inflicted by someone else. In a society like ours, which presumes the innocence of persons accused of wrongdoing, such

---

Chart 13–2 Satisfactory Explanations of Suspicious Injuries

An inference of abuse is countered by a *believable* parental explanation establishing that

- The child's apparent injuries are actually manifestations of an undiagnosed illness.
- The child's injuries were more likely to be ordinary injuries of childhood and are consistent with the parents' explanation.
- The child was not in the parents' custody during the time when the injuries were sustained.
- Someone other than the parents inflicted the injuries, and the parents' inattention or indifference was not a contributory factor.

Doubtful situations should be resolved in favor of protecting the child. The law, after all, requires reports of *suspected* child maltreatment.

---

mistakes are unavoidable. Some abusive parents have had long experience lying, and they do it convincingly.

There is no excuse, however, for accepting farfetched, illogical, or contradictory explanations. Robin M, a 43-day-old infant, was brought by her mother to a hospital in a coma with multiple fractures of the skull, a subarachnoid hemorrhage, and contusion of the brain. The injuries were so severe that Robin died the next day. Her mother claimed that Robin had "fallen out of bed." You do not need a medical degree to be suspicious of such explanations.[6]

Although your assessment of a parent's explanation is often a matter of judgment, there are a number of guidelines that can be provided. First, you should not accept explanations that are at variance with visual observations and clinical findings. In fact, sufficiently implausible explanations can be inculpatory,[7] and injuries that are inconsistent with the parents' explanation are a common reason for making a report. For example, the parents' claim that a child pulled a pot of hot water off a stove does not explain extensive splash burns on the child's back (which were more likely suffered as the child tried to run away from the parent).

Black eyes are frequently explained as resulting from a fall. With one black eye, you may not be able to tell if this is true. But "two black eyes with no accompanying damage to the nose are highly suspect, since it is virtually impossible to sustain accidental injuries of this type."[8] The only alternate explanation for two black eyes is a severe injury to another part of the head. If no such injury is found, you should consider the black eyes to have been inflicted. If there is a head injury, that injury must be assessed to determine if it appears to have been inflicted.

Likewise, numerous bruises on different parts of the body—and at different stages of healing—conflict with a parent's claim that the child "ran into a coffee table." They imply repeat beatings. As Schmitt noted:

> Most falls give bruises on just one body surface. Bruises on multiple body planes are usually inflicted, unless there is a history of a tumbling accident. It is true that tumbling accidents often cause minimal bruises and abrasions, but if there are many, they will predominate on the elbows, knees, and shoulders. "Falling down a stairway" is commonly offered as a last minute explanation for unexplained bruises on a child. However, the lack of bruises in the above locations makes this explanation doubtful.[9]

Second, information that the parents abused the same child or a sibling or that there is a history of questionable injuries is a strong reason to disbelieve the parents' explanation. As the New York Court of Appeals explained, "the credibility of the 'accident' explanation diminishes as the instances of similar alleged 'accidental' injuries increase."[10] Chart 13–3 describes how to gauge the relative age of bruises.

Rose B's father ran out of implausible explanations for her suspicious injuries:

> The respondent's explanation was patently feeble. Although he stated he was completely unaware of his daughter's condition until it was brought to his attention by the school authorities, he attributed the presence of the sores on her body to excessive scratching of insect bites and to allergies. As to the presence of linear abrasions, he assigned the wearing of too tight a belt as the reason, a theory clearly belied by the color photographs in evidence. He had no explanation for the blackened eyes save for the mention of the possibility that Rose had fallen from her bed. While respondent generally denied striking the infant, he did concede that some time before the discovery of her condition he had disciplined her with his belt.[11]

Third, a parent's claims that a child's injuries were self-inflicted should be assessed within the context of the child's age and stage of development and the likelihood of the claimed behavior. Few six-month-olds can climb out of a crib and few one-year-olds can fill a tub with scalding hot water. As Schmitt stated:

> The child who is under six months of age is unlikely to be able to

Chart 13–3 **Gauging the Relative Ages of Bruises**[12]

A bruise results from an injury or trauma to the body that breaks the small blood vessels beneath the skin; it is the external manifestation of this subsurface bleeding. Over time, a bruise changes color as this subsurface blood changes color. The exact dating of bruises is difficult because different bruises and different people heal at different speeds. Nevertheless, the following chart will help you determine the relative age of bruises:

Age	Color
0–2 days	swollen, tender
0–5 days	red, blue, purple
5–7 days	green
7–10 days	yellow
10–14 days	brown
14–28 days	clear

induce any accident. Absurd stories, such as the baby rolled over on his arm and broke it, or he got his head caught in the crib and fractured it, are pure nonsense. Histories implying that the child is masochistic are also uniformly false, such as the child who hurts himself badly during a temper tantrum, gets subdural hematomas by hitting himself with a bottle, climbs up onto a hot radiator, or burns himself up to the elbow by immersing his arm in hot water. Children rarely injure themselves deliberately.[13]

Fourth, it is always possible that someone other than the parents inflicted the child's injuries. If this explanation is accepted, no report should be made unless the parents failed to take adequate steps to protect the child from further injury. On the other hand, you should report parents who blame a child's injuries on an unidentified baby-sitter or a mysterious stranger whose name and address they do not know. Although their story could be true, it is up to the child protective agency to determine the credibility of such unsupported claims.

Similarly, a parent's claims that the child's injuries were caused by another child should be assessed within the context of the other child's ability to cause the kinds of injuries involved. Often, medical evidence is needed to assess such claims. In one criminal prosecution, for example, "two Nassau County medical examiners, one of whom was a karate expert, testified that the death dealing blows to the child's liver and kidneys were caused by karate chops or fingers poked into the abdominal area and that the child's siblings, aged five and eight years, could not have caused the fatal injuries."[14]

Finally, a visual examination of the site of an alleged accident also can assist in the assessment of the parent's explanation:

For example, a 2-year-old boy was examined with a burn on his right buttock that allegedly occurred when he fell onto the stove while trying to get cookies out of a kitchen cabinet. A home evaluation found it was impossible for the boy to have sustained the injury as described.[15]

Relatively few potential reporters will be in a child's home or be able to visit it, but, if there, you should not miss the opportunity to gain valuable information and to document it fully through a written summary and photographs, if possible.

BEHAVIORAL INDICATORS

Unsatisfactory explanations of suspicious injuries should be rejected and a report should be made. But some childhood injuries are of ambiguous origin; an accidental cause may be as likely, or almost as likely, as an inflicted one. And some parental explanations are sufficiently consistent with the nature of the injuries that they cannot be dismissed out of hand. In these ambiguous situations, the behavior of either the child or the parent can help you decide whether to report.

Behavioral indicators are not, in themselves, grounds for a report. Over the years, many behavioral "profiles" of abusive parents have been developed. These behavioral profiles are uniformly *unreliable* when used to identify abusive parents *before* the child has been assaulted. Not only do they falsely label many innocent parents as abusive, they also miss many actual abusers.[16]

Nevertheless, the behavior of abused children and of abusive parents tends to fall within certain recurrent patterns. For example, abusive parents often delay seeking medical help for their children for fear of being discovered; because of indifference to the child's needs; or, perhaps "hoping that the event never occurred, or that the injury will not require medical care."[17] As Schmitt noted:

Normal parents come in immediately when their child is injured. Some abused children are not brought in for a considerable period of time despite a major injury. In extreme situations, children are brought in nearly dead. One study showed that 40 percent of children weren't brought in until the morning after the injury. Another 40 percent came in one to four days after the injury.[18]

Certain behavioral indicators can be used to help assess ambiguous situations. Although not an independent ground for a report of abuse, the presence of one or more of the parental behaviors described in Chart 13–4 or of the child behaviors described in Chart 6–1 reinforces the significance of suspicious or ambiguous injuries and turns an ambiguous situation into one that should be reported. (Their absence, however, does not necessarily mean that the child has not been abused.) And, of course, even in the absence of suspicious injuries to the child, they can be a sign for you to explore possible family problems.

One further caveat about using these behavioral indicators: While they are designed for use by all potential reporters, laypersons should use them with great care. Even experts have difficulty judging the significance of many parent and child behaviors.

Chart 13–4 **Parental Behaviors Used to Assess Ambiguous Injuries**[19]

There is no behavioral profile of abusive parents that does not falsely label many innocent parents while also missing many actual abusers. Nevertheless, the behavior of many abusive parents tends to fall within certain recurrent patterns. Hence, although *not an independent ground for a report of abuse,* the following extremes of parental behavior can assist you in the assessment of ambiguous injuries and parental explanations that are of borderline plausibility.

Suspicious Actions

Abusive parents often behave in a way that suggests that they are trying to conceal a child's injury or how it was received:

- Abusive parents often respond inappropriately to the seriousness of the child's condition either by overreacting (seeming to be hostile or antagonistic when questioned even casually) or by underreacting (showing little concern or awareness and seeming to be more preoccupied with their own problems than those of the child).
- Abusive parents often are unable to explain how a child was injured; they frequently claim that they just "don't know what happened."
- Abusive parents often give explanations for their children's injuries that are farfetched or at variance with clinical findings. They also often change their explanations (and social histories) on close questioning.

Parental Behaviors Used to Assess Ambiguous Injuries

- Abusive parents often blame their children's injuries on a baby-sitter or a stranger whom they cannot identify.
- Abusive parents often attempt to conceal the extent of their children's present and past injuries; they frequently refuse to consent to diagnostic studies.
- Abusive parents often delay seeking medical help, which suggests that they fear being discovered or that they have little concern for the child's welfare; they frequently seem to hope that the child will recover without medical care.
- Abusive parents often bring their children to a hospital late at night for what they claim are accidental injuries. The lateness of the hour, however, suggests that the child was abused for not going to bed, that the child was awakened and abused during a parent's violent rage, that the parents delayed seeking help in the hope that the child would recover, or that the parents realized that the child's condition was worsening.
- Abusive parents often change hospitals or physicians in the hope that their abuse will not be discovered through knowledge of past injuries (or, ironically, they may be looking for someone who will notice their problems and offer help).
- Abusive parents often seek medical assistance for minor or nonexistent ailments as a way of seeking help; they frequently bring a child in for a cold, a headache, or a stomachache when the child has serious physical injuries.

Personality Characteristics

Although less reliable than suspicious actions, certain personality characteristics—revealed by the following parental behaviors—are sufficiently associated with child abuse to be useful in assessing ambiguous situations:

- Abusive parents often have rigid and unrealistic expectations of their children. They expect or demand behavior that is beyond the child's age or ability and frequently are unaware of the normal developmental stages and milestones of childhood.
- Abusive parents often have little understanding of their children's physical and emotional needs; they may ignore their child's crying or react with impatience.
- Abusive parents often are overcritical of their children and seldom, if ever, discuss their children in positive terms. They frequently describe their children, even infants, as unloving or ungrateful. In more extreme cases, they

(continued on next page)

Parental Behaviors Used to Assess Ambiguous Injuries (*continued*)

sometimes describe their children as "different," "bad," "all trouble," "a monster," or "a witch." (Some mothers will say that a male child is "just like his father," who, often, will have deserted her.)

- Abusive parents often are isolated from social support, such as friends, relatives, neighbors, and community groups. They may consistently fail to keep appointments and may discourage social contact and never participate in school activities or community events.
- Abusive parents sometimes blame their children for their own problems.
- Abusive parents sometimes vigorously defend their right to punish misbehaving children, even if the children have been seriously injured.
- Abusive parents sometimes seem unable to relate to their children; they may avoid touching or looking at them.
- Abusive parents sometimes describe how they were abused or neglected as children.
- Abusive parents sometimes are unable to describe their young children's eating habits or daily activities.
- Abusive parents sometimes seem to encourage a parent/child role reversal, with the child being expected to comfort the parent.
- Abusive parents sometimes misuse alcohol or drugs.
- Abusive parents sometimes live in situations of chronic family discord, financial problems, or other personal stresses.
- Abusive parents sometimes have recently undergone a major personal crisis, such as the loss of a job or of a loved one.
- Abusive parents sometimes appear to lack control or to fear that they will lose control.
- Abusive parents sometimes are of borderline intelligence or are psychotic or psychopathic. Such diagnoses should be made only by qualified mental health professionals, but even the lay observer can sometimes make an initial determination that the parent seems intellectually incapable of child rearing, exhibits generally irrational behavior, or seems excessively cruel and sadistic.

In weighing the significance of the behaviors described in this chart, you should remember that the parent is being observed in an obviously stressful situation. You should also take into account the parent's social situation and likely inexperience with and fear of authority figures and quasi-law enforcement processes. To be useful in assessing the significance of the child's injuries, the parent's behavior should be extreme. In addition, you should always consider explanations for the parent's behavior other than abuse.

MAKING A DECISION

Chart 13–5 summarizes the questions that you should ask yourself before accepting a parent's explanation. In the great majority of cases, the parent's explanation can be satisfactorily judged by reference to the questions listed there. In some cases, though, ambiguous injuries or parental explanations of borderline plausibility make a definitive determination impossible. *As a general rule, doubtful situations should be resolved in favor of protecting the child.* The law, after all, requires reports of *suspected* child maltreatment.

Chart 13–5 **Judging Parental Explanations**

- Does the parent have an explanation for the child's suspicious injury? A claim of ignorance is no explanation.
- Is the parent's explanation inconsistent with the nature of the injuries? For example, does the parent claim that the child sustained a fractured skull or a serious subdural hemorrhage from falling off a bed or a changing table? Does the parent claim that a child with scalding burns on the buttocks (but not the feet) "stepped into a tub of hot water?"
- If the parent claims that the injuries were the result of an accident, is the parent's description of the child's behavior or other circumstances plausible? For example, does the parent claim that injuries on an apparently docile infant were self-inflicted? Or, is the physical setting of the claimed accident inconsistent with the nature or severity of the child's injuries? (Injuries that result from the parent's gross negligence also should be reported.)
- Do other situational factors suggest that the parent's explanation should not be accepted? For example, does the parent describe difficulties in toilet training or disciplining a young child who is suffering from immersion burns to the perineum or buttocks?
- In situations in which the origin of the injuries is ambiguous or the parent's explanation is of *possible* plausibility, does the behavior of either the child or the parent suggest abuse? For example, when pressed for details, does the parent give contradictory descriptions of the same events?

Doubtful situations should be resolved in favor of protecting the child. The law requires reports of *suspected* child maltreatment.

Moreover, even if the parent's explanation is believed, there still may be reason to report. In telling what happened, the parent may have described gross inattention to the child's need for safety that amounts to reportable physical endangerment, [20] as described in Chapter 10. Or, the parent may have described how no action was taken to protect the child from a dangerous adult. Such conduct suggests that the child is in continuing danger of further injury and must be reported.

PART

THREE

The Reporting Process

14

Preserving Evidence

E vidence of maltreatment is often more available at the time of the
report than at any other time in the process. You should do your
best to preserve it—even before making a report. Like the prior chapter,
this one is largely directed to professionals, but anyone may come upon
evidence of child abuse and should know what to do about it.

PHYSICAL EVIDENCE

More often than is realized, physical evidence exists to document the
suspected abuse or neglect. Be alert to the possibility of such evidence
and attempt to obtain and preserve it, especially if you are in the family's
home.

Physical evidence of abuse may include the instrument used to beat
the child (such as a whip, a belt, a stick, or a wire or cord), the object
used to burn the child (such as a cigarette lighter, an iron, a space
heater, or an electric grill or hot plate), or clothing worn by the child
showing blood, other stains, or damage. In cases of sexual abuse, most
physical evidence is obtained from a physical examination of the child,
the child's clothes, and laboratory tests. Such evidence may include
the alleged perpetrator's semen, blood, or pubic hair on the child's genital,
anal, or oral areas or on the child's clothes or other belongings. Sexual
exploitation may be documented in photographs, films, or videotapes.
Physical evidence of neglect may include illegal drugs found in the
parent's possession or dangerous items, such as guns, knives, or poisons,
found within the child's reach.

All physical evidence should be carefully labeled and put away for
safekeeping. It should be described in your records and, as soon as
appropriate, turned over to the child protective agency, the police, or
other investigating authority. (Obtain a receipt.)

Medical facilities have a special obligation toward the child. As part
of their management of the child's case, they should carefully evaluate

Chart 14–1 **Hospital Management of Suspected Child Abuse and Neglect**

A. Report the case by telephone to the mandated state agency. This report is to be made by the examining physician, nurse, or other health professional (as per the state law). Record the name of the individual to whom the report is given as well as the date and time.

B. Complete a written report as soon as possible.

C. Admit the child if there is any question about the safety of his/her home environment, even if there does not appear to be a clear "medical" indication for hospitalization of the child.

D. Admission Orders:
   1. Social Service consultation.
   2. Psychiatric consultation: Mandatory in cases of sexual/physical abuse; otherwise, optional unless the child is exhibiting behavior of concern to the staff.
   3. Occupational Therapy consultation: Initially for developmental screening as a baseline in young children and repeated during the hospital course for comparison.
   4. Skeletal Survey: Mandatory for children suffering from physical abuse or if any history of prior trauma is elicited.
   5. Obstetric and Gynecology consultation: Mandatory in cases of sexual molestation or genital trauma in female children.
      a. VDRL serology.
      b. Gonococcal cultures of the vagina/penile, rectal, and oral areas.
      c. Chlamydial cultures (as per gonococcal cultures).
   6. Photographs should be taken, as soon as possible, of any manifestations of physical injury (burns, lacerations, bruises, old scars), as well as any manifestations of failure to thrive, neglect, malnourishment, or

the child's general physical and developmental condition. They should also begin the process of case planning and treatment. (See Chart 14–1.)

PHOTOGRAPHS AND X RAYS

Unfortunately, the child's physical condition is often the best evidence of abuse or neglect. However, after weeks of hospital or foster care, even the most seriously abused or neglected child may show no signs of past maltreatment. Cuts and bruises may have healed. The child may have gained weight and muscle tone; in fact, the child's entire physical appearance may have changed. A previously battered or emaci-

Chart 14–1 Hospital Management of Suspected Child Abuse and Neglect (*continued*)

severe dehydration. While awaiting photographic documentation, representative drawings should be placed in the chart along with a pertinent narrative on the initial history and physical examination form.

7. Recreational Therapy consultation: To obtain a practical assessment of the child's behavior, as well as to incorporate all potential modalities available as diagnostic aids.

8. Samples of urine, emesis, and blood should be sent for analysis in cases of known or suspected ingestions.
   a. Screening for the specific drug (if known).
   b. General drug screening (if unknown).

9. In cases of Failure-to-Thrive (FTT):
   a. The weight, height, and head circumference at the time of admission should be plotted on appropriate growth charts and included in the medical record.
   b. The birth weight, as well as pertinent perinatal information, should be recorded.
   c. The name of any hospital/clinic/physician providing prior medical care should be noted.
   d. Accurate daily weights should be charted at a predetermined time and utilizing the same scale.
   e. Dietary consultation is often of pivotal importance.

SOURCE: H. B. Levy and S. H. Sheldon, "A Hospital's Response to the Increasing Incidence of Abuse and Neglect in an Inner-City Population," *Mount Sinai Journal of Medicine* 51:2 (1984), 161–64.

ated child may have been transformed into a healthy, flourishing one. Under such circumstances, it may be difficult to convince child protective officials—and judges—of the need for protective measures.

Long after memories have faded, photographs and X rays can provide graphic and incontestable evidence of the severity of a child's injuries at the time of their discovery. Thus, more than half the states explicitly authorize the taking of photographs and X rays without parental consent. Some of these states authorize *any* mandated reporter to take the photographs or X rays or to arrange to have them taken, but most limit this authorization to physicians or other medical personnel, law enforcement officials, and child protective workers. A few states *require* the taking of photographs and X rays by the head of a school, medical facility, or a similar institution.

Chart 14–2 **Guidelines for Taking Photographs**

- Put the child at ease. Be supportive and explain what is happening. The child is already in a traumatic situation, and great care should be taken to prevent the child from becoming more distressed.
- If the child has to be undressed, even partially, say so in advance. Limit the time the child must be undressed.
- For older children, it is advisable to have an adult of the same sex in the room.
- Generally, the sooner a photograph is taken, the more accurately it portrays the injury. However, contusions (black and blue marks) grow more visibly serious as time goes by, and you may thus decide to photograph them when they have reached their peak intensity. When in doubt about timing, take a photograph as soon as possible. Later, if the bruises become more apparent, they can be rephotographed.
- If medical treatment will lessen the visible severity of the injury, try to photograph the child before such treatment. However, the child's health and well-being comes first, and needed emergency treatment should not be delayed.
- Color film should be used, if possible, because black and white film does not portray the severity of the injury as clearly.
- Make sure the area is well lighted.
- Position the child against an uncluttered background, neutral in color. Infants and toddlers are most easily photographed while being held in someone's arms, while in the lap, or while being held from under the armpits.
- Start with a series of identifying photographs of the front, sides, and back of the child in full length. This series will identify the subject of your photographs and will pinpoint the location of injuries. After this series of shots, take close-ups of particular injuries.
- Photographs of actual injuries should not cover too large an area. A full-body picture may be helpful to show the child's overall condition, but it will make specific injuries too small to evaluate properly. As a general rule, areas no larger than the back, torso, or extremities should be photographed at one time.

To encourage the taking of photographs and X rays, many states have laws that protect against lawsuits as long as the person taking the photographs or X rays acted in good faith. A few states also authorize the child protective agency to provide reimbursement for their costs.

To help ensure that the photographs and X rays reach the appropriate

Chart 14–2 **Guidelines for Taking Photographs (*continued*)**

- Photographs of the child should include a body landmark to establish the anatomical location and size of the injury. (If an extreme close-up is necessary, take another photograph at a greater distance away, so the injury is shown in relation to the landmark.)
- The child's face should also be photographed, so there is no question about his or her identity.
- Take more than one photograph of each area or injury. (Shoot the pictures at different angles and vary the shutter speeds, if the camera is so equipped.) There is always the possibility that a picture will be over or underexposed, out of focus, distorted, or otherwise misleading. There is no reason to be penny-pinching when taking pictures. Film is inexpensive compared to the cost of unusable pictures.
- Photographs of the home require a similar approach. It is impossible for one photograph to depict an entire room without distortion. Plan your shots carefully, selecting a good vantage point. Take a series of three or four photographs in a clockwise sequence, covering the entire area. Photograph from eye level so that the proper perspective is achieved. If a particular area is to be shown in a detailed close-up, photograph the general area first, then the detail. This will identify the location of the detailed area.
- To corroborate the fairness and accuracy of the photographs, describe the child's condition or that of the home in writing and place the description in the file.
- The conditions under which the photographs were taken also should be described in writing and made part of the file.
- Clearly label the photographs with the child's name (or a description of the home area that was photographed), the date and time of the photograph, and the names of the photographer and any other persons who were present.
- For the photographs to be admitted into evidence, the photographer or some other witness who was present must be able to establish that the photographs are a "fair and accurate representation" of the condition of the child or home.

decision makers, some states require that the child protective agency be notified that they were taken; many state laws also require that copies be forwarded to the agency. Even if you are not required to do so, you should certainly inform the child protective agency about any photographs or X rays.

This is a fluid area of state law, however, and you should contact your local child protective agency to determine whether you are authorized—or required—to take photographs and X rays. If not, the agency should determine whether they are necessary and arrange for them to be taken.

Photographs should be taken whenever evidence of suspected abuse or neglect is visible on a child's body. Such evidence includes signs of malnutrition and failure to thrive, as well as all bruises, lesions, scabs, burns, or other marks.

There is little difficulty in using photographs taken by professional photographers, especially those with forensic experience. (Photographs taken in medical photography studios, for example, are of a higher quality because of controlled lighting and special equipment.) But it is unrealistic to expect all hospitals, let alone other agencies, to have a professional photographer available.

You need not be a professional photographer to take acceptable pictures of a child's injuries. Photographs taken by "amateurs"—physicians, nurses, schoolteachers, social workers, police officers, and child care workers—can also be used as evidence in subsequent court proceedings if they fairly and accurately portray the child's injuries. Chart 14-2 provides general guidelines for photographing maltreated children and their homes that, if followed, should make the photographs diagnostically valuable and admissible in any possible court action. (Photographic methods are described in greater detail in various technical publications, which you may wish to consult.)[1]

Photographs of home conditions also may be helpful. They can document health or physical hazards, such as exposed wiring; extreme filth; and inadequate sleeping, eating, plumbing, or washing facilities. If the parents claim that the child was injured in an accidental fall, a photograph of the area where the accident allegedly occurred may be a crucial element in establishing a contrary cause for the child's injuries.

X rays should be taken whenever there is sufficient reason to believe that they will detect or document internal or skeletal injuries that are suggestive of maltreatment. Multiple old and new injuries are strong indicators of child abuse. Many of these injuries will be visible on the child's body; others can be detected only by a full-body bone scan. Thus, X rays can do more than preserve evidence of abuse or neglect. They often discover it, by revealing telltale past injuries.

"Every child who has a serious unexplained injury should have x-rays taken of the long bones, ribs and skull. This is the physician's most important tool. The x-ray findings often speak for the child," advised

Dr. Vincent Fontana, chairman of the New York City Mayor's Task Force on Child Abuse.[2]

Of course, X rays should be taken only by qualified medical personnel, preferably those who know how to detect and document signs of maltreatment. If standard procedures are followed, there is little problem in using X rays as evidence in subsequent court proceedings.

Ordinarily, the parents will consent to their child being X-rayed. Their refusal to consent is suspicious behavior and is a ground to report (assuming, of course, that the child has a traumatic injury of "suspicious" or ambiguous origin). The same would be true, by the way, for parental refusals to consent to other diagnostic procedures.

CAREFUL RECORD KEEPING

Many months often elapse between the making of a report and its final resolution. If the case reaches court, you may be called to testify about the conditions that led to the report and what happened afterward. (You may also be called to testify in those rare situations in which parents file a lawsuit alleging that the report was made in bad faith.)

A written record of what transpired at the time of the report will help refresh memories of events long past and may be used, under certain circumstances, as evidence to bolster the testimony of witnesses. In addition, records are a form of institutional memory, which usually can be introduced into evidence if the original maker of the record is unavailable to the court. (This can be especially important for those institutions, such as urban hospitals, that have a high turnover of staff.)

Rules concerning the admission of records vary widely among states. For more information, you should contact the attorney for the state's child protection agency or another legal counselor. In some states and under certain conditions, medical records that were "certified" by the head of the hospital can be introduced into evidence without calling the physician as a witness.

Major decisions not to report should also be recorded and documented. Doing so may assist in the assessment of subsequent questionable circumstances, and it may prove invaluable in a later lawsuit for the failure to report.

Since this book is designed for a national audience of both laypersons and professionals from many disciplines, it is impossible to specify the form or content of the records that should be maintained. In general,

Chart 14–3 **Description of Injuries: Example of a Medical Report**[3]

PATIENT'S NAME: D.F.

BD: 2/26/72

CGH#: 444555

History: The child and both parents were brought to [hospital] on 29 April 73 at 3:00 p.m. by the police. The child was admitted for intensive burn therapy. At 8:00 a.m. on this day, the father reports that he bathed this 14-month-old baby because she had "messy" pants. It is known that the parents are currently trying to toilet train this child. Despite her crying, he admits to holding her in the bathwater continually for 15 to 20 minutes. When he took her out, he noted the burn. Allegedly she usually cries during the bath, so this did not alarm him. Also, the father states that "he can't tell hot from cold water." He states that the bruise on her cheek is probably from a fall off the sofa yesterday. He states he did not notice the bruise until we pointed it out. The parents deny easy bruisability in the child.

Physical Exam:

1.   70-80% body burn up to midchest and involving both forearms. Many blisters present ranging in size from 1" to 8". No open burns.

2.   2-3 cm., round, fading bruise on left cheek and scattered bruises of left earlobe, less than 0.5 cm. These are yellow-blue and at least 5 days old.

Trauma X-rays: normal

Conclusion: This burn is a classic dunking burn, probably inflicted as punishment for resistance around toilet training. The forearm burns are from struggling to get out of the tub. The child is old enough to climb out unless forcibly held. The bruise on the left cheek and ear is the type that usually results from being slapped, and is older than the father's description.

_____   _____

(Date)   M.D.

---

the records should include as much of the information listed on Chart 16–1 as possible. As described in Chapter 16, follow-up written reports often call for all or most of this information; they should be made part of the agency's record, as should any photographs or X rays taken of the child.

Special care should be taken to record the child's physical condition and the nature and extent of any visible injuries, whether or not photographs and X rays have been taken (*see* Chart 14–3).

In describing the injuries, avoid words that are open to interpretation, such as an "old bruise" or "severe cut." Instead, use coloring, measurements, and precise adjectives to describe the subject. Avoid deductive descriptions on the diagram, such as "deep purple bruise caused by a belt." This type of description would render the diagram inadmissible in court unless you could prove the bruise was caused by a belt. If you suspect the cause of an injury, include that suspicion in your case narrative, not on the diagram.[4]

Illustration 14–1 **Diagram of Injuries**[5]

VICTIM _____ DATE OF OFFENSE _____ CASE # _____

DATE OF BIRTH _____ HEIGHT _____ WEIGHT _____ HAIR _____ EYES _____

ADDRESS WHERE EXAMINED _____ SKETCHED BY _____ DATE _____

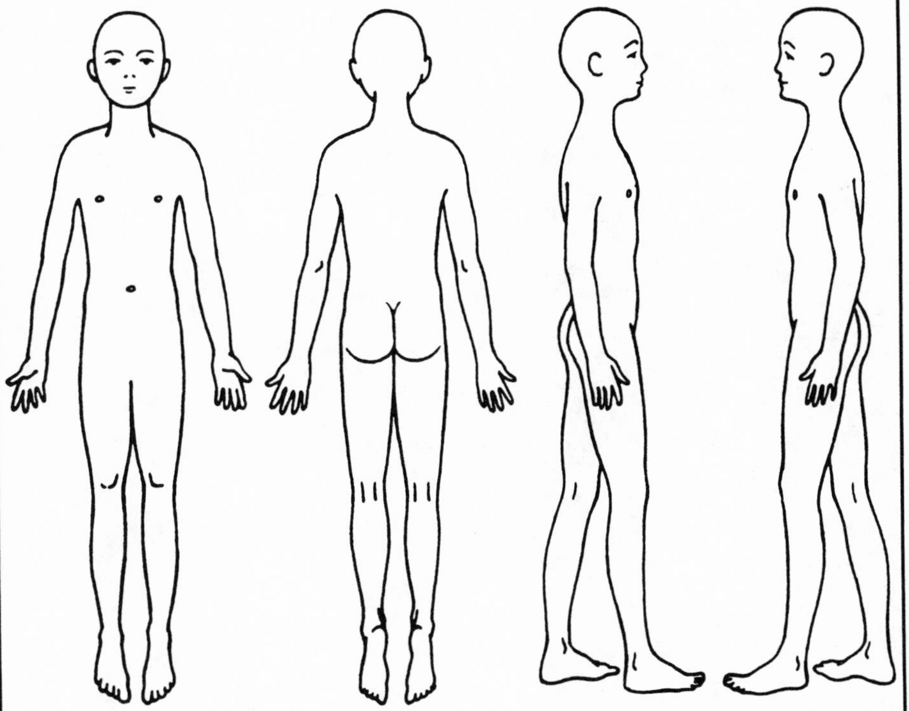

WITNESSES: _____ TITLE: _____

_____ TITLE: _____

Proceed as follows: (1) Fill in the identifying information at the top of the diagram. (2) Examine the child for injuries or defects. (3) Mark the location of injuries on the silhouette. Try to approximate the shape and relative size. (4) Write a brief description of the injury next to the silhouette. (5) Connect the description to the injury it describes with a line. If several injuries are similar, one written description and several connecting lines will do.

A sketch or drawing of the injury is often more accurate than is a layperson's description of anatomical parts. (*See* Illustration 14–1.) If properly completed, the diagram is acceptable evidence in court, but it must be attested to by the person who made it.

All records of suspected child maltreatment or other private family matters should be kept confidential. Only persons with a sufficient "need to know" should have access to them.

15

Emergencies

M ost situations can be handled by an oral report to the child protective agency or the police, who will see to the child's safety and welfare. Some children, however, need immediate protection. To emphasize that you may have to take emergency action before actually making a report, these situations are discussed first.

IMMEDIATE MEDICAL ATTENTION

Maltreated children sometimes suffer from illnesses or injuries that, if not treated promptly, could cause lasting harm and even death. Whether or not the result of the parents' abuse or neglect, some conditions require immediate medical attention.

Children who seem to need medical care should be seen promptly by a physician. You should not be overly conservative in deciding to seek medical assistance. Remember, you need not decide whether the child actually needs medical treatment, only whether a physician should see the child. Even apparently minor black and blue marks on the abdomen may signal severe internal injuries that need immediate treatment. (*See* Chart 15–1.)

Ordinarily, parents will consent to the needed treatment. But if the parents refuse or if they are unavailable, you are not powerless to help the child. Most states have Good Samaritan laws that authorize medical personnel to provide needed emergency treatment. (The hospital's authority is not diminished in those cases in which the parents' refusal is based on their religious beliefs, as discussed in Chapter 9.) In less urgent situations, an authorization usually must be obtained from a judge. The hospital can ask the local child protective agency for assistance in seeking a court order. (Some states empower the child protective agency, itself, to authorize medical care for children placed in protective custody.)

Chart 15–1 **Conditions Requiring Immediate Medical Attention**[1]

- Loss of movement in an extremity or other evidence of a broken bone
- Severe or unusual bleeding
- Severe or unusual burns
- Severe or unusual bruises (especially to the head or abdomen)
- Head injuries
- Unconsciousness or prolonged and unexplained dizziness
- Unexplained seizures
- Prolonged and severe diarrhea or vomiting
- Symptoms of severe malnutrition or failure to thrive
- Signs of sexual abuse (as much to preserve the evidence as to treat the injuries)
- Serious but apparently unattended medical problems, such as high fever or difficulty breathing

Remember, you are not deciding whether the child actually needs medical treatment, only whether a physician should see the child.

Even when medical care is being provided without the parents' consent, hospital staff should seek to understand and reduce the parents' resistance. As much as appropriate, the parents should be encouraged to cooperate with the diagnostic and treatment process.

PROTECTIVE CUSTODY

Some abused and neglected children are in immediate danger of serious and perhaps irreparable injury. Unless their safety can be assured by some other means, they must be placed in protective custody as soon as possible. Put bluntly, this is a life-or-death decision.

In a surprising number of cases, the parents will consent to protective care. (In fact, the majority of placements are voluntary.) Some parents have highly ambivalent feelings about their children and may welcome the relief that placement provides. (If the child can be protected adequately through a placement with friends or relatives, the parents' agreement may be more likely.)

Recognizing that unnecessary legal coercion can be detrimental to later treatment efforts, many states have specific laws or administrative regulations requiring that the parents' consent be sought before involuntary protective custody is invoked. This does not minimize the element of coercion inherent in such "voluntary" resolutions; the parents may sense—or be told—that their failure to consent may result in formal court action. Nevertheless, there is a qualitative difference between situations in which parents agree to cooperate, for whatever reason, and those in which they do not.

Frequently, though, the child must be removed from the home against the parents' wishes. This decision should be made with extreme caution. The child's removal from the home is a major intrusion on the family's integrity that can leave lasting psychological scars. Moreover, the great majority of maltreated children do not need to be removed from their parents' custody, especially not on an emergency basis. Most forms of maltreatment do not pose the threat of immediate serious injury. The danger they pose, though great, arises from the *long-term consequences* of inadequate child care. There is usually time to work with parents so they can care adequately for their children.[2]

Children who are in immediate danger of serious injury should be removed from their parents' custody on an emergency basis. Deciding whether emergency removal is needed involves a balancing of the possible danger the child faces (taking into account the ability of in-home services to protect the child) against the possibly traumatic effects of removal from the parents' care. In some cases, the danger to the child is so great that the need for protective custody is beyond question. But in less severe situations, decision making is much more difficult. As in so many areas of child protection, there are no hard-and-fast rules. The competing considerations are impossible to quantify and the factual information on which they are based is too uncertain. Chart 15–2 lists the most common situations that *suggest* the need for emergency protective custody.

The preferred method of removing a child is by a court order. As in all situations in which individual discretion is paramount, there is always the danger of the careless or automatic, though well-meaning, exercise of power. Prior court review lessens such dangers by ensuring that a judge, an outsider, reviews the administrative decision to place a child in custody.[3] Indeed, even when the police and child protective agencies have the legal authority to remove a child against the parents' wishes, they often seek court approval before doing so. (When the court is not in session, for example, at night or on weekends, they may obtain such authorization by telephoning a judge at home.)

Nevertheless, sometimes removal must occur before court review is

Chart 15–2 **Situations Suggesting the Need for Protective Custody**

- The child was severely assaulted, that is, hit, poisoned, or burned so severely that serious injury resulted or could have resulted. (For example, the parent threw an infant against a wall, but somehow the infant was not seriously injured.)
- The child has been systematically tortured or inhumanely punished. (For instance, the child was locked in a closet for long periods; forced to eat unpalatable substances; or forced to squat, stand, or perform other unreasonable acts for a long time.)
- The parent's reckless disregard for the child's safety caused serious injury or could have done so. (For example, the parent left a young child in the care of an obviously irresponsible or dangerous individual.)
- The physical condition of the home is so dangerous that it poses an immediate threat of serious injury. (For instance, exposed electrical wiring or other materials create an extreme danger of fire or upper-story windows are unbarred and easily accessible to young children.)
- The child has been sexually abused or sexually exploited.
- The parents have purposefully or systematically withheld essential food or nourishment from the child. (For example, the child is denied food for extended periods as a form of punishment for real or imagined misbehavior.)
- The parents refuse to obtain or to consent to medical or psychiatric care for the child that is needed immediately to prevent or treat a serious injury or disease. (For instance, the child's physical condition shows signs of

possible. The police in all states are authorized to take a child into protective custody *without a court order.*[4] In about half the states, child protective agencies also have this power. (However, as a practical matter, child protective agencies normally do not attempt a forcible removal of the child without police assistance because of the potential danger to their workers.) Many state laws place two limitations on when a child may be taken into protective custody without a court order: (1) the child must be in imminent danger and (2) there must be no time to apply for a court order.[5]

Authorized persons who remove children in good faith have legal immunity. Many states have laws that explicitly grant immunity, but specific legislation is not really needed. Under general legal doctrines, anyone with the legal authority to place a child in protective custody is protected from liability as long as the removal was accomplished in accordance

Chart 15–2 **Situations Suggesting the Need for Protective Custody** (*continued*)

severe deterioration to which the parents seem unwilling or unable to respond.)

- The parents appear to be suffering from mental illness, mental retardation, drug abuse, or alcohol abuse so *severe* that they cannot provide for the child's basic needs. (For example, the parents are demonstrably out of touch with reality.)
- The parents have abandoned the child. (For instance, the child has been left in the custody of persons who have not agreed to care for the child for more than a few hours and who do not know how to reach the parents.)
- There is reason to suspect that the parents may flee with the child. (For example, the parents have a history of frequent moves or of hiding the child from outsiders.)
- There is specific evidence that the parents' anger and discomfort about the report and the subsequent investigation will result in retaliation against the child. (Such information could be gained through a review of the parents' past behavior, the parents' statements and behaviors during the investigative interview, or reports from others who know the family.)
- The parents have been arrested (for any reason) and there is no one to care adequately for the child.

In any of these situations, the younger the child, the greater the presumable need for protective custody.

---

with legal requirements. Even if it turns out that the child was not actually in danger, there is no liability unless the decision to remove the child was made maliciously, recklessly, or, in some circumstances, negligently.

There may, though, be liability for leaving children in dangerous situations. The police, child protective agencies, and hospitals (and their staffs) have been successfully sued for failing to place children in protective custody.[6]

If you think that a child is in immediate danger, promptly inform the authorities. Ordinarily, you should call the child protective agency, which, then, will decide what should be done. If it appears that the parents will injure or flee with the child in the time it will take for the child protective agency to respond, you should call the police. You should also call police if you have reason to fear for your safety.

Under the common law of most states, all citizens have the legal authority to use force to protect a third party.[7] A child who is in imminent danger of serious injury could be placed in protective custody under this general authority. (In addition, in most states, almost anyone may request the appropriate court to issue an order authorizing protective custody.) Only in rare instances, however, should someone other than a police officer or child protective worker consider placing a child in protective custody (the major examples being when the child is already out of the home, perhaps in a hospital, at school, or in a day care center and it appears that the child will be at great risk if sent home). Even then, it is probably more practical to consider *delaying* the child's return home until the police or child protective worker arrives. The child protective agency or the police should be immediately notified of any child who is placed in protective custody.

Hospitals often have special authority to "hold" a child. There is one major exception to the general rule that only the police and child protective agencies should place a child in protective custody. Laws in about half the states also give hospitals, similar medical institutions, and sometimes individual physicians the authority to hold endangered children against the parents' wishes—as a stopgap measure to give other components of a community's child protection system enough time to mobilize.

Actually, the authority granted to medical institutions is usually much broader than that granted to the police and child protective workers: a child can be placed in protective custody whenever "the facts so warrant." Such open-ended discretion is designed to give medical personnel a flexible tool with which to protect children when there is no time to apply for a court order or to obtain help from the police. For example, children often are brought to the hospital in the middle of the night for the treatment of inflicted injuries. When the parents realize that the hospital staff is suspicious, they sometimes try to take the child out of the hospital. At such times, the hospital needs the legal power to retain custody of the child without having to decide whether there is reasonable cause to suspect child abuse. As in the case of any removal, the hospital should try to convince the parents to consent to the child's continued hospitalization before invoking its legal authority to "hold" the child.

Because of the unfettered nature of this authority, state laws limit the time during which a hospital may hold a child to twenty-four, forty-eight, or seventy-two hours, or until the next sessions of the local family or juvenile court. If, after this initial period, the child requires continued protective custody, a court order is necessary. (Generally, it is not the hospital's responsibility to obtain the court order. However, if the police or child protective agency fail to obtain such an order, responsibility may fall on the hospital to protect the child by seeking the court order.)

Protective custody is only the beginning of the child protective process. The local child protective agency should be notified of the removal as soon as possible so it can initiate the necessary legal and social service efforts. Some appropriate person, preferably from the child protective agency, should tell the parents where the child was taken—and why— to calm their fears and to enable them to maintain contact with their child. (In the case of a "hospital hold," the senior treating or attending physician should tell the parents.) Only in unusual or severe cases, for example, when there is a danger that parents will forcibly interfere with the child's care, should they not be told of the child's exact whereabouts. (In such cases, contact between the child and the parents may have to be limited to highly structured situations.)

Children who are placed in protective custody may be taken to a medical facility for evaluation and treatment (this may be an emergency need, as already described) or to a foster home or juvenile shelter. In many communities, the dearth of suitable facilities for the temporary care of abused and neglected children has led to their placement in a jail or a facility for the detention of criminal or juvenile offenders. Only as a last resort should maltreated children be placed in adult detention facilities while in protective custody. Indeed, the practice is statutorily prohibited in some states.[8] Of course, such prohibitions do not apply to situations in which abused or neglected children require secure detention because of their misconduct and there is independent legal authority for detaining them.

Whatever the initial basis for placing a child in protective custody, it is essential for a court to review the correctness of the initial administrative decision. That decision may have been wrong—based on incomplete or misunderstood facts—or the situation may have changed since the decision was made—for example, counseling, homemaker, day care, or housing services may have succeeded in making it safe for the child to return home. Therefore, all states require that a child abuse or neglect petition be filed in the juvenile court within a short time after a child is placed in protective custody, so a custody hearing can be held. Although many states put no time limit on protective custody before review, some require the review to be held promptly, generally in one to three days.[9] At the custody hearing, a judge will review the protective custody status and either order it to be continued pending the adjudicatory hearing or revoked and the child returned home.

Chart 15–3 **Special Hospital Procedures for Abused and Neglected Children**[10]

- The child should be placed in a room near the nurses' station so visitors can be watched.
- Permission from the attending physician should be required before anyone other than pediatric ward personnel examine the child or view the injuries.
- If not done so already, photographs, X rays, and blood studies should be taken as soon as possible.
- The child's medical chart should be kept at the nurses' station, so access to it can be controlled.
- Charts and records should be available only to those who have a legitimate need to know their contents.
- Visitors should be restricted, as directed by the attending physician, to decrease rumors and avoid information seekers.
- Only designated hospital staff should release medical information to outsiders.
- Hospital staff should try to relate to the parents in an accepting and supportive manner to facilitate the development of a more positive relationship between the parents and the child.

Protective custody should not be treated as a final disposition of the case; the ultimate goal of a child protective action is to help the parents care adequately for their child. Bear in mind that subsequent treatment efforts may be impaired if the parents are not accorded full due process, not treated fairly, or not fully informed about what is happening. All these goals, of course, are important in themselves.

Unless doing so will endanger the child, the parents should be encouraged to visit frequently and to take over the care of their child during these times. Since the appropriate disposition may depend on the parents' involvement with the child, an exact record should be kept of the number of visits, the duration of the visits, and what each parent does during the visits.

Thus, for example, when a maltreated child is hospitalized—with or without the parents' consent—special procedures are needed to protect the child, to safeguard the family's privacy, and to reinforce treatment efforts with the parents (see Chart 15–3). If the parents do not regularly visit their hospitalized child, a public health nurse or social worker should try to help the parents overcome the problems that prevent them from visiting the child.

Hospitalization can be confusing and stressful for children, even if the parents visit regularly. Hence, the hospital should provide these children with a nurturing and supportive environment. Whenever possible, volunteers, such as foster grandmothers, or selected ward nurses should be assigned as parent surrogates for these children.

This discussion of protective custody should not be concluded without mentioning that temporary protective custody can turn into long-term care because of breakdowns in the planning process, overburdened child protective staffs, backlogged courts, inadequate long-term alternatives, weak management procedures, and the absence of a host of other needed services. Children can be temporarily "parked" for months and even years in foster homes, shelters, and hospitals where, if they are medically ready for discharge, they are called "boarder babies." This is all the more reason to be extremely careful about removing children from their parents.

ARE THE POLICE NEEDED?

The police play an important role in the child protective process. Even the best child protective agencies may be unable to respond to some aggravated or emergency situations. The police should be involved whenever their assistance would be helpful. Their legal authority to protect citizens and to seek evidence, their operational capabilities, and the skills and expertise of individual officers make them an important resource for investigating child abuse and neglect. Indeed, the failure of some state reporting laws to recognize the important role of the police in child protective cases is a serious deficiency in existing legislation.

Although an increasing number of child protective agencies can respond to reports twenty-four hours a day, seven days a week, some cannot—even in emergencies. A few state laws require that children who need immediate protection be reported to the police when the child protective agency is not available.[11] But even in the absence of such a law, you should notify the police whenever it appears that a child will be endangered in the time it will take for the protective agency to respond.

In addition, the police are sometimes needed to help the child protective agency perform its functions. Although most maltreating parents are willing to cooperate with child protective workers, some are not. For instance, the police may be needed to deal with parents who do not allow access to their children or who refuse to permit their children to

---

Chart 15–4 **Reports to the Police**

- When someone other than a parent has abused the child
- When the child protective agency cannot be reached (such as at night or on weekends and holidays) *and* an immediate response is needed
- When speed is essential and the proximity of the police to the child gives the police faster access than the child protective agency
- When assistance is needed to protect a child from injury (usually by gaining access to a home or by placing the child in protective custody against the parents' wishes)
- When it appears that the suspected perpetrator should be arrested (usually, only in serious cases when there is reason to believe that he or she may flee)
- When assistance is needed to protect the person reporting or otherwise to maintain order (for example, when the parent becomes belligerent or physically threatening)
- When assistance is needed to preserve evidence

The foregoing factors are not the same as those used by the police to decide whether to make an arrest or to begin criminal prosecution—decisions that the person who is reporting does not make.

---

be examined by a physician or to be placed in protective custody. A few parents can be dangerous to the person who reports them, the child protective worker, and others who cooperate with the investigation. Hence, when a parent becomes belligerent or physically threatening, the police may be needed to maintain order. Situations of actual danger are rare, but when they arise, the presence of the police can prevent a tragedy.

Last, in serious cases in which there is reason to believe that the suspected perpetrator may flee, the police should be contacted so they can decide whether an arrest would be appropriate. This is not, however, the same as deciding that a criminal prosecution is needed—a decision that should be made by the child protection agency and the police (if they are otherwise involved).

Whether or not the state's reporting law recognizes these realities by expressly authorizing reports to the police, you must do so. Chart 15–4 lists the conditions under which a report should be made to the police. Depending on the circumstances, either the person who reported the case or the police should make a follow-up report to the child protective agency.

ARRESTING PARENTS

Although the social service approach is the most appropriate response in most cases, for some abusive or neglectful parents, criminal penalties are a needed community statement that such behavior toward children is not countenanced. Arrest and criminal penalties can also be more effective in protecting certain children and deterring their further maltreatment. As former police inspector Jack Collins wrote:

> The arrest of child-beating suspects accomplishes an important result—namely, an immediate change in the environment. Although this change is often temporary, it removes the offending adult from the environment, allowing the police to protect the child from continued abuse and affords other agencies in the community an opportunity to initiate a more permanent rehabilitation program.[12]

Furthermore, foster care is often used when it would be better to jail the offender. For example, some children are placed in foster care because the mother's live-in boyfriend has abused the child and she seems unable to prevent him from returning to the home.

An arrest of one or both parents may be necessary to protect the child or to uphold community values. The Attorney General's Task Force on Family Violence recommended that "family violence should be recognized and responded to as a criminal activity." It also recommended that law enforcement agencies "presume that arrest, consistent with state law, is the appropriate response to situations of serious injury to the victim . . . or other imminent danger to the victim."[13]

"Probable cause" is the ordinary standard for arrests by the police. For that purpose, it is defined as the reasonable belief that a crime has been committed and that the suspected person committed it.[14] But since all forms of child abuse, no matter how minor, are crimes, this is only the first step in deciding whether to arrest a parent.

The conditions that can lead to an arrest are listed in Chart 15–5. The major reason for an arrest, of course, is that a criminal prosecution is deemed appropriate, although a prosecution can be commenced without an arrest. An arrest may also be made in some circumstances without

Chart 15–5 **Conditions Suggesting the Need for an Arrest**

Subject to the provisions of state law and the existence of probable cause to believe that a crime was committed and that it was committed by the suspect, the following situations suggest the need to arrest the parent or other suspect:

- When an arrest is needed to initiate a criminal prosecution
- When a criminal prosecution seems likely (especially if there is reason to believe that the suspect will flee)
- When the arrest of the suspect is the only way to reasonably ensure the child's safety
- When the arrest of the suspect will sufficiently protect the child so the child need not be removed from the home
- When an arrest may assist in the interview of the suspect
- When the suspect's arrest is necessary to preserve the peace.

For the purposes of this chart, arrest includes any time that an individual is placed in police custody, whether or not a criminal prosecution has been decided upon. Moreover, in some circumstances, arrests are made when there was no initial intention to do so. For example, a parent may be arrested for resisting efforts to gain entrance to the home to assess the child's situation.

---

the intent of presenting the case to the prosecutor. For example, a parent may be arrested if he or she resists efforts to gain entrance into the home to assess the child's situation.

An arrest with no follow-up, that is, if the parent is simply released, may further endanger the child because it can suggest that what the parent did was not really wrong or that the parent can get away with abusing his or her children. Therefore, an arrest must be approached with utmost care, and alternatives, like protective or restraining orders to keep the alleged abuser out of the home, should be considered. Given these concerns, although the decision to arrest a parent is basically within the province of the police and prosecutors, they should try to consult with the child protective agency before making the arrest.

16

Making a Report

In almost all communities, reporting procedures have been streamlined so a report should take only a few moments of your time. This chapter describes where to report and whether to notify the police, whether to make an oral or a written report or both, and whether to tell the child and the parents about the report.

WHERE TO REPORT

The 1963 model child abuse reporting law, promulgated by the U.S. Children's Bureau, recommended that reports be made to the police (see Reporting Laws in Chapter 2). The police were chosen not because criminal prosecutions were deemed the most appropriate response but because police agencies were available to investigate reports. Most states agreed and, in adopting mandatory reporting laws, required that reports be made to the police. The expansion of specialized child protective agencies, however, has obviated the need to rely on the police to investigate reports of suspected child maltreatment.

In keeping with society's therapeutic response to child maltreatment, most reports should be made to child protective agencies. You have little choice in about half the states; the law requires that reports be made to a child protective agency (usually part of a public social service agency called the Department of Social Services, Department of Public Welfare, Department of Children and Family Services, or Department of Human Services). In the other states, the law gives you a choice; it allows reports to be made to either a child protective agency or the police. But even in these states, most reports should be made to the child protective agency, which can obtain help from the police, if necessary. The police will usually refer the case to a child protective agency, anyway.

Emergency or especially serious cases should be reported to law enforcement agencies. Some cases require an immediate law enforcement re-

171

sponse, and, for this purpose, you should make a report directly to the police. For example, an immediate police presence may be needed to make after-hours, emergency investigations. Since not all after-hours reports involve immediate danger to the child, you should consider whether an investigation can wait until regular office hours. (These issues are discussed in Chapter 15.)

WHO MAKES THE REPORT

Many potential reporters work in hierarchical agencies or institutions. Recognizing this, some state laws require professionals to report their suspicions to the head of their agency or institution,[1] who is then responsible for making the report. This procedure is meant to allow agencies to coordinate and systematize the reports they make.

Unfortunately, such provisions are sometimes used to prevent staff members from reporting. The head of the agency may refuse to file a report, no matter how well documented. For this reason, some states make *both* the head of the agency and the individual staff member responsible for reporting.[2] Under such laws, when there is disagreement about the need for a report, the staff member is required to report, no matter what the supervisor says, unless the staff member is truly persuaded that his or her original concerns were unfounded. (In practice, such conflicts usually are resolved by an anonymous report.)

ORAL REPORTS AND HOTLINES

In almost all states, the law specifically requires that initial reports be made orally. These statutes usually mandate that oral reports be made "immediately," "promptly," or "as soon as possible." All states, though, encourage oral reports.

An Arizona social worker was criminally prosecuted for not reporting a case "immediately." When the client, an incest victim, told her about the "past molestation" of her own daughter by a family friend, the social worker "immediately urged" the client to report the incident to the police.[3]

The social worker did not report the incident herself because she feared that doing so against the wishes of her client "could result in a serious remission to her former state of emotional upheaval" and cause her to "flee therapy." She also believed that no case could be made against the molester without the client's involvement and that encouraging the client to report complied with the law. When she interviewed her client's daughter (at the client's request), she found that the girl had not suffered any "lasting emotional damage" from the molestation and was no longer in danger of being molested because "the client had broken off contact with the molester's family."

Eventually, the client reported the incident to the police, and the social worker "followed up on that call as was agreed, but was not contacted by the police for some time."

The social worker was criminally prosecuted because she failed to report "immediately," as required by state law. The reporting law, similar to that in most states, makes no exceptions, not even when a therapist determines that it would be better if the mother were to make the report. The requirement of "immediate" reporting is designed to (1) prevent the would-be reporter's procrastination (and, perhaps, ultimate failure to report) and (2) help ensure prompt protection for the child. In justifying the charges in this case, the prosecutor is reported to have said that "any delay in reporting—even if well intentioned—leaves time for other children to be victimized." Only after almost eight months were the charges dropped and then only because, according to her lawyer, the state's "haphazard" record-keeping system precluded proof that a report was not made in a timely manner.

To facilitate "immediate" oral reports, many local communities have established special telephone numbers, sometimes called "reporting hotlines." Hotlines encourage people to report cases of child abuse and neglect by simplifying the process, by having an easily publicized telephone number, and by ensuring that qualified personnel answer the phone twenty-four hours a day, seven days a week.

At different times, all hotlines have difficulty managing an unpredicted increase in reports. As a result, you may get a busy signal when you call, be put on hold for five minutes (or more), or be told that someone will call you back. Do not be discouraged. Unless you persist in trying to report your concerns, no one will know about the child's plight.

Appendix B lists the child protective agencies for each state. For the fifteen or so states that have statewide hotlines, toll-free telephone numbers are listed. For the other states, consult your local telephone directory to find the telephone number of the particular agency. (In many communities, the telephone number is also listed under "Child Abuse.")

On the phone, an intake worker will try to obtain as much information as possible from you. Although anonymous reports are not encouraged, they will be accepted, as discussed in Chapter 3. The worker will ask

Chart 16–1 **Contents of an Oral Report**

A person who reports suspected child maltreatment will be asked to supply as much of the following information as possible:

- The child's (or children's) name, age, sex, ethnic background, and permanent address
- The child's (or children's) present condition and the possible need for emergency action
- The child's (or children's) present location and the location where the incidents occurred, if different from the permanent address
- The name of the parents or other persons who are responsible for the child's (or children's) care (and address, if different from the permanent address of the child)
- The name and address of the person or persons who are alleged to be responsible for the abuse or neglect
- The siblings' names, sex, ages, and present location
- The names, ages, sex, and relation to the child of other adults in the home
- The nature and extent of the suspected abuse or neglect
- Any other evidence of the alleged maltreatment
- The reason or reasons for suspecting abuse or neglect, including the physical or emotional condition of the child (or children) and statements of a child or parents
- Any other relevant statements made by the parents, the child, or significant others
- Any available information about previous injuries to the child or siblings (or other evidence of prior maltreatment)
- The names, addresses, and telephone numbers of possible witnesses to the alleged maltreatment
- Other individuals or agencies that may have information about the alleged maltreatment
- Any actions taken by the reporting source or others (such as placing the child in protective custody or taking photographs or X-rays)
- The reporter's name, telephone number, address, and occupation if the reporter is willing to provide this information
- The relationship of the reporter to the child and family
- Any other information that the reporter believes may be helpful.

Chart 16–2 **Basis of Reports**

Direct Evidence

- Eyewitness observations of a parent's abusive or neglectful behavior
- The child's description of being abused or neglected, unless there is a specific reason for not believing it
- The parent's description of abusive or neglectful behavior, unless it is long past
- Accounts of child maltreatment from a spouse or other family members
- Films, photographs, or other visual material depicting a minor's sexually explicit activity
- Newborns who are denied nutrition, life-sustaining care, or other medically indicated treatment
- Children in physically dangerous situations
- Young children who are left alone
- Apparently abandoned children
- The parent's demonstrated disabilities (for example, mental illness or retardation or alcohol or drug abuse) that are severe enough to make child abuse or child neglect likely
- The parent's demonstrated inability to care for a newborn baby.

Circumstantial Evidence

- "Suspicious" injuries that suggest physical abuse
- Physical injuries or medical findings that suggest sexual abuse
- For young children, signs of sexual activity
- Signs of severe physical deprivation on the child's body that suggest general neglect
- Severe dirt and disorder in the home that suggest general neglect
- Apparently untreated physical injuries, illnesses, or impairments that suggest medical neglect
- "Accidental" injuries that suggest gross inattention to the child's need for safety
- The parent's apparent indifference to a child's severe psychological or developmental problems
- The parent's apparent condonation of or indifference to the child's misbehavior that suggests improper ethical guidance
- Chronic and unexplained absences from school for which the parent is apparently responsible
- A newborn who shows signs of fetal exposure to drugs or alcohol.

NOTE: Behavioral indicators, by themselves, are not a sufficient basis for a report.

about the alleged maltreatment, the child's condition and whereabouts, the composition of the family, and other information needed to evaluate the report and conduct the investigation. The worker should also ask whether the child appears to be in such immediate danger that an emergency investigation should be conducted. (The worker's questions are usually based on a printed form especially designed for this purpose.)

Although practices vary, Chart 16–1 lists the information that is commonly requested from callers. This list is provided to assist you in preparing to report. Your inability to provide all the information listed is no reason for not reporting; the child protective agency will understand if you do not have some of the information. (The reasons why reports are rejected are discussed in Chapter 17.)

Expect to be asked what specific evidence of abuse or neglect you have. Be prepared to make specific reference to one or more of the forms of evidence listed in Chart 16–2.

Given the type and scope of information that must be provided, the person who makes the call should be the one who observed the behavior or condition being reported. The child protective agency, before proceeding with its investigation, probably will want to speak to this person, anyway. However, a report may be based on information supplied by a co-worker or a reliable eyewitness. For example, a physician may arrange to have the initial report made by a nurse or social worker on the hospital staff or the police may relay a report made by a neighbor. When a report is relayed, though, the police (or whoever relays the report) should have good reason to trust the reliability of the informant.

REJECTED REPORTS

Child protective agencies must accept and investigate *all* reports that are properly made to them. Reporters do not have to prove, on the phone, that a child has been abused or neglected; they need only show that there is a reasonable basis for suspecting that the child is maltreated, as described in Chapter 6 (see also Chart 16–2). Iowa's attorney general explained the rationale for limiting discretion: "We will never know if a report of child abuse is valid or not until the appropriate investigation is made."[4]

Yet, hotlines receive calls from tens of thousands of strangers, so they must screen reports. Investigating all reports, regardless of their validity, would be patently improper, since workers would be immobilized by the burden of investigating so many cases of no apparent danger to children. Such investigations would also be a violation of family rights and would invite lawsuits. Child protective agencies that carefully screen calls have lower rates of unsubstantiated reports and expend fewer resources investigating inappropriate calls. Thus, agencies have the duty to screen out reports for which an investigation would be clearly unwarranted.

One real danger is that reports that should be accepted will be rejected. In Arizona, for example, the child protective agency was successfully sued for the wrongful death of Messeret Mammo after the agency refused to accept and investigate a report from her father.

Messeret Mammo was the youngest of three children. When her parents divorced, the mother received custody of her, Sirgute (age 3), and Tamiru (age 1). Every weekend, the father kept the two older children for an entire day, but because Messeret was an infant, he would visit her only briefly before taking the other children.

Over two weekend visits, Mr. Mammo noticed bruises on the two older children. Tamiru told him that all three children had been beaten by their mother and her live-in boyfriend. The father was particularly concerned for the safety of Messeret because he had not been allowed to see her on these two visits, so he went to the police. The police reported his allegations to the Arizona Department of Economic Security (DES) and told him to keep the two older children with him. DES said they would send an agent to see him the next day. On the following day, Mr. Mammo spoke with an intake unit supervisor for Child Protective Services (after calling the agency himself), but DES would take no action except to recommend that he get himself an attorney and try to gain custody of the children.

Mr. Mammo did get a lawyer, who immediately filed a motion to gain custody. A hearing was set, but Messeret remained with her mother. When the mother did not show up for the hearing, her lawyer told the judge that she and the baby were vacationing out of state, and a new hearing was set for about two weeks later. Four days before that hearing was to take place, however, Messeret was found dead. According to the police, she had been killed either by her mother or her mother's live-in boyfriend.[5]

The father filed a wrongful death action against the Arizona DES, claiming that it was negligent and breached its statutory duties to accept and investigate reports. After a trial, the jury returned a verdict for $1 million. The trial judge, deciding that the award was excessive, reduced it to $300,000;[6] the award was affirmed on appeal.

Although it is somewhat unfair to make a judgment based only on the court's description of what happened, it appears that the child protective agency viewed Mr. Mammo's report as the exaggerated concerns of a disgruntled spouse (at best) or as a tactical maneuver in a custody battle (at worst), rather than as a sign of serious danger to the child. In effect, the father's report was being screened in accordance with a well-known fact: the vast majority of reports from noncustodial parents prove to be unfounded.

Overreacting to cases like *Mammo v. Arizona*, some child protective agencies assume that they should not screen reports at all; that is, that they must assign all reports for investigation. This is a mistake. The proper lesson to be drawn from *Mammo*, and cases like it, is not that screening reports is wrong, but that decisions to reject a report must be made with great care. In *Mammo*, whether because of a heavy workload or careless decision making, the agency seems not to have made an individual assessment of the report. The father's report was simply disregarded—even though his claims were corroborated by the bruises on the bodies of the two older children and by the actions of the investigating police officer.

Child protective agencies should adopt specific policies concerning the screening of inappropriate reports. Reports should be rejected when the allegations fall outside the agency's definitions of "child abuse" and "child neglect," as established by state law. (Often, the family has a coping problem for which they would be more appropriately referred to another social service agency.) Reports should also be rejected when the caller can give no credible reason for suspecting that the child has been abused or neglected. And, reports in which insufficient information is given to identify or locate the child should likewise be screened (although the information may be kept for later use if a subsequent report about the same child is made).

The foregoing examples are relatively easy to apply. More difficult to assess are reports that appear to be falsely and maliciously made by an estranged spouse, by quarrelsome relatives, by feuding neighbors, or even by an angry or distressed child. As a general rule, unless there are clear and convincing grounds for concluding that the report is being made in bad faith, any report that falls within the agency's legal mandate must be investigated. Reports from questionable sources are not necessarily invalid; many anonymous reports are substantiated by the investigation.

Even a history of past unsubstantiated reports is not a sufficient basis, on its own, for automatically rejecting a report. There may be a legitimate explanation for why previous investigations did not substantiate the reporter's claims. Therefore, a subsequent report that contains a sufficient statement of facts to bring the case within statutory definitions must be

Chart 16–3 **Reports that Should Be Rejected**[7]

- Reports in which the allegations clearly fall outside the agency's definitions of "child abuse" and "child neglect," as established by state law. (Prime examples include children beyond the specified age, alleged perpetrators who are not within the legal definition, and family problems that do not amount to child abuse or neglect.)
- Reports in which the caller can give no credible reason for suspecting that the child has been abused or neglected. (Although actual proof of the maltreatment is not required, some evidence is.)
- Reports whose unfounded or malicious nature is established by specific evidence. (Anonymous reports, reports from estranged spouses, and even previous unfounded reports from the same source should not be automatically rejected, but they need to be carefully evaluated.)
- Reports in which insufficient information is given to identify or locate the child. (This is not technically a rejection; moreover, the information may be kept for later use should a subsequent report be made about the same child.)

NOTE: In questionable circumstances, the agency should recontact the caller before deciding to reject the report. When appropriate, rejected reports should be referred to other agencies that can provide services that the family may need.

---

investigated—unless there is clear and convincing evidence of its malicious or untrue nature. The key, in such questionable situations, is to insist that the person who is reporting provide the specific information that aroused his or her suspicion. If the agency determines that the report is being made maliciously, it should consider referring the case for criminal prosecution or notifying the parents so they can take appropriate action.

The conditions under which protective agencies should consider rejecting a report are listed in Chart 16–3. In questionable circumstances, a child protective worker should recontact the caller before deciding whether to reject the report.

Many of the reports that are rejected because they do not amount to child abuse or neglect nonetheless involve serious individual and family problems. For example, the rejected report may involve:

- Custody disputes in which there is no indication of abuse or neglect

- Behavioral problems of adolescents (such as truancy, delinquency, school problems, and sexual acting out) that are not caused by abuse or neglect
- Children who need specialized education or residential placement
- Parent-child conflicts in which there is no indication of abuse or neglect
- Marital conflicts that do not result in the maltreatment of a child, or
- Chronic problems involving property, unemployment, inadequate housing, or the poor management of money

That such situations have not resulted in the abuse or neglect of a child does not reduce the family's need for assistance. Hence, all hotlines should be equipped to refer callers to another, more appropriate, social service agency and should be reasonably sure that these other agencies *will* provide the necessary services. (Unfortunately, such referrals frequently are made without notifying the other agency of the practice and without checking to make sure that the agency can help the person referred.)

This kind of intake decision making cannot be done by clerks or untrained caseworkers, as is often the case. A sophisticated judgment about the child's need for protection must be made. In a growing number of communities, therefore, hotlines are staffed with highly trained personnel who can provide information and assistance to parents who seek help on their own; refer inappropriate reports to other agencies that are better suited to deal with a family's problems; advise potential reporters about the law and child protective procedures in general; assist in the diagnosis and evaluation; consult about the necessity of photographs, X rays, and protective custody; and help reporters deal with distressed or violent parents. All hotlines should be staffed in this way.

WRITTEN REPORTS

Most states require that written reports follow oral reports, although this requirement is often limited to mandated reporters. Depending on the state, written reports are due from twenty-four hours to seven days after the initial oral report. Most states have developed special reporting forms that are easy to use, ask only for necessary information, and include instructions regarding where they should be sent (see Chart 16-4). Copies of these forms may be obtained from your local child protective agency.

Chart 16–4 **Typical Reporting Form**

REPORT OF CHILD ABUSE OR NEGLECT

Name of Child	Date of Birth or Age of Child	Today's Date

Child's Home Address (Street,City, State, ZIP)

NAMES OF PARENTS OR PERSONS RESPONSIBLE FOR CHILD	RELATIONSHIP TO CHILD

Does the child have any brothers or sisters? . . . . ☐ Yes ☐ No ☐ Don't Know

When and where can the child be seen? (give dates and places): _____

_____

Type of Child Abuse or Neglect
☐ Burning ☐ Beating ☐ Fracture ☐ Sexual Abuse ☐ Abandonment ☐ Malnutrition ☐ Internal Injuries
☐ Physical Neglect ☐ Medical Neglect ☐ Lack of Supervision ☐ Other (specify):

Briefly describe the situation and/or condition of the child: _____

_____

_____

Has this report already been called in? . . . . ☐ Yes, to local Child Protective Services ☐ Yes, to Child Abuse Hotline ☐ No

If yes, date: _____ To whom? _____

PERSON MAKING THIS REPORT (Anonymous reports are accepted, but DHS staff will be able to do a better investigation if they can contact you.

Name	Place of Employment

Work Address (Street, City, State, ZIP)	Work Telephone

OR, I prefer to be contacted at home: ⟩ Home Address (Street, City, State, ZIP)	Home Telephone

Source: Texas Department of Human Services

Although some professionals think written follow-up forms are a nuisance, these reports perform many important functions. Because potential reporters are required to put their suspicions in writing, they tend to be more careful about making a report (although, as was just mentioned, mandated reporters are usually the only persons who are required to file written reports). Moreover, a subsequent written report provides added assurance that the initial oral report will be investigated because it is a physical record of the first report. In addition, since it is made sometime after the initial report, it provides the reporter with an easy way to give the child protective agency more up-to-date information about the family's situation.

There is another reason for written reports. The record-keeping practices of many public and private agencies and institutions leave much to be desired; often, there may be no clear written summary of what happened or what was observed. When there are no agency records or the records are hard to locate or vague, a written report may provide the only recorded evidence of the child's condition at the time. Keeping a copy will guarantee that you have a specific, detailed record of your observations to refer to during discussions with the child protective agency or in preparation for court testimony.

The written report, moreover, may be admissible in court. (Of course, a written report is not presumptive evidence that a child has been abused or neglected, and the court can attach whatever persuasive weight to the report that it deems appropriate.) Many states have specific laws that make such reports admissible, but these laws vary widely. Some are limited to mandated reports, and others to reports only from physicians; some require that the report first be examined *in camera* by the judge and others require that the admission of the report conform to the rules of evidence. Even if your state does not have such a law, the written report will probably be admissible as evidence (under what is called the "business records" exception to the hearsay rule or to refresh your memory).

The person (or agency) who makes the report should keep a copy, placing it in an appropriate file on the child or family. (Sometimes, agency procedures require that reports be placed in a special file to ensure that only those who have a "need to know" can gain access to them.) Many of the printed forms provided by child protective agencies have a precarboned attachment for the reporter's convenience. If your state's form does not have one, make a photocopy before you send the filled-out form to the child protective agency.

INFORMING THE CHILD AND THE PARENTS

Many of us feel anger and outrage toward abusive parents. We expect parents to be caring and concerned and have difficulty relating positively to parents who are not. There is a natural fear of relating to volatile and often violent people. It is important to admit that these feelings exist, so they can be dealt with in a way that does not compromise the safety of the child or later efforts to rehabilitate the parents.

If there is any reason to believe that doing so will place the child in greater danger, do not tell the parents that you are about to make a report. The parents may blame the child for the report and maltreat him or her more or may flee the community with the child. In addition, if there is reason to believe that the parents may react violently toward you, it is likewise inadvisable to tell them about the report.

Besides the potential danger to the child or you, it may simply be inappropriate to tell the child or the parents about the report. For example, the child may be too young to understand what is happening, or knowledge of the report (and the need to keep it secret) may make the child feel disloyal to the parents. Also, it is normally inappropriate for nonprofessional reporters (such as friends, neighbors, and relatives) to tell the parents that they have made a report. Even when such situations do not pose a physical danger to the reporter, they are inherently embarrassing for all involved. To a much lesser extent, the same can be true for some professional reporters, such as schoolteachers, who continue to see the family in informal settings.

In many situations, though, the child or the parents should be told that a report has been made. For example, if an adolescent has told a schoolteacher about being sexually abused, knowledge that the teacher has taken action can help reassure the child and prepare the child for the subsequent investigation. In the same way, parents who are involved in an ongoing relationship with a professional may feel betrayed if they are not warned that a child protective worker will visit their home and they later discover that the professional made the report. The result may be angry parents who come to school, for example, demanding to know why someone is telling them how to raise their children. When this happens, it may be all but impossible for the professional to rebuild a trusting relationship with the parents. Finally, in some situations, there is no way to prevent the parents from learning that a report has been made. For example, if the child is placed in protective custody by a hospital, someone must explain what is happening.

Few parents are happy to be reported to the authorities for abuse or neglect, and you should expect a hostile or at least a passive-aggressive reaction. (Again, parents who you think may become violent should not be told about the report.) However, many maltreating parents realize they have a problem and, if approached sympathetically, may even feel relieved that outsiders will become involved. Maintaining a sympathetic posture is understandably difficult. It is natural to feel angry at parents who have maltreated their children, but expressing this anger may further endanger the child and will certainly lessen the possibility of parental cooperation.[8] It sometimes helps to remember that most of these parents are lonely, anxious, depressed, or otherwise needy people.

A straightforward and honest approach is generally the best one to take. You should tell the child, the parents, or both of your suspicions and of the need to make a report. "The notification is firm, but kind. It states the legal authority for the report, and casts no blame."[9] (If you are under a legal mandate to report, it may be helpful to tell the parents this.) For hospital-based physicians, the National Center on Child Abuse and Neglect recommends the following approach:

Tell the parents the diagnosis and the need to report it. One can state: "Your explanation for the injury is insufficient. Even though it wasn't intentional, someone injured this child. I am obligated by (your State) law to report all suspicious injuries to children." The physician should do this, if the case is reported on the basis of the physician's medical findings or if he has a relationship with the parents. In fact, after all diagnostic studies are completed, the physician should review the interpretation of the actual cause of each specific injury in a way that is supportive to the family. This convinces the parents that we know what actually happened and permits them to turn their attention to therapy. The physician should be willing to discuss the general content of the medical report. The overall outlook should be positive and emphasize that this problem is treatable, that the CPS worker will be involved (preferably not the police, unless required by the law of the jurisdiction), that the matter will be shared only with professionals (will not appear in the newspapers), and that everyone's goal is to help them find better ways of dealing with their child (not to punish the parents). If the parents become argumentative, they can be advised to seek legal counsel.[10]

Describing what will happen next is often helpful. You can explain that the purpose of the report is not to punish the parent but to help protect the child, that a caseworker will visit the family to determine whether the child's needs are being met, and that the worker will offer the parents assistance in caring for their child.

Schools that have instituted this procedure report good results. Parents are less hostile and resentful when they understand that the school has a legal obligation it must fulfill. In addition, they often appreciate an expression of concern or an offer of support at a time which, after all, is a very difficult one for them.[11]

If the parents seem receptive, you may encourage them to seek help on their own, as described in Chapter 19. Although their doing so does not relieve you of the legal obligation to report, it may give them an early start on treatment and help convince the child protective agency of their amenability to assistance. One approach frequently used, especially by Parents Anonymous groups, is to tell the parents that a report will be made the next day and that it would be better if the parents called the protective agency before then. (Of course, this approach can be taken only if the child does not appear to be in immediate danger and it does not seem that the parents will flee.)

There will be times when you misjudge the parents' response to being told about the report. Hence, you should choose a location for the discussion that, although private, is not so isolated that you cannot easily obtain help. If the parents become agitated, you should try to calm them before calling for help. You should "empathize with the parents' feelings, and point out your professional and legal responsibilities to the child. Emphasize that you have no power to make custodial decisions, but rather, you are mandated by law to report certain types of biosocial situations. Be quick to point out that environments that appear to be adverse or unsafe on first glance can later be judged satisfactory after more careful scrutiny."[12] It often helps to remind parents that, except for placing the child in emergency protective custody, nothing can be done without their consent unless a court order is obtained and that they have a right to legal counsel.

Whatever its outcome, the entire discussion with the parents should be well documented in agency or office records and made available to the child protective agency. It is especially important to do so if, during the discussion, the parents admit to having abused or neglected the child or if they give information that suggests that they did so.

Telling the child, the parents, or both about the report and its consequences should be only the first step in an ongoing process of support and encouragement. Knowledge of their problems gives the professional an added responsibility to respond to the family's special needs. Depending on the situation, the professional should offer continuing support and encouragement to both the child and parents. Schoolteachers and child care professionals, for example, should be sensitive to the child's need for advice and support during the subsequent stages of the child protective process; they should make themselves available to the child and should encourage the child to come to them for help. Similarly, mental health professionals should be aware that the parents are under great emotional stress (as is the child) and they should be prepared to help family members deal with their problems. Finally, even if it turns out that your concerns about possible abuse or neglect are unfounded, the parents may still need the assistance of a social service agency—and you should help them get it.

17

Monitoring Investigations

E ach day, child protective agencies make a herculean effort to investigate the thousands of reports that they receive. But reports are
increasing faster than these agencies can handle them, so protective
investigations are often backlogged and poorly performed. Depending
on the community, 25–50 percent of all child abuse fatalities involve
previously reported children.[1]

Your *legal* obligation toward abused children ends when you make a
report. But since making a report does not guarantee that the child
will be protected from further abuse, you have a deeper responsibility
to do as much as you can to ensure that the proper steps are taken. If
you are going to make a difference, though, you need to understand
the child protective process.

UNDERSTANDING THE PROCESS

Almost all communities now have specialized child protective agencies
to receive reports (usually via highly publicized hotlines) and then to
investigate them. These agencies perform essentially the same functions,
as Chart 17–1 portrays. They receive and screen reports (intake); investigate
reports and determine whether child protective intervention is needed
(investigation); determine whether the child requires immediate protection
(emergency services); decide what long-term protective measures and
treatment services are needed and seek the parents' consent for them
(case planning and referral); supervise the parent's care of the child and
monitor the provision of treatment services when a maltreated child is
left at home or is returned home after having been in foster care (case
monitoring); and close the case after the parents seem to be able to
care properly for the child or after parental rights have been terminated
and the child has been placed for adoption (case closure).

To the fullest extent possible, the child protective agency seeks the

Chart 17–1 **Standard Child Protective Procedures**

Intake
- Receive reports
- Screen reports
- Assign reports to individual caseworkers

Investigation
- Collect information
- Verify reports

Emergency Services
- Assess need for immediate protective measures
- Implement emergency services
(either with parents' consent or through court order)

Case Planning and Implementation
- Determine appropriate case plan
- Implement case plan through direct provision of services
or referral to other agencies
(either with parents' consent or through a court order)

Case Monitoring
- Supervise parents' care of child
- Continually monitor implementation of case plan
(to determine whether the case plan remains appropriate,
a new case plan is needed, or the case can be closed)

Case Closure
- Close case because parents can care properly for the child
or
- Close case because parental rights were terminated
and child placed for adoption

parents' voluntary consent to the protective measures and treatment services it deems necessary. If the parents do not agree to the agency's plan, the agency may seek court authority to impose it on the parents (court action). Child protective agencies differ only in the degree to which these functions are separated and assigned to different staff units, which, in turn, is usually determined by the size of the agency. Larger agencies are more likely to have specialized units because it is more efficient for them to do so.

Thus, a report of suspected child maltreatment is only the first step in the child protective process. The report must be investigated promptly and appropriate protective action taken. Unfortunately, the press of cases and administrative breakdowns often prevent child protective agencies from doing so. These agencies are so overburdened that some reports actually go uninvestigated, and many more are delayed, often for days. Agencies attempt to identify emergencies that need immediate investigation, but they often miss situations of real danger.

Expect a follow-up call for further information and be concerned if you do not get one. The initial telephone report rarely elicits all the information that a reporter has about a family. Moreover, in the time between the report and the beginning of the investigation, the reporter may have learned more about the alleged maltreatment (either in support or contradiction of the initial report). Therefore, the caseworker should recontact you (preferably before seeing the family), even if only a few hours have elapsed.

Although practice varies, the worker will seek to obtain more detailed and more up-to-date information about the situation. When appropriate, the worker also will discuss the situation with any of your associates who also know the child and the parents. For example, if the report was made by a physician on a hospital staff, nurses and other hospital personnel may be questioned about the family. At this time, the worker also may determine your willingness to be identified to the parents as the source of the report and whether you are willing to cooperate with subsequent aspects of the case, such as preparing and implementing a treatment plan and testifying in court.

Friends, neighbors, or relatives are usually interviewed in person to obtain a complete picture of the situation, especially when there is a question about the appropriateness of the report. An in-person interview is essential when there is reason to suspect that the report was made in bad faith. Follow-up interviews of professionals are ordinarily performed by telephone, except (1) when the report has come from an institution in which others may have information to contribute and (2) when the reporter has placed the child in protective custody, in which case the worker will need to see the child anyway.

The absence of a follow-up interview suggests that the report is not being investigated properly or at all. If you have not been contacted, you *definitely* should call again. It may be that no one was assigned to the case. In one Massachusetts case, for example, the family was reported twice in the same year. The first report was not investigated because the agency was shorthanded. When the second report was made, eleven months later, the agency still did not have enough workers, so a supervisor conducted the investigation. The supervisor found that "the father had come home one evening intoxicated and repeatedly stabbed the mother in front of her six children." He also found "blood on the walls and floor, in addition to poor health conditions, lice, and a strong stench of urine." But even after these gruesome findings, no caseworker was assigned to the family. Instead, "a technician, who is not a social worker, was assigned because the workers were already carrying too many cases."[2] This is not how to protect endangered children.

FEEDBACK

Feedback to reporters is essential to the long-term success of a community-wide, child protective reporting system. Persons who report suspected child abuse or neglect naturally want to know the disposition of their reports and whether the investigation verified their suspicions. The fact that you made a report demonstrates that you care about the child. Moreover, potential reporters need to know whether reporting will accomplish anything.

If persons who report are not told what happened, they may conclude that the agency's response was ineffective or even harmful to the child, and the next time they suspect that a child is maltreated, they may decide not to report. In addition, finding out whether their suspicions were valid also refines their diagnostic skills and thus improves the quality and accuracy of their future reports. Reporters also need such information to interpret subsequent events and to monitor the child's condition. Finally, feedback to the reporter increases the likelihood that the agency will make an accurate assessment of the child's situation because it allows the reporter to correct any misleading information obtained during the investigation.

In Pueblo, Colorado, a child protective worker and her supervisor were criminally prosecuted for failing to respond adequately to a report of maltreatment and, thus, for allowing the child to die. The child had previously been placed in foster care and then returned to her parents' custody. During the time when the caseworker was on medical leave, the agency received new reports of suspected abuse from the child's school and the school nurse.

According to the indictment against the supervisor, the reports consisted of "telephone contacts . . . wherein a report was made of cigarette burns on the child, wounds to [the] arms of the child, bruises and scratches to a large portion of said child's back, scars from apparent large burns to the child's back, and other injuries."[3] With her doctor's permission, the caseworker, who had a BSW degree and ten years of experience with the agency, returned to the office for one day to arrange a psychological evaluation of the child, but made no attempt to verify the nature or extent of the reported injuries. The worker claimed that she was not told of the school reports.[4] Shortly thereafter, the child died of apparent neglect. (The convictions of both the caseworker and her supervisor were overturned on appeal because of legal issues not related to their guilt.)[5]

Seek feedback about the report and the investigation. By your continuing involvement, you can prevent such tragedies. Another call from the school might have prevented the case from being mishandled.

Unfortunately, child protective agencies frequently fail to provide feedback to reporters, usually because of high caseloads and a general insensitivity to the legitimate needs of those who report. Some agencies claim that they cannot provide such information because their records and investigations are confidential. But this is not true. There is no legal impediment to telling reporters about the general results of the investigation. After all, the reporters made the report in the first place. Furthermore, they are under a continuing legal obligation to report subsequent abuse or neglect. To say that they cannot be told what happened is to adopt an overly legalistic interpretation of confidentiality. To override this hesitancy, a few states have enacted laws that require that the reporter is to be notified of the investigation's results, although such provisions are technically not needed.

Persons who have made a report should be told whether the investigation verified their suspicions and how the agency handled the situation. In certain circumstances, the child's future safety may depend on their having this information. If the child protective agency does not automatically provide such feedback, reporters should feel free to ask for it.

However, the right of reporters to know what happened is not absolute. In deciding what information to provide, child protective agencies must balance the reporter's need to know against the family's right to privacy. If the reporter is a friend, neighbor, or relative of the family, he or she should receive only limited information. The National Center on Child Abuse and Neglect recommends that if the report appears to be valid, such persons should be told something along the following lines:

> "The family does have some problems."
>
> "We are working with the family."
>
> "We think you did the right thing to refer the family; we are staying in there."
>
> "We find it to be a very complex situation."
>
> "I can't give you specific facts but want you to know we are looking into the situation."[6]

Professionals who report should be given more information, including a clear indication of whether the report was valid and whether the child appears to be in any immediate danger. Only with such information can the reporter be expected to detect situations that deteriorate further. In addition, if the reporter (or his or her agency) will be involved in treatment efforts, as many are, much more information must be provided. A clear picture of the family's dynamics, including its strengths and weaknesses, is needed for successful treatment.

18

Being Prepared

When a possibly abused child comes before you is the wrong time to start learning about how to handle such situations. If you regularly see children who may be abused or neglected, you have a responsibility to learn the signs of suspected maltreatment and your legal powers and obligations to protect endangered children—before you face a potential emergency.

ONGOING TRAINING

Although professional awareness of child abuse is at an all-time high, there are still major gaps in understanding and knowledge. Better education on reporting responsibilities continues to be the single most effective method of encouraging more complete and accurate reporting. Recognizing this, almost half the states have specific statutes that mandate professional training and public awareness efforts.[1] California goes further, requiring all those who enter employment as a "child care custodian [which includes teachers], health practitioner, or with a child protective agency" to sign a statement indicating an understanding of the state's mandatory reporting provisions.[2] Of course, legislation is not required for a state to provide public and professional education, and most do.

Professional education programs should sensitize all child-serving professionals to the occurrence of child abuse and should instruct them in how and when to report. They should cover all forms of child abuse and neglect, including institutional abuse and neglect, explaining that child protective procedures are not punitive in nature and that their purpose is to protect the child and rehabilitate the parents. The general focus should be on the reporting process, conveying the community's reliance on professional reporting of suspected child abuse and neglect and describing professional responsibilities, powers, and immunities un-

192

Chart 18–1 **Topics for Training**

- Persons who *must* report
- Persons who *may* report
- Definitions of child abuse and neglect in state law
- Liability for failing to report
- Protections for those who report
- Sources of information
- Indicators of child abuse and neglect
- How to handle emergencies
- Preserving evidence
- Reporting procedures
- Working with the child protective agency and other human service agencies
- Respecting parental rights and sensibilities

---

der state reporting laws. The specific focus should be on how to identify maltreated children and the mechanics of reporting.

Professional education programs should also seek to improve cooperation and coordination among all agencies that serve children and families. Thus, they should explain the interrelated responsibilities of child protective agencies, law enforcement agencies, the courts, and community human service agencies. Chart 18–1 lists the basic topics that should be covered in any program of professional education.

Although child protective agencies have the major responsibility for educating both the public and professionals, all child-serving professions and agencies should conduct their own training and educational programs to supplement the efforts of state and local child protective services. Professional education should start in graduate schools and proceed through in-service or continuing education programs. Agencies should provide a clear understanding of what is expected of employees. For example, employees should know what actions they can take on their own initiative (and the considerations involved) and what actions require the approval of supervisors or administrators.

Ultimately, though, all professionals, whether on their own or working in agencies, must take the responsibility to learn about child abuse and what they can do about it. This means reading professional literature, seeking and taking advantage of educational opportunities, consulting with others, and maintaining membership in professional groups and organizations.

ADOPTING A FORMAL POLICY

An increasing number of public and private agencies are adopting formal policies about reporting suspected child abuse and neglect. Some state laws mandate them. Florida, for example, requires all administrators of hospitals and public health service agencies to develop a method of informing their employees of the duty to report.[3]

The primary purpose of these policies, or agency protocols, is educational: to inform staff members of their obligation to report and of the procedures to be followed. They are also an implicit commitment by agency administrators to support frontline staff members who decide to report; the very process of drafting a written document can clarify previously ambiguous or ill-conceived agency policies.

A broad cross section of agency officers, staff, and relevant outsiders should be consulted in the drafting process. This will make the policy more effective and more acceptable to those who are bound by it. The policy should be written within the context of the agency's resources, competence, and legal mandate; great care should be taken to ensure that the policy does not ask the staff to do the impossible.

The particulars of a policy depend on the provisions of state law, the nature of available child protective services, and the type and size of the agency involved. The following generalizations can be made, though:

1. The policy should clearly state the legal requirements for reporting, as well as the penalties and protections established in the law. (These portions of the policy should be reviewed by the agency's attorney or the appropriate child protective agency.)

2. The policy should describe where and how to report. (These provisions should also be reviewed by the child protective agency.)

3. The policy should delineate the duties and responsibilities of different types of staff members in the agency; in other words, it should describe *who* should do *what*. For example, a school's policy may require that all reports be routed through the principal's office; sometimes this is required by state law. The policy may also give the principal responsibility for informing the child, the parents, or both about the report. In larger agencies, a specific staff member (or unit) may be made responsible for providing case consultation, for coordinating child protective activities within the agency, and for being the contact person for outside agencies.

4. Agency policies also may have provisions concerning record keep-

ing, confidentiality of records, ongoing staff training, and the participation of staff in multidisciplinary teams and public awareness campaigns. Chart 18–2 lists some of the more common elements of agency policies, together with sample wording.

A well-received and clearly written policy can greatly upgrade an agency's response to child abuse and neglect. But to be effective, a policy must be known. Copies of the policy should be distributed to all staff members. In addition, copies or appropriate summaries should be posted in key locations, such as staff lounges or cafeterias. (Florida law, for example, requires all schools to post notices informing teachers of their reporting obligations.)[4] Moreover, even the most comprehensive and well-written policy must be buttressed by regular staff training on the identification and reporting of suspected child maltreatment.

MULTIDISCIPLINARY TEAMS

Assessing situations of possible child abuse or neglect frequently entails a complex weighing of medical, psychological, child development, and legal considerations. You should feel free to call on the appropriate child protective agency for guidance about whether particular conditions justify a report. Colleagues are also an important source of advice, but because more extensive assistance is regularly needed, a large number of agencies have established a formal source of help. "Multidisciplinary child protection teams," based on the original Denver model,[5] focus the collective expertise of relevant professionals on the identification and treatment of child maltreatment. They can provide a "holistic approach to families, thereby minimizing confusion for the family, overlapping of services, and the likelihood of families being under or inappropriately served."[6]

Located in a variety of medical and social service settings, multidisciplinary teams now exist in many communities. About half the states have laws that either authorize or require the creation of such teams.[7] No law is needed, however, to allow a hospital, a school, or any other agency to establish a team.

"Every medical center should have a child abuse committee," according to Dr. Vincent J. Fontana, medical director of the New York Foundling Hospital and a national expert on child abuse and neglect. Fontana recommends that the committee serve as a "team of consultants, headed by a senior pediatrician to assist the house staff, a psychiatrist, a social worker and hospital administrator."[8]

Chart 18–2 **Model Agency Policy for Reporting Suspected Child Abuse and Neglect**

Statement of Support	To protect children from abuse and neglect, this agency supports the identification and reporting of such endangered children to the proper governmental authorities.
Legal Mandate	The laws of this state require the following persons to report a child if they have reasonable cause to suspect that a child is abused or neglected: . . .

Reportable Conditions	In this state, "child abuse" is defined as . . .
	   "Child neglect" is defined as . . .
	   "Sexual abuse" is defined as . . .

Who Should Report	All staff members who have reasonable cause to suspect that a child is abused or neglected should report. *Optional:* [You should contact the head of this agency, who shall make the report.]
How to Report	As soon as possible, a report should be made by calling the local child protective agency at . . . A written report must be submitted within forty-eight hours.* [Reporting forms can be obtained from . . .]
Emergencies	Bring any child who needs to be placed in protective custody or to receive medical care to the immediate attention of the child protective agency (or the head of this agency). If it appears that the parents may become violent or attempt to remove the child forcibly, consider calling the police at . . .
Information Required	The person who is reporting need not prove that the child has been abused or neglected, only that there is reasonable cause for suspecting maltreatment.

* This is a requirement in some states.

Chart 18–2 **Model Agency Policy for Reporting Suspected Child Abuse and Neglect (*continued*)**

	Be prepared to give the following information: the name, address, and age of the child; the name and address of the parent or caretaker; the nature and extent of the injuries or a description of the maltreatment; and any other information that may help establish the cause of the injuries or condition.
Protection for Reporting	Anyone who makes a report in good faith is immune from civil or criminal liability for reporting.
Penalties for not Reporting	Persons who fail to report when they have reasonable cause to suspect abuse or neglect are subject to criminal prosecution and a civil lawsuit. In addition, failure to report may result in a disciplinary action by this agency.
Informing the Child and/or the Parents	The decision to inform the child and/or the parents about the report should be made by. . . .
Preserving Evidence	All statements and visible signs of maltreatment should be documented fully and carefully. Diagram any injuries. Attempt to preserve physical evidence. *Optional:* Arrangements for photographs and x-rays can be made through . . .
Record Keeping	A careful record should be kept of the report, the conditions that led to it, and its outcome. A copy of the written report should be included in this agency's records.
Confidentiality	To protect the family's privacy, all records concerning the report should be kept confidential. Staff members should discuss the report only with persons who have a "need to know" about it.
Consultation	Advice on reporting requirements and procedures, as well as consultation on particular situations is available from . . . This person also serves as the liaison with the child protective agency.

Chart 18–3 **Functions of Multidisciplinary Teams**[9]

Case Diagnosis and Planning

- Assess cases of suspected child abuse and neglect
- Report suspected cases to the child protective agency or police
- Consult on the diagnosis and treatment of difficult cases
- Manage the treatment of individual families
- Educate professionals in the institution and in the community
- Assist other agencies to develop child abuse teams
- Participate in community activities related to the prevention, identification, or treatment of child abuse and neglect.

Program Planning and Coordination

- Plan communitywide approaches to treatment
- Educate professional and lay groups in the community
- Identify gaps in services for families and propose ways to fill them
- Advocate for improved and expanded programs
- Implement new projects.

Depending on the community and the circumstances of individual cases, multidisciplinary teams include representatives of the relevant medical, mental health, law enforcement, and social service agencies. (Most teams also include a representative of the local child protective agency, in recognition of its legal mandate to investigate reports and to provide needed therapeutic services.) Although their primary purpose is to provide diagnostic and case planning consultations, many teams also help manage treatment efforts and perform a variety of coordinating and educational functions[10] (see Chart 18–3).

The substance and outcomes of all case consultations, whether with a child protective agency, colleagues, or a team, should be written down and filed for future reference. Any and all evidence and information about possible maltreatment should be preserved and documented, as described in Chapter 10.

FOUR

A
Word
to
Parents

19

Is Your Child Abused?

U p to now, this book has focused largely on what to do when you suspect that someone else's child may be abused. However, your family may be more immediately touched by child abuse. You may think that someone may have abused your child or that you are losing control and may be hurting your own child.

IF IT HAPPENS TO YOUR CHILD

You must be alert to the possibility that your child may have been abused by a baby-sitter, a teacher or a custodian at your child's school, a day care worker, the older sibling of a playmate, a relative, a spouse or ex-spouse, or his or her companion. It can happen to anyone's child. Here is one mother's story:

> When my daughter was 2½ she casually mentioned, in her own words, that her babysitter (a woman) had been sexually molesting her. My immediate reaction was to assure my daughter that I believed her and that she had done nothing wrong. Those next few weeks are a blur in my memory. Physically I felt nauseous and was barely able to eat or sleep. Emotionally I shifted into "cruise control." I performed all the routine household duties required of me, took care of my daughter, and technically continued functioning. But I was in a state of shock. The babysitter was someone I had considered to be a friend, so the violation and betrayal carried over to me.[1]

Focus on your child's needs. As this mother's account demonstrates, you will feel many powerful emotions if your child is abused, ranging from anger to bitterness to betrayal; you may even feel vengeful towards the perpetrator. But your prime concern must be your child, who, with your help, will have the opportunity to recover.

Vent your feelings to a good friend, a clergyman, or a mental health professional. Never direct them to your child, who may already be afraid and confused. Your child's response may be shaped by your reaction, especially in sexual abuse cases, in which some children tell only part of what happened, holding back the rest to see how you react; if you react too strongly, you may not learn the whole story. It helps to remember that once the victimization has come to light, it will probably stop.

Begin by supporting your child. Commend him or her for telling you about the abuse. One of a child's worst fears is that he or she is somehow to blame for the incident. Alleviating this guilt is of utmost importance. A child also needs to know that it is alright to talk about the abuse. Tell your child that you are glad he or she told you about the situation, so you could help. Be direct. Say, "I'm glad you told me," or "I'll do my best to protect you."

Assure the child that you will do your best to make sure that this does not happen again. Be sure not to make this promise, however, unless you can keep it. The loss of trust is a major consequence of sexual abuse, and the child needs to regain the ability to rely on adults. Empty promises cannot do that.

Address your child's other questions and concerns. Try to allay any fears about threats the abuser may have made, such as that the child will go to jail. Make sure that the child knows that this could never happen. Uncertainty is stressful for us all, but especially for children. As best as you can, tell your child about any medical, legal, or counseling process that he or she may need to go through.

Respect your child's privacy. Do not share the details of the abuse with many people. To do so may stigmatize him or her, with the effects felt long after the crisis. Tell your child that you will only tell people who need to know—the people who are going to help.

Verify the facts as best you can. Some experts assume that the child is telling the truth when they report child abuse. After all, children rarely lie about being sexually abused; to know much about it, they generally have to go through the experience. Nevertheless, you must keep open the possibility that there may have been a mistake or misunderstanding or even that your child could be lying.

If your child tells you of an incident, question him or her carefully. You could ask, for example, "Is someone touching you in a way that makes you feel uncomfortable?" Do not pressure your child and *absolutely* do not ask leading questions. While leading questions can help a child open up and talk about an uncomfortable situation, they can also implant your worst fears into the mind of an impressionable young child. (See

Chapter 6.) If others tell you they suspect that something has happened to your child, ask for specific details.

If the incident occurred at a day care center, you may ask friends who also have a child there whether they have noticed any unusual behavior or physical symptoms in their children. But if you believe that your child was abused, do not go to the center to talk about your concern. Instead, make a report to the appropriate licensing agency or the police.

Having your child confront the accused perpetrator is not a good idea because it could be an overwhelmingly stressful and damaging experience. (There may be times during an investigation that the child and the perpetrator will be in the same courtroom, but every effort will be made to help the child feel comfortable and safe.) The only time that you should even consider a confrontation is when your child has accused a close family member and you have such serious misgivings about your child's veracity that you have *already* decided not to file a report. (In such cases, consider having your child seen by a professional. Making an untrue allegation of sexual behavior is neither common nor normal.)

Get a medical examination for your child. The child may require treatment or evidence may need to be preserved. Do not assume that an examination is unnecessary merely because the child seems all right. For example, when a child reports that someone "touched me," the abuse may have been more severe. It is usually best to have the examination immediately after disclosure, provided, of course, that the child's emotional state allows it.

In cases of sexual abuse, the purpose of a medical examination is to assure the child that he or she is all right, to determine the extent of abuse, to check for sexually transmitted diseases or any injuries that may need attention, and to gather evidence. In older girls, it may also be necessary to check whether they are pregnant.

Get a physician with the experience and training to detect and recognize sexual abuse when you seek a special medical examination for your child. The best sources for referrals are sexual abuse treatment programs in the community, children's hospitals, and medical societies.

Report the abuse. The best way to protect your child—and other children—from the same perpetrator is to make a report. Suspected abuse by a baby-sitter, day care personnel, or any other nonhousehold member should be reported to the police immediately. Suspected abuse by a parent, stepparent, guardian, or any other household member should be reported to the child protective agency or the police, in accordance with the considerations discussed in Chapter 6.

A MOTHER'S FEELINGS ABOUT DISCOVERING INCEST[2]

1. Usually her first reaction is one of horror, shock, and the disbelief that comes from feeling disgraced and wanting intensely for it not to be true. She feels numb, confused, guilty, betrayed. She suddenly feels cut off from both her husband and her daughter. Her well-established emotional ties have been fractured and there follows a period during which she flounders, wondering what to do.

2. She fears public disclosure and embarrassment, and she may feel guilty and inadequate as wife and mother, wondering if this is all her fault.

3. She is caught in the middle, having to choose between her husband and her child, and she stands to lose a lot no matter how she chooses. Most mothers feel victimized by a situation they had no direct part in yet must shoulder major responsibility for resolving. This situation generates a lot of frustration leading to anger and sometimes rage, which, whether expressed or suppressed or repressed, is always there.

4. She fears destruction of her family. Her partner or spouse may go to jail. Her child may go to a foster home.

5. She fears loss of economic support, has anxiety about supporting the family on her own.

6. She may herself have been sexually abused as a child and discovering it in her own family may dredge up old unresolved feelings which compound her present problems.

7. Some mothers may feel jealous of their daughter, and may wonder if the daughter engaged in seductive behavior.

8. Nearly all mothers experience some degree of ambivalence, not toward the act of incest (which they abhor), but toward

To protect your child's interests, you will need to learn about the child protective system. The aftermath of a report can be frightening and frustrating for both you and your child. As one mother explained: "I reported my daughter's abuse and we were immediately thrown into the various systems: interviews with social services, therapists, an officer from the sensitive crimes unit of the police department, and the District Attorney's office."[3]

their partner and their child. In the past, professionals have assigned at least part of the blame to the mother (she "unconsciously promoted" sexual abuse by setting up conditions so the incest could happen) in nearly all cases. While this may be true in a few instances, it is our opinion that the mother has not learned until now the **need** to protect her child from her partner. What was termed ambivalence is an untenable characterization of the mother's plight. Rather, in the shock and confusion of finding out about the incest, it takes time for the mother to absorb the fact that she must in some way physically intervene to stop the abuse. As others have said, how can a mother know before the fact of incest that her child needs to be chaperoned with her own father? The ambivalence toward her mate stems from her abhorrence for what he has done, and her continuing caring for him, and she feels this is irrational. Her ambivalence toward her daughter relates to points 6. and 7. above, plus her reaction to the fact that the daughter may be blaming the mother for not protecting her. A few mothers have no ambivalence at all.

9. Nearly all mothers have some degree of denial upon first learning about the incest. It is a disservice to think of this as resistance. Denial is a survival tool: It helps dilute the sense of debasement, it helps to absorb the intense fear and anger. It buys valuable time until the person can feel strong enough to face the problem for herself.

10. She has anger toward human services systems, partly as displacement, but mostly through her experience of feeling accused and/or misunderstood, sometimes believing she's being told what to do without regard for her feelings and anxieties.

Although most of the professionals assigned to your case will be concerned about you and your child, they probably will be too busy to explain everything that is happening or everything that will happen. Also, they may not tell you about the options in how the case can be handled. See Chapter 17 and Chart 17–1 for a better idea of what to expect.

Consider counseling for your child and for yourself. Some children need counseling to remediate the effects of the abuse. Dealing with such issues as soon as possible could prevent problems from developing later. Be sure to select a therapist with the appropriate expertise.

Worry about yourself, too. Talk the situation over with someone. You will have many feelings about the abuse, feelings that need to be expressed to someone you trust. By using another adult as an outlet, you will be better able to help your child. You may also consider seeking professional help.

But most important, do not blame yourself. Sexual abuse is an unpleasant reality in our society. The vast majority of abuse occurs in situations in which the child knows and trusts the adult. You cannot protect your child from all risks.

SELF-HELP

As a society, we have traditionally relied on self-help and voluntarily accepted social and psychiatric services to deal with personal problems. The passage of mandatory reporting laws reflects the reality that most abusive and neglectful parents will not seek help on their own. But this does not mean that we should abandon our commitment to self-help in these cases.

Therapeutic programs are most effective when they are entered voluntarily. Moreover, self-help may be the only way to protect a large number of children who would otherwise not receive help. Many cases are not recognized or reported by outsiders until it is too late. These children can only be protected if family members seek assistance.

If parents understand their need for help, they may seek it on their own or be more willing to accept it when it is offered, as the following case illustrates:

> Ruth, the mother of a 3-year-old daughter and a year-old son, was feeling overwhelmed trying to manage her children. She said that she screamed at her daughter and found herself kicking and throwing the child. Ruth has received individual counseling and she and her husband are undergoing marriage counseling. Ruth attends . . . monthly parent informational meetings and has attended the parent education classes, during which time transportation and babysitting were provided. Her daughter was enrolled in a day care program for abused children, which gave Ruth some relief from child care and some time to herself.

Ruth has identified the abuse she received as a child as a factor in her abuse of her daughter. She has worked very hard and enthusiastically on her problems and has decreased significantly the abuse to her daughter. Ruth is still working on improving her life and feels very proud and relieved. She has also referred a friend to [the program] and given a brochure on it to another friend.[4]

Many programs are now using the mass media to give a direct message to parents who may need help to care adequately for their children. These media campaigns seek to persuade parents that they are not alone in their difficulty and to inform them where they can get help.

That such parents have sought help for themselves probably means that they will accept the services offered. However, they are understandably fearful about identifying themselves to a public agency and are easily frightened by a harsh, unsympathetic response. Because the children of such parents may be in great danger, it is imperative that agencies support and reinforce the parents' decision to seek help. To ensure that these calls are handled with the requisite sensitivity, many states train their hotline workers to help parents get assistance. All states should do so.

ARE YOU LOSING CONTROL?

The first step is to recognize that you have a problem. The next step is to do something about it. If you think that you may be hurting your child or that you may do so, seek help. (Chart 19–1 lists some of the steps you might consider.)

Knowing what to expect from children can put things in perspective. Many communities offer classes and workshops that cover such topics as how children grow up, why they act the way they do, and how to discipline them. You may learn, for example, that your own children do not misbehave any more than do others. Look for these programs in day care centers, hospitals, public libraries, and churches.

Talking with someone about how you feel can be helpful. This person may be a close friend or family member who listens well or even a parents' "hotline" where trained volunteers will help you work out some of your problems. Family or individual therapy can also help. Many communities have support groups that give parents a chance to meet with other parents who are having similar problems dealing with their kids.

Chart 19–1 **Are You Hurting Your Child?**[5]

If you think that you may be hurting your child by what you say or do, you can:

- *Stop.* Think about what you are doing. Why are you so upset? Are you really mad at the child? Or are you mad about something else? How would you feel if someone said these words or did these things to you?
- *Think back.* Is it so important that the children always do things your way? After you've lost control, how do you really feel about yourself? Can you really "make it up" to them?
- *Take time out.* When you are angry, calm down before you respond to the child.
- *Talk to someone.* Tell someone you trust about the problem. Talk to a good friend. Talk to someone in the family. Maybe they have problems with their children, too. What do they do when they are upset? It helps just to know that other people have the same problems. Or, talk to your pastor, a teacher, your doctor, or someone else you trust. They may have some good ideas about other ways to handle the problem rather than blowing up at the child.
- *Take a parenting or discipline class.* Good parenting and teaching skills can be learned. Children behave better when they are praised for doing a good job.
- *Join a parents' group.* Parents Anonymous, Parents United, and other groups for parents provide support and insight into how to handle problem situations.
- *Seek professional help.* If you improve your own life, you will be better able to care for your children. A mental health professional may help you deal with your problems, instead of taking them out on the children you love. (Chart 19–2 describes how to find help.)

One such support group is Parents Anonymous (PA), the nation's leading self-help organization for parents who are afraid of their anger toward children. PA started in 1970 with a small group of mothers who met once a week in each other's homes. By 1988, it had become the nation's largest provider of direct services to abusive parents, with over 1,200 individual chapters in 42 states, as well as chapters in Australia, Canada, England, and West Germany. PA currently serves over 30,000 families a year with a variety of programs, including programs for children, prisoners, teenage mothers, minority families, and other special popula-

Chart 19–2 **How to Find Help**[6]

Many different programs provide help for parents who have problems caring for their children. Call them to find out more about what they offer. Most programs will not even ask your name. Many are free or will make special arrangements if it is hard for you to pay. If the program you call is not right for you, feel free to ask for help in finding one that is.

Parents Anonymous (PA) is a self-help group for parents who have taken out their anger on their children or feel that they may do so. Find the telephone number of the chapter in your community in the white pages of your local telephone book or by calling (800) 421–0353 (outside California) or (800) 353–0386 (inside California).

Parents United provides self-help for sexually abusive parents, as well as child and adult victims of sexual abuse. For information, call (408) 280–5055.

Yellow pages. Look under the heading "Social Services Organizations." Most of these organizations will have a name that includes the word "Family," "Families," "Parents," "Parental," "Child," or "Children." Also, many local mental health associations have information about group and individual counseling services.

Public Libraries. Some public libraries offer information and referral services to help you find out what is available in your community. If your library does not, the reference librarian may have this information at hand or know where to find it quickly.

Church Counseling Services. You may feel more comfortable talking with someone with a religious orientation. See what your church offers. Besides counseling, it may have inexpensive child care programs and discussion groups for parents.

Public Social Service Agencies. The telephone number for the public programs in your community are in the white pages of your local telephone book under the name of the county and then under the "Department of Social Services," "Human Services," "Human Resources," or "Public Welfare." There may be a special listing for "children's programs" or "child welfare services."

When you call: If you cannot tell the purpose of a program by its name, call and **ask what it does.** If you do not feel comfortable with what a program says it does, **call another one.** If you do not know where else to call, **ask for the names of agencies that may be able to help you.** Someone may not be available the minute you call, but **do not give up.**

REMEMBER: Most human service progressionals are required to report suspected child abuse and neglect. If your situation seems serious enough, they will make a report to the local child protective agency.

tions. There are more than 250 active children's programs, for example. In 1985, PA received the President's Volunteer Action Award.

Membership in PA is free. PA chapters usually meet weekly to give parents support and insight into how to handle problem situations. Fathers as well as mothers meet in mutual-support discussion groups. Chapter meetings are led by the chairperson who is a parent, with a volunteer mental health professional acting as a "chapter sponsor." During meetings, the parents share their experiences and their feelings in a noncritical, mutually supportive atmosphere. The group becomes a kind of surrogate family, providing support for members during times of stress. Between meetings, if parents feel their emotions are getting out of hand and are afraid that they may abuse their children, they can call each other (parents exchange telephone numbers) or the chapter sponsor.

PA maintains a national office to support its local chapters. Parents who need advice or information can call the national office from 9 AM to 5 PM Pacific Time, Monday through Friday. The telephone number of its crisis and referral line is (800) 421–0353 and from California only: (800) 352–0386.

PA also invites professionals to call its national office for further information about the program. The office will identify chapters in a professional's locality; if there are no chapters nearby, national office staff will help the professional (or parents) to start one. In addition, program materials may be purchased from the national office.

Sometimes it is necessary to take a break from being a parent. Particularly during hectic or frustrating periods in your life, you should think about getting help in caring for your children from baby-sitters, friends, or relatives. This does not mean you have failed as a parent; even the best parents need to get away from their children once in a while.

Some communities have a crisis nursery where parents can bring their children when they feel they are going to abuse them. Most communities have activities for children—day care centers, "drop-in" centers, play groups, and Big Brother/Big Sister organizations—that are fun for the children and provide "time out" for parents. Chart 19–2 describes how you can find out more about these and other programs.

20

If You Are Reported

The first indication that you have been reported is likely to be when a child protective worker or a police officer knocks on your door. You may feel relieved that someone knows about your problem and seems willing to help or you may feel that you have done nothing wrong and that the report is completely unjustified. Either way, you need to know how to respond.

COOPERATION IS THE BEST DEFENSE

Child protective investigators are legally required to investigate reports thoroughly. They must question parents and children, often extensively, about the most intimate personal and family matters. And it is often necessary to interview friends, relatives, and neighbors, as well as school-teachers, day care personnel, physicians, clergy, and others who know the family. Chart 20–1 describes what to expect in the investigation.

Child protective agencies and the police have broad powers to investigate reports. If you do not allow them to enter your home or to see your child, they can seek a search warrant. One will be issued if "probable cause" exists to believe that the child may be in danger. Even an anonymous report can establish probable cause. In emergencies, protective action can be taken without a warrant.[1]

Anything that you say to the investigator may be used against you in subsequent court proceedings, including indirectly inculpatory statements, as described in Chapter 13, as well as outright confessions. Because child protective investigations are civil in nature, caseworkers (and in some states, the police) do not give *Miranda* warnings.[2]

Whether or not you are guilty of anything, it is normal to be upset about being reported. "Just being accused of abuse can be such a devastating blow that the accusation alone can make you feel guilty," wrote James Strickland and Stuart Reynolds. "If just being accused of abuse isn't enough to damage your self confidence, the investigation that follows

Chart 20–1 **What to Expect in an Investigation**

Although practices vary, a comprehensive child protective investigation includes the following elements:

- The investigator will talk to any child who is old enough to provide information and probably will physically examine him or her. This interview may be conducted at any reasonable time and place, including the child's school. Your child may be interviewed before you are.
- The investigator will tell you about the report and let you know what to expect during the child protective process. You will not be told who made the report. In some states, your legal rights will also be described.
- The investigator will seek your explanation of how your child was harmed. Also, you will probably be asked a series of wide-ranging questions about your family and personal situation, including questions about how you care for your children, relations between you and your spouse or other adults in the house, and your employment history.
- The investigator will visit your home to see what it reveals about the child's care. At that time, all your other children will be interviewed and, perhaps, physically examined.
- The investigator will interview any other person alleged to have abused or neglected your child.
- The investigator will interview your friends, relatives, and neighbors, as well as schoolteachers, day care personnel, physicians, clergy, and others who know the family.
- The investigator may ask for a medical, psychological, or psychiatric examination of your child. You may be asked to submit to one as well.

probably will be." As one accused—but innocent—"abuser" described it: ". . . having 'that person' wandering around asking my friends, co-workers and parents questions like 'have you ever noticed . . . doing anything with the children?' just made me feel creepy."[3]

It is natural to feel "creepy," "all sick inside," "depressed," and "lost."[4] Nevertheless, it is important that you do not overreact.

Unless you are concerned about the direction of the investigation, you should cooperate with it. You are under no legal obligation to answer the investigator's questions and to allow your child to be examined,[5] but it is wise to do so. Most child abuse investigators have an open mind about the validity of reports (as witnessed by the high rate with which they declare reports to be unfounded), so unless you have something to hide, it makes sense to cooperate.

Chart 20–1 **What to Expect in an Investigation (*continued*)**

- If abuse or neglect is identified, you will be offered services to help solve your problems and to help you care for your child. These services may include counseling, day care, parent aide and homemaker services, education in child rearing, and, in extreme cases, foster care.
- The agency cannot force you to use the services it offers, but if you refuse the services, a court petition may be filed to ensure that your child gets adequate care and protection.
- If your child has been placed in protective custody, you will be told where the child will be staying and when you may visit, unless doing so will endanger the child. Whether or not you consent to your child's placement, you may be required to pay its cost.
- You will have the right to a court hearing to determine whether your child should be returned home.
- If the case goes to court, you will have the right to be represented by an attorney. If you cannot afford to hire a lawyer, one will be appointed for you. Ordinarily, however, no lawyer will be appointed to assist you during the investigation.
- In court, you will have the right to confront and cross-examine the witnesses against you and to call witnesses on your own behalf.
- All information collected about you will be kept confidential, available only as specified by law.
- The agency's records will reflect the final outcome of the investigation. In many states, records of unfounded reports are destroyed, expunged, or sealed.

In fact, refusing to do so will be held against you. Rightly or wrongly, it will be interpreted as a sign that the child may be in danger. Merely saying that you want to consult a lawyer before answering any questions will be taken negatively. Parents who refuse to cooperate with the investigations sometimes lose custody of their children until the facts can be sorted out.

Even when the report is not dismissed, your cooperation will probably prevent severe action being taken against you. Less than 10 percent of all reports result in either court action against parents or the child's placement in foster care.[6] Many cases result in the provision of in-home services to help parents solve their problems and learn methods of child care and discipline that do not harm their children.

Many parents accept such services as a way to get the child protective agency "out of their lives." This is often a wise response, especially since most of us could use assistance raising our children. Realize, however, that unless you are clear on the subject, your acceptance of such services may be seen as an implicit acknowledgment that you are having problems caring for your children. Also, whether or not you consent to your child's placement in foster care, many states require parents to pay the cost of foster care, even if it is for an adolescent who wants out of the house.

Although it is difficult, try to be patient about the process. Investigating reports of suspected child abuse and neglect is not a pleasant job. If you doubt this, just put yourself in the caseworker's shoes. It helps to remember that there are seriously abused children who need protection. An understanding response from you will go a long way in shaping the caseworker's assessment of you and your situation. But you need not passively accept everything that the investigators do. If you do not understand—or like—what is happening, ask questions. And, when necessary, object.

YOU HAVE RIGHTS

You have a right to object if the investigation becomes unreasonably threatening or intrusive. The investigator's right to interview parents and children is not a license to conduct an inquisition. You have a right to courteous treatment. Investigators cannot step beyond the bounds of proper interviewing—to harass, threaten, or browbeat the parents. An Alabama court allowed a trial on the mother's claim that a police officer unlawfully took her into custody and forced her to confess by confining her "in a small isolated room at Police Headquarters, . . . by threat of physical harm, and by threat to take her eight day old child into custody."[7]

You have a right to a confidential and discreet investigation. In Virginia Beach, Virginia, for example, the child protective agency agreed to pay $4,000 to settle a father's claim that he was subjected to "a course of conduct amounting to harassment, including threats of prosecution for crimes and conduct of which the plaintiff was innocent." He also alleged that the workers "maliciously and falsely addressed remarks to third persons, the substance of which were that the plaintiff was an alcoholic; that the plaintiff was mentally unstable and was a 'very sick man'; that he was guilty of child molestation; that they were going to take his child or children away from him; and that he would be prosecuted criminally."[8]

Any physical examinations of your children should be conducted in a way that minimizes the inherent emotional trauma involved, as described in Chapter 6. The authority to look for signs of maltreatment on a child's body is not license to embarrass or humiliate the child. Illinois parents, for example, alleged that the male worker completely undressed their two-year-old daughter in the presence of her four-year-old brother and a neighbor. They further alleged that he "held her up to a light, spread-eagled, for visual inspection of her vaginal area. [He] then placed [her] on a couch and lifted her over his head to make a visual inspection of her anus."[9] The agency defended the worker's action on the ground that such strip searches are an appropriate investigative practice. It is impossible to judge what actually happened and whether the worker's alleged conduct was necessitated by the circumstances, but such actions would have been a deeply disturbing experience for the parents—and the little girl.

You should also be concerned if the investigator seems to have prejudged your case. Some agencies intervene on the most tenuous evidence, especially in cases of sexual abuse. It is almost as if the presumption of innocence had been suspended in these cases. Thus, lawsuits for the unjustified removal of children have been settled for amounts ranging from $10,000 to $35,000.

If your child is removed from your custody, you will be encouraged to visit your child to reassure and support him or her and to maintain family ties. In fact, your failure to visit regularly and as scheduled will be seen as an indication that you do not care about your child. So, be sure your child protective worker knows when conditions outside your control prevent you from visiting. Your visitation rights may be restricted if your conduct during visits is deemed harmful to the child or others (see Chart 20–2).

Finally, if someone else has abused your child and you either did not know it or you took appropriate steps to stop it, you have a right to be treated as an innocent victim (see Parental Responsibility, Chapter 3). For a while, the professional literature blamed all mothers for "allowing" their daughters to be sexually abused by their husbands or boyfriends. It is true that some mothers are subconscious accomplices to their spouses' abuse, but many are not. Unless there is evidence against you, you have a right to be treated as a loving and responsible parent. Thus, if the charge is that your husband abused your children, ask whether he can be ordered from the house (or, in aggravated cases, placed in custody), rather than having your children taken from you and put in foster care.

There are many things that you can do to defend yourself against

Chart 20–2 **When Your Visiting Rights May Be Restricted**[10]

In most cases, child protective agencies encourage parents to visit their children who are placed in foster care. Parents' visits help reassure and support the children and maintain family ties. However, your visitation rights may be restricted:

- If you arrive for an unauthorized visit. Most visits must be prearranged with the caseworker *and* foster parent.
- If you visit while under the influence of drugs or alcohol.
- If you insist that an unauthorized individual visit your child with you.
- If you insist on visiting longer than the authorized time.
- If you talk to your child about the case or the reasons he or she was removed.
- If you try to influence your child's testimony.
- If you cause your child to become upset during the visit.
- If you express anger or threaten your child, the caseworker, foster parent, or any member of the placement staff.
- If you pose a danger to the safety or security of the shelter or foster home.
- If you threaten to remove your child.

NOTE: Failure to visit your children regularly and as scheduled will be seen as an indication that you do not care about them. Therefore, be sure your child protective worker knows when conditions outside your control prevent you from visiting.

---

untrue charges. You may want to have a physician or psychologist of your own choosing examine the child, even if the agency or court also had the child examined. You may want to take a lie detector test. (This often convinces prosecutors of a parent's innocence in ambiguous cases of sexual abuse.) There are also things that you can do to minimize the intervention. Many children, for example, can be safely placed with relatives rather than with strangers in foster care. And, if the case is dismissed, you will want the agency's records about you to reflect this determination or to be destroyed.

Unfortunately, these and other defensive strategies cannot be discussed responsibly in a book like this. The variations among cases and communities are too great. Real advice on what to do must come from someone who is familiar with local practices and your situation. For example, some experts recommend that you tape record all discussions with investigators. But, given the investigator's likely adverse reaction to your doing so, there is no way to decide whether this is a good idea without knowing the facts of your case.

The best advice that I can give is that you should find out as much as you can about your state's child abuse law, the local child protective agency's policies, and your rights and obligations generally. You should certainly seek advice from others, such as friends, relatives, experts, or members of Parents Anonymous, VOCAL, and other similar parents' groups. You may want to join one of these groups. Ultimately, you may decide that you need a lawyer, as described at the end of this chapter.

ACCESS TO AGENCY RECORDS

As a matter of fundamental fairness, if not constitutional right, parents should know what information a government agency is keeping about them. Furthermore, only if they have access to the records can they seek to have inaccuracies corrected.

Although hesitantly and after some delay, most child protective agencies will allow parents access to the records about them. When agencies refuse to do so, courts generally support the parents' right to see the records.[11] In addition, some states have laws that specifically guarantee parents' access to data in a central register.[12]

The parents' right of access to child protective records is not absolute. The identity of any persons who made the report or who cooperated with the subsequent investigation, including neighbors, baby-sitters, teachers, and other persons who are in regular contact with the parents, is usually withheld if disclosure would likely endanger them or if it would adversely affect their day-to-day interaction with the parents.[13] In some situations, the detriment to the person who reported or is cooperating in the investigation may entail potential psychological or social harm, as opposed to physical injury. For example, the disclosure to a parent that a grandparent or spouse reported the case or cooperated in the investigation could so disrupt family life as to be contrary to the interests of all concerned.

In addition, the agency may seek to withhold information that may be harmful to the subject of a report. Such information may involve statements of relatives, psychiatric reports, or other information that, if known by the subject of the report, could cause mental anguish or harm. The authority to withhold such information is provided by specific statutory provisions in some states. In others, information is withheld pursuant to the agency's regulations or protective court orders obtained by the agency.

Utmost care, however, must be exercised so that such authority is not used as an excuse for improperly withholding information about the report and the investigation. And, as a general rule, no information should be withheld concerning reports made in bad faith.

CENTRAL REGISTER RECORDS

All but a few states have established central registers of child protection cases.[14] These central registers receive, store, and make easily accessible basic information about all reports of suspected maltreatment in the state. Depending on the state, a central register helps a child protective agency perform a number of functions, including case diagnosis, case management, program monitoring, research, and program planning. The uses to which a central register can be put depend on its contents; some registers perform sophisticated case management and program monitoring based on follow-up reports filed by child protective workers.[15]

The ease with which information in a central register can become widely available justifies the concerns over personal rights (and "Big Brotherism") that such information systems arouse. The laws against improper disclosure, just discussed, are the primary way in which states seek to protect the confidentiality of these records. However, such laws are not an absolute guarantee against improper disclosure. There is also the danger that information, though disclosed in accordance with legal restrictions, will be misused. About half the states have passed laws and many others had adopted administrative procedures for sealing, expunging, removing, and correcting information in their central registers.

Sealed records are not destroyed and, in accordance with legal procedures, may be reopened at a later time; usually, they are removed from the regular record-keeping area and placed in a locked file. *Expunging* records means erasing or obliterating information, generally the names of and other identifying information about the child; the parents; and, under certain circumstances, the reporter or other persons who cooperated with the investigation. *Removing, destroying,* and *correcting* records means just what these words suggest. (Such procedures usually apply only to records in the central register; they are not considered necessary for the case records of local agencies, which have much less potential for misuse than do the records in centralized data banks.)

Procedures vary too widely for detailed discussion here. Some laws require that the entire record be destroyed if the investigation determines that the report was "unfounded." Others allow the records to be retained (for the purposes of data gathering and policy review) but require that the names and other information identifying the subjects of the report be expunged.[16]

There is a growing movement to give parents a statutory right to request the modification of records in central registers. Many state laws require that parents be told of the record about them, and some give parents an express right to request that the record be amended, sealed, or expunged. Often, the parents are given the right to an administrative hearing if their request is denied. But even in the absence of such specific legislation, most agencies recognize the parents' right to correct misleading or inaccurate information in agency records. If all else fails, parents usually can seek redress through a lawsuit.

In addition, almost half the states *automatically* expunge, seal, destroy, or otherwise limit access to reports after a specified period. Most do so after the child reaches age 18, some do so after the child reaches age 20 or 28, and others do so after 7 or 10 years have elapsed since the last report. (Retaining records after children reach maturity and are presumably able to protect themselves is designed to make the records available in case a sibling of the named child is reported or in case the named child, as a parent, is reported for maltreating his or her own children.) Last, a few states give child protective agencies generalized authority to amend, expunge, or seal records "upon good cause shown" and with notice to the child and the parents named in the record, although this power is probably within their administration discretion.

IF NECESSARY, GET A LAWYER

Most parents who are reported do not need a lawyer. Lawyers are expensive and may not be needed to have the case go your way. Most reports, after all, even most substantiated ones, are resolved without court action and without lawyers. But, sometimes, you may need a lawyer to defend yourself against a charge of abuse, to gain protection for your child against someone else, or to gain access to records about you or to have them corrected or destroyed.

Certainly, if either a civil or criminal court proceeding is filed, you need a lawyer, and one will be appointed if you cannot afford to hire your own.[17] (Financial eligibility depends on local rules.)

The problem is knowing whether you need a lawyer during the investigation. Early representation by a lawyer can be crucial to preventing a court action. It is much easier to convince investigators and prosecutors not to seek an indictment than it is to have them dismiss one. Many court actions are filed because of a simple breakdown in communication. A lawyer may be able to convince investigators that you are innocent or that the case is better resolved informally.

No jurisdiction, however, will provide a lawyer before the initiation of a court case against you. (In rare instances, legal services attorneys can be convinced to represent low-income parents at this stage.) Hence, if you want legal representation during the investigation, you will have to pay for it yourself. Legal fees are expensive: Expect hourly charges of $75 to $200, with a required retainer of $1,000 to $5,000.

You should consider hiring a lawyer whenever you are unhappy with the direction the investigation is taking. For example, you should probably have a lawyer if you are asked to appear before a grand jury, especially if the prosecutor is vague about the purpose of your testimony. And, like the Heaths in Chapter 2, a series of unfounded reports may be a warning that you need to talk to a lawyer.

Aside from a criminal prosecution, your biggest concern should be whether your child will be removed from your custody and placed in foster care. If you have advance warning that this may happen, you may need a lawyer's advice immediately. It is many times easier to prevent a child's placement than to obtain the same child's return home, for, the momentous step having been taken, decision makers are less hesitant about keeping the child in care because doing so is only maintaining the status quo. Since removal will lead to a court hearing, a lawyer will be appointed if you cannot afford to hire your own.

Any lawyer you hire should have experience with criminal or child protective matters. Do not depend on your Uncle Joe, who usually handles real estate cases. A lawyer who never handled a criminal case or who has insubstantial experience is simply not competent to represent you. The same is true for a lawyer who never practiced in the juvenile or family court and is not familiar with child protective procedures, which are often informal and based more on social considerations than on legal ones. The stakes are too high to have your lawyer learn while on your case.

Basically, selecting a lawyer is like choosing a physician. Personal recommendations from friends and colleagues are the best way to identify a qualified professional. Ask around. Find other parents who have been reported (perhaps through the local VOCAL chapter) and ask who represented them and whether they were satisfied with the representation they received. Do not be shy. Ask what the result was and how much the lawyer charged.

Lawyer referral services can also help. But they must be used with care. The quality of referral services varies widely. Although some maintain minimum standards for listing—such as a specified amount of experience in an area—most do not. Referral services that are sponsored by local bar associations (which can be located by looking up the local bar association in the telephone directory) are usually more reliable than are commercial ones.

Be wary of legal advertising. A television commercial or newspaper or magazine advertisement may make the lawyer seem impressive, but it does not provide an accurate picture of the lawyer's qualifications.

Comparison shopping is important. If there is time, you should interview the top two or three candidates. Use the interview to get a feel for the lawyer—you have to like your lawyer—and to gain basic information about the lawyer's practice, approach to cases like yours, and fees. Prepare for the interview by drawing up a list of questions you want to ask before and during the interview. Chart 20–3 contains a checklist of questions to ask.

Most lawyers offer to hold such exploratory interviews for free; some will charge. Before you arrange the interview, ask if there will be a charge. The amount of the fee may help you decide whether this is an attorney you would be interested in hiring.

During the interview, try to get a sense of what it would be like to work with the lawyer. Discuss the details of your case. Does the lawyer listen well? Does he or she ask probing questions? Are you comfortable with the lawyer's style and approach? Court proceedings often go badly for long periods; the two of you will probably have some tense moments. It is important that you begin your relationship with a sense of rapport.

Make sure to discuss fees. Ask for an estimate of what it would cost to defend your case. Although the lawyer cannot provide more than a general idea of total costs, the answer will help you evaluate your situation and the lawyer. Also ask the lawyer to describe the various ways that billing and payments can be handled. You will find that most lawyers bill on either an hourly basis or at a flat rate for specific steps in the litigation (such as pretrial discovery) or a combination of both. Find out whether the lawyer charges more for time spent in court. Most do.

Feel free to question the amount the lawyer wants to charge. Many lawyers are not so busy that they can afford to turn away clients who are unwilling to pay their maximum rate. They will negotiate fees.

Chart 20–3 **Questions to Ask When Selecting a Lawyer**[18]

Before the Initial Interview

- Do you ordinarily handle this type of case?
- Are you currently available to handle this case?
- Do you perceive a possible conflict of interest? If so, what is it?
- How quickly should I retain an attorney?
- Will there be a charge for the initial, exploratory interview?

During the Initial Interview

- What kind of practice do you have? What kinds of clients do you have?
- What kind of experience do you have with cases like mine? How many have you handled? How many do you handle each year? Could you give me some examples? What was the outcome, and about how much did you charge? Could I have the names and telephone numbers of these clients and your permission to call them? (This last question may be difficult to answer because the lawyer's clients may wish to guard their privacy.)
- Is there anyone else I could call for a reference?
- What other background or experience makes you particularly qualified to handle my case?
- How would you handle my case? At this point, what legal and procedural approaches do you think advisable?
- Would you be doing all the work? If not, will you introduce me to the other people who may be working on my case? What kind of supervision would you provide?
- How long do you think my case may take to be resolved? What do you think will be the likely result?
- What would be your fee arrangement for handling my case? Can you give me an estimate of the total legal costs?
- What is your billing procedure? Do your bills itemize the legal work done?
- How will you keep me apprised of the progress of my case?
- Would you provide me with a contract or letter of engagement describing the fee and billing arrangements to which we have agreed?

There are few hard-and-fast rules about how to decide which lawyer is best for your needs. Nevertheless, some lawyers should be avoided.

- Avoid a lawyer who seems too busy to give your case the requisite time and attention.
- Avoid a lawyer who guarantees a favorable outcome; even the strongest cases can unexpectedly deteriorate.
- Avoid a lawyer who is vague on the subject of fees.
- Avoid a lawyer who refuses to provide a contract or letter of engagement which spells out billing arrangements.
- Avoid a lawyer who tries to impress you with legal jargon.
- Avoid a lawyer who refuses to give you any references.[19]

The ultimate decision about selecting a lawyer is intensely personal. Besides differences in types of cases, different clients need lawyers with different styles. Based on everything you have learned—and your "feelings" about the lawyer—only you can decide whether this is the lawyer for you.

After you have engaged a lawyer, place the case in his or her hands. *All* inquiries should be referred to the lawyer.

21

Conclusion

This book has focused on the reporting of suspected child abuse and child neglect. It has attempted to provide guidelines for deciding when to report and when not to report. Nevertheless, reporting is only one aspect of what must be a multifaceted, communitywide, and long-term effort to prevent and treat this serious problem.

In recent years, major progress has been made in building such a comprehensive system. In all parts of the country, there are programs that protect children and help their parents to care adequately for them. Health, social service, education, and law enforcement agencies, as well as individual professionals, increasingly see themselves as jointly, not separately, responsible for protecting children and, wherever possible, preserving and strengthening families. New resources have been identified, useful family support systems have been tried, and some simplistic definitions and solutions have been discarded. Statistics, definitions, and procedures are being standardized and upgraded. More concretely, the quality and scope of treatment services have been greatly improved.

But we still face enormous gaps between what is being done to protect children and what needs to be done. Too many children are processed through the system with only a paper promise of help. Too often, the only treatment alternatives available to child protective agencies are infrequent and largely meaningless home visits or overused and sometimes abusive foster care. The agenda is clear:

We need *better research* on child abuse and neglect so that service providers can apply the best state-of-the-art knowledge to improve their programs.

We need to upgrade reporting practices, child protection agencies, and courts to ensure the *immediate protection* of all endangered children.

We need to develop cost-effective *treatment* approaches that can break the cycle of abuse and neglect.

We need to protect *individual* and *family rights* to privacy and cultural diversity during the process of involuntary protective intervention.

We need to commit ourselves to a *prevention* program that seeks to strengthen family life in America.

We need to recognize and combat child abuse and neglect in *residential care-giving institutions*.

We need to work continuously to *coordinate* public and private programs related to child abuse and neglect to maximize their impact and minimize the duplication of efforts.

All around the country, groups are working together to achieve these goals. (For information and materials on the subject, contact the national organizations listed in Appendix A.) In the meantime, the shortcomings of existing child protective programs dramatically underscore the responsibility that society places on individuals when it allows (and, in many situations, mandates) them to report suspected child abuse and child neglect. This book has sought to aid the professionals and private citizens who must make this fateful decision. Nevertheless, no book can provide all the answers. The decision to report is an intensely personal one that requires the exercise of discretion and sound judgment.

I remember vividly a child protective case that I handled as a young prosecutor almost twenty years ago. A little Chinese girl had been found by her Chinese neighbors with her fingers dreadfully infected and her forearms swollen. The neighbors immediately took the child to a hospital. The mother, a recent immigrant from Hong Kong, was unknown in the neighborhood of mostly U.S.-born Chinese-Americans. She spoke a dialect of Chinese for which the court had no interpreter, and we were only able to piece together a vague story of her sticking pins into her daughter's hands and arms, which we took to be some form of dreadful torture. It was not until President Nixon's visit to China two years later that Americans learned about acupuncture. To this day, I do not know whether that mother was attempting to harm her daughter.

Protecting the welfare of children and the rights of parents cannot be accomplished by easy formulations and superficial slogans. We need informed professionals and a supportive citizenry who understand the need to protect maltreated children and the dangers of overreporting. This book has sought to increase such understanding.

Appendix
A

National Organizations Combatting Child Abuse

The following national organizations provide educational and consultative services and written materials on various aspects of the identification, reporting, prevention, and treatment of child abuse and neglect.

American Bar Association
National Legal Resource Center on
   Children and the Law
Suite 200
1800 M Street, N.W.
Washington, DC 20036
(202) 331–2250

American Humane Association
American Association for Protecting
   Children
9725 East Hampden Avenue
Denver, CO 80231
(303) 695–0811
(800) 227–5242

American Public Welfare
   Association
810 First Street, N.E.
Suite 500
Washington, DC 20002
(202) 682–0100

Childhelp USA
6463 Independence Avenue
Woodland Hills, CA 91367
(800) 4-A-CHILD
(800) 422–4453

Child Welfare League of America
440 First Street, N.W.
Suite 310
Washington, DC 20001
(202) 638–2952

C. Henry Kempe Center for
   Prevention and Treatment of
   Child Abuse and Neglect
1205 Oneida Street
Denver, CO 80220
(303) 321–3963

National Association of Counsel for
   Children
1025 Oneida Street
Denver, CO 80220
(303) 321–3963

National Committee for Prevention
   of Child Abuse
332 South Michigan Avenue
Suite 950
Chicago, IL 60604
(312) 663–3520

National Association of Social
  Workers
7981 Eastern Avenue
Silver Spring, MD 20910
(301) 565–0333

National Center for Missing and
  Exploited Children
1835 K Street, N.W.
Suite 700
Washington, DC 20006
(800) 843–5678
(202) 634–9821

U.S. National Center on Child
  Abuse and Neglect
Department of Health and Human
  Services
P.O. Box 1182
Washington, DC 20013
(202) 245–0586

Parents Anonymous
6733 South Sepulveda Boulevard
Suite 270
Los Angeles, CA 90045
(213) 410–9732
(800) 421–0353 or (800) 352–0386
  (California only)

Parents United/Daughters and Sons
  United/Adults Molested as
  Children United
P.O. Box 952
San Jose, CA 95108
(408) 280–5055

Victims of Child Abuse Laws
  (VOCAL)
P.O. Box 11335
Minneapolis, MN 55412
1–800–84VOCAL

Appendix

B

State Child Protective Agencies

Alabama:
Alabama Department of Human Resources
Division of Family and Children's Services
Office of Protective Services
64 North Union Street
Montgomery, AL 36130–1801
During business hours, make reports to the county's Department of Human Resources, Child Protective Services Unit. After business hours, make reports to the local police.

Alaska:
Department of Health and Social Services
Division of Family and Youth Services
Box H-05, Juneau, AK 99811
Ask the operator for Zenith 4444 to make reports in state. Out of state, add area code 907. This telephone number is toll free.

American Samoa:
Government of American Samoa
Office of the Attorney General
Pago Pago, AS 96799

Make reports to the Department of Human Resources at (684) 633–4485.

Arizona:
Department of Economic Security
Administration for Children, Youth and Families
P.O. Box 6123
Site COE 940A
Phoenix, AZ 85005
Make reports to local offices of the Department of Economic Security.

Arkansas:
Arkansas Department of Human Services
Division of Children and Family Services
P.O. Box 1437
Little Rock, AR 72203
Make reports in state to (800) 482–5964.

California:
Office for Child Abuse Prevention
Department of Social Services
714–744 P Street, Room 950
Sacramento, CA 95814

SOURCE: U.S. National Center on Child Abuse and Neglect, *Child Abuse and Neglect: A Shared Community Response* (Washington, DC: U.S. Department of Health & Human Service, March 1989), pp. 16–23.

Make reports to the county's
Department of Welfare and the
Central Registry of Child Abuse
(916) 445–7546, maintained by the
Cal. Department of Justice.

Colorado:

Department of Social Services
  Central Registry
P.O. Box 181000
Denver, CO 80218–0899

Make reports to the county's
Department of Social Services.

Connecticut:

Connecticut Department of
  Children and Youth Services
Division of Children and Protective
  Services
170 Sigourney Street
Hartford, CT 06105

Make reports in state to (800) 842–
2288 or out of state to (203) 344–
2599.

Delaware:

Delaware Department of Services for
  Children, Youth and Their
  Families
Division of Child Protective Services
330 East 30th Street
Wilmington, DE 19802

Make reports in state to (800) 292–
9582.

District of Columbia:

District of Columbia Department of
  Human Services
Commission on Social Services
Family Services Administration
Child and Family Services Division
500 First Street N.W.
Washington, DC 20001

Make reports to (202) 727–0995.

Florida:

Florida Child Abuse Registry
1317 Winewood Boulevard
Tallahassee, FL 32301

Make reports in state to (800) 342–
9152 or out of state to (904) 487–
2625.

Georgia:

Georgia Department of Human
  Resources
Division of Family and Children
  Services
878 Peachtree Street, N.W.
Atlanta, GA 30309

Make reports to the county's
Department of Family and Children
Services.

Guam:

Department of Public Health and
  Social Services
Child Welfare Services
Child Protective Services
P.O. Box 2816
Agana, GU 96910

Make reports to the Child Protective
Services Agency at (671) 646–8417.

Hawaii:

Department of Social Services and
  Housing
Public Welfare Division
Family and Children's Services
P.O. Box 339
Honolulu, HI 96809

Make reports to each island's
Department of Social Services and
Housing Child Protective Services
reporting hotline.

Idaho:

Department of Health and Welfare
Field Operations Bureau of Social
  Services and Child Protection
450 West State, Tenth Floor
Boise, ID 83720

Make reports to regional offices of
the Department of Health and
Welfare.

Illinois:

Illinois Department of Children and
  Family Services
Station 75
State Administrative Offices
406 East Monroe Street
Springfield, IL 62701

Make reports in state to (800) 25–
ABUSE or out of state to (217) 785–
4010.

Indiana:

Indiana Department of Public
  Welfare—Child Abuse and
  Neglect
Division of Child Welfare–Social
  Services
141 South Meridian Street
Sixth Floor
Indianapolis, IN 46225

Make reports to the county's
Department of Public Welfare.

Iowa:

Iowa Department of Human
  Services
Division of Social Services
Central Child Abuse Registry
Hoover State Office Building
Fifth Floor
Des Moines, IA 50319

Make reports in state to (800) 362–
2178 or out of state (during business
hours) to (515) 281–5581.

Kansas:

Kansas Department of Social and
  Rehabilitation Services
Division of Social Services
Child Protection and Family
  Services Section
Smith-Wilson Building
2700 West Sixth Street
Topeka, KS 66606

Make reports to area offices of the
Department of Social and
Rehabilitation Services.

Kentucky:

Kentucky Cabinet of Human
  Resources
Division of Family Services
Children and Youth Services
  Branch
275 East Main Street
Frankfort, KY 40621

Make reports to the county offices
in fourteen state districts.

Louisiana:

Louisiana Department of Health
  and Human Resources
Office of Human Development
Division of Children, Youth, and
  Family Services
P.O. Box 3318
Baton Rouge, LA 70821

Make reports to the parish's
Protective Service Unit.

Maine:

Maine Department of Human
  Services
Child Protective Services
State House, Station 11
Augusta, ME 04333

Make reports to the regional Office
of Human Services, in state to (800)
452–1999 or out of State to (207)
289–2983. Both operate 24 hours
a day.

Maryland:
Maryland Department of Human
  Resources
Social Services Administration
Saratoga State Center
311 West Saratoga Street
Baltimore, MD 21201
Make reports to the county's
Department of Social Services or to
local law enforcement agencies.

Massachusetts:
Massachusetts Department of Social
  Services
Protective Services
150 Causeway Street
Eleventh Floor
Boston, MA 02114
Make reports to the department's
area offices or the Protective
Screening Unit or in state to (800)
792–5200.

Michigan:
Michigan Department of Social
  Services
Office of Children and Youth
  Services
Protective Services Division
300 South Capitol Avenue
Ninth Floor
Lansing, MI 48926
Make reports to the county's
Department of Social Services.

Minnesota:
Minnesota Department of Human
  Services
Protective Services Division
Centennial Office Building
St. Paul, MN 55155
Make reports to the county's
Department of Human Services.

Mississippi:
Mississippi Department of Public
  Welfare
Bureau of Family and Children's
  Services
Protection Department
P.O. Box 352
Jackson, MS 39205
Make reports in state to (800) 222–
8000 or out of state (during business
hours) to (601) 354–0341.

Missouri:
Missouri Child Abuse and Neglect
  Hotline
Department of Social Service
Division of Family Services
P.O. Box 88
Broadway Building
Jefferson City, MO 65103
Make reports in state to (800) 392–
3738 or out of state to (314) 751–
3448. Both operate 24 hours a day.

Montana:
Department of Family Services
Child Protective Services
P.O. Box 8005
Helena, MT 59604
Make reports to the county's
Department of Family Services.

Nebraska:
Nebraska Department of Social
  Services
Human Services Division
301 Centennial Mall South
P.O. Box 95026
Lincoln, NE 68509
Make reports to local law
enforcement agencies or to local
social services offices or in state to
(800) 652–1999.

Nevada:
Department of Human Resources
Division of Welfare
2527 North Carson Street
Carson City, NV 89710
Make reports to the local offices of
the Division of Welfare.

New Hampshire:
New Hampshire Department of
Health and Welfare
Division for Children and Youth
Services
6 Hazen Drive
Concord, NH 03301–6522
Make reports to the district offices
of the Division for Children and
Youth Services or in state to (800)
852–3345 (ext. 4455).

New Jersey:
New Jersey Division of Youth and
Family Services
P.O. Box CN717
One South Montgomery Street
Trenton, NJ 08625
Make reports in state to (800) 792–
8610. District offices also provide 24-
hour telephone services.

New Mexico:
New Mexico Department of Human
Services
Social Services Division
P.O. Box 2348
Santa Fe, NM 87504
Make reports to the county's social
services offices or in state to (800)
432–6217.

New York:
New York State Department of
Social Services
Division of Family and Children
Services

State Central Register of Child
Abuse and Maltreatment
40 North Pearl Street
Albany, NY 12243
Make reports in state to (800) 342–
3720 or out of state to (518) 474–
9448.

North Carolina:
North Carolina Department of
Human Resources
Division of Social Services
Child Protective Services
325 North Salisbury Street
Raleigh, NC 27611
Make reports in state to (800) 662–
7030.

North Dakota:
North Dakota Department of
Human Services
Division of Children and Family
Services
Child Abuse and Neglect Program
State Capitol
Bismarck, ND 58505
Make reports to the county's Social
Services Office.

Ohio:
Ohio Department of Human
Services
Bureau of Children's Protective
Services
30 East Broad Street
Columbus, OH 43266–0423
Make reports to the county's
Department of Human Services.

Oklahoma:
Oklahoma Department of Human
Services
Division of Children and Youth
Services

Child Abuse/Neglect Section
P.O. Box 25352
Oklahoma City, OK 73125

Make reports in state to (800) 522–3511.

Oregon:

Department of Human Resources
Children's Services Division
Child Protective Services
198 Commercial Street, S.E.
Salem, OR 97310

Make reports to the local offices of the Children's Services Division and to (503) 378–4722.

Pennsylvania:

Pennsylvania Department of Public Welfare
Office of Children, Youth and Families
Child Line and Abuse Registry
Lanco Lodge, P.O. Box 2675
Harrisburg, PA 17105

Make reports in state to CHILDLINE (800) 932–0313 or out of state to (713) 783-8744.

Puerto Rico:

Puerto Rico Department of Social Services
Services to Family With Children
P.O. Box 11398
Fernandez Juncos Station
Santurez, PR 00910

Make reports to (809) 724–1333.

Rhode Island:

Rhode Island Department for Children and Their Families
Division of Child Protective Services
610 Mt. Pleasant Avenue
Bldg. 9
Providence, RI 02908

Make reports in state to (800) RI-CHILD or 742–4453 or out of state to (401) 457–4996.

South Carolina:

South Carolina Department of Social Services
1535 Confederate Avenue
P.O. Box 1520
Columbia, SC 29202–1520

Make reports to the county's Department of Social Services.

South Dakota:

Department of Social Services
Child Protection Services
Richard F. Kneip Building
700 Governors Drive
Pierre, SD 57501

Make reports to the local social services offices.

Tennessee:

Tennessee Department of Human Services
Child Protective Services
Citizen Bank Plaza
400 Deadrick Street
Nashville, TN 37219

Make reports to the county's Department of Human Services.

Texas:

Texas Department of Human Services
Protective Services for Families and Children Branch
P.O. Box 2960, MC 537-W
Austin, TX 78769

Make reports in state to (800) 252–5400 or out of state to (512) 450–3360.

Utah:
Department of Social Services
Division of Family Services
P.O. Box 45500
Salt Lake City, UT 84110
Make reports to the district offices
of the Division of Family Services.

Vermont:
Vermont Department of Social and
Rehabilitative Services
Division of Social Services
103 South Main Street
Waterbury, VT 05676
Make reports to the division's district
offices or to (802) 241-2131.

Virgin Islands:
Virgin Islands Department of
Human Services
Division of Social Services
P.O. Box 550
Charlotte Amalie
St. Thomas, VI 00801
Make reports to the Division of
Social Services (809) 774-9030.

Virginia:
Commonwealth of Virginia
Department of Social Services
Bureau of Child Protective Services
Blair Building
8007 Discovery Drive
Richmond, VA 23229-8699
Make reports in state to (800) 552-
7096 or out of state to (804) 281-
9081.

Washington:
Department of Social and Health
Services
Division of Children and Family
Services
Child Protective Services
Mail Stop OB 41-D
Olympia, WA 98504
Make reports in state to (800) 562-
5624 or to local offices of the
Department of Social and Health
Services Offices.

West Virginia:
West Virginia Department of
Human Services
Division of Social Services
Child Protective Services
State Office Building
1900 Washington Street East
Charleston, WV 25305
Make reports in state to (800) 352-
6513.

Wisconsin:
Wisconsin Department of Health
and Social Services
Division of Community Services
Bureau for Children, Youth, and
Families
1 West Wilson Street
Madison, WI 53707
Make reports to the county's Social
Services Office.

Wyoming:
Department of Health and Social
Services
Division of Public Assistance and
Social Services
Hathaway Building
Cheyenne, WY 82002
Make reports to the county's
Department of Public Assistance and
Social Services.

Notes

Acknowledgments

1. Republished in D. Besharov, *Protecting Children from Abuse and Neglect: Policy and Practice* (Springfield, Ill.: Charles C Thomas, 1988), chap. 13.

2. See, e.g., U.S. National Center on Child Abuse and Neglect, *State Child Abuse and Neglect Laws: A Comparative Analysis* (1986). See also L. Younes and D. Besharov, "State Child Abuse and Neglect Laws: A Comparative Analysis," in Besharov, Appendix, *supra* n. 1.

Chapter 1
You Can Make a Difference

1. A. Sedlak, *Study of National Incidence and Prevalence of Child Abuse and Neglect* (Bethesda, Md.: Westat, December 1987).

2. Compare ibid., p. 2–2, Table 2–1, estimating 1,100, *with* National Committee for Prevention of Child Abuse, *Child Abuse and Neglect Fatalities: A Review of the Problem and Strategies for Reform* (Chicago, Ill.: 1988).

3. Based on comparison data from *Vital Statistics of the United States for 1980: Advanced Report of Final Mortality Statistics* (U.S. Bureau of the Census, 1980).

4. U.S. National Center on Child Abuse and Neglect, *Impact of Federal Law on Provision of Child Protective and Related Services* (1981), p. 1, citing M. Mewshaw, *Life for Death* (New York: Avon, 1980).

5. See, e.g., R. Hunner and Y. Walker, eds., *Exploring the Relationship between Child Abuse and Delinquency* (Totowa, N.J.: Allanheld, 1981).

6. *Child Abuse and Neglect Reporting and Investigation: Policy Guidelines for Decision Making*, republished in D. Besharov, *Protecting Children from Abuse and Neglect: Policy and Practice* (Springfield, Ill.: Charles C Thomas, 1988), chap. 13.

7. See, e.g., U.S. National Center on Child Abuse and Neglect, *State Child Abuse and Neglect Laws: A Comparative Analysis* (1986). See also L. Younes and D. Besharov, "State Child Abuse and Neglect Laws: A Comparative Analysis," in Besharov, Appendix, *supra* n.6.

Chapter 2
A Balanced Approach

1. Holter and Friedman, "Child Abuse: Early Case Finding in the Emergency Department," *Pediatrics* 42:1 (July 1968).

2. Cited in New York State Assembly Select Committee on Child Abuse, *Report* (April 1972), p. 25; reprinted in R. E. Helfer and C. H. Kempe, eds., *The Battered Child*, 2nd ed. (Chicago: University of Chicago Press, 1974).

3. Ibid., p. 24.

4. *Initial Quarterly Progress Report to New York City Criminal Justice Coordinating Council, Child Abuse Grant C55934* (January 1972), p. 8.

5. E. Elmer, "Hazards in Determining Child Abuse," *Child Welfare* 45 (1966), p. 28.

6. V. Fontana and D. Besharov, *The Maltreated Child*, 4th ed. (Springfield, Ill.: Charles C Thomas, 1979), p. 6.

7. U.S. Children's Bureau, *The Abused Child—Principles and Suggested Language for Legislation on Reporting of the Physically Abused Child* (1963).

8. M. Paulsen, "The Legal Framework for Child Protection," *Columbia Law Review* 66 (1966), pp. 679, 711.

9. U.S. Children's Bureau, *Juvenile Court Statistics* (1966), p. 13.

10. Source: American Association for Protecting Children, *Highlights of Official Child Abuse and Neglect Reports: 1985* (Denver, Colo.: American Humane Association, 1987) p. 3, Figure 1. Data for 1986 obtained by telephone from John Fluke, American Association for Protecting Children, July 8, 1988. Data for 1987 obtained by telephone from Robin Alsop, American Association for Protecting Children, July 7, 1989.

11. A. Sedlak, *The Supplementary Analyses of Data on the National Incidence of Child Abuse and Neglect* (Rockville, Md.: Westat, May 1989) p. 2–2, Table 2–1.

12. New York State Department of Social Services, *Child Protective Services in New York State: 1979 Annual Report*, Table 8 (1980).

13. R. S. Kempe and C. H. Kempe, *Child Abuse* (Cambridge, Mass.: Harvard Univ. Press, 1978), p. 8.

14. Sedlak, p. 3–19, *supra* n. 11.

15. Region VI Resource Center on Child Abuse, *Child Abuse Deaths in Texas*

(Austin: University of Texas Graduate School of Social Work, 1981), p. 26.

16. An analysis of child fatalities in one state described how "in two of the cases, siblings of the victims had died previously. . . . In one family, two siblings had died mysterious deaths that were undiagnosed. In another family a twin had died previously of abuse." Confidential material held by the author.

17. See, e.g., P. Levin, "Teachers' Perceptions, Attitudes, and Reporting of Child Abuse/Neglect," *Child Welfare* 62 (January/February 1983), pp. 14, 19.

18. There are no exact national statistics on unfounded reports. The 65 percent estimate is based on the author's state-by-state analysis. Cf. American Association for Protecting Children, p. 12, *supra* n. 10, which projected, on incomplete data, a 58 percent unfounded rate.

19. Cf. *National Analysis of Official Child Neglect and Abuse Reporting* (1976) (Denver, Colo.: American Humane Association, 1978), p. 11.

20. Memorandum to Sandy Berman from Charles Root, New York State Department of Social Services, September 14, 1984.

21. C. Mouzakitis, "Investigation and Initial Assessment in Child Protective Services," in W. Holder and K Hayes, eds., *Malpractice and Liability in Child Protective Services* (Longmont, Colo.: Bookmakers Guild, 1984), pp. 71, 75.

22. Derived from "For the Love of Baseball," VOCAL *National Newsletter* 1:3 (September/October 1985), p. 7.

23. R. Wexler, "Invasion of the Child Savers," *The Progressive* (September 1985), pp. 19, 20–22.

24. N. Thoennes and J. Pearson, "Difficult Dilemma: Responding to Sexual Abuse Allegations in Custody and Visitation Disputes," in D. Besharov, *Protecting Children from Abuse and Neglect* (Springfield, Ill.: Charles C Thomas, 1988), pp. 91, 93; L. Berliner, "Deciding Whether a Child Has Been Sexually Abused," in *Sexual Abuse Allegations in Custody and Visitation Cases* (Chicago: American Bar Association, 1988); and D. Jones, "Reliable and Fictitious Accounts of Sexual Abuse in Children," *Journal of Inter-personal Violence*, Issue 3 (1986), Table 2, which estimated that 8 percent of sexual abuse reports are falsely made (2 percent by children and 6 percent by adults).

25. J. Alfaro, "What Can We Learn from Child Abuse Fatalities: A Synthesis of Nine Studies," in Besharov, chap. 9, *supra* n. 24.

26. *Buege v. Iowa*, No. 20521 (Allamakee, Iowa, July 30, 1980). See also Jury Research, "Case Summary" (Solon, Ohio, March 3, 1982); and *State v. Hilleshein*, 305 N.W.2d 710 (Iowa 1981), a criminal prosecution in the same case.

27. J. Alfaro, *Impediments to Mandated Reporting of Suspected Child Abuse and Neglect in New York City*, May 1984, (New York: Mayor's Task Force on Child Abuse and Neglect), p. 66.

28. "Greasy Kid Stuff," *The New Republic*, May 13, 1985, p. 4.

Chapter 3
Reporting Obligations

1. Cal. Penal Code § 11166(a) (West 1989).

2. Cal. Penal Code § 11165.7a (West 1989).

3. See, e.g., Pa. Stat. Ann. tit. 11, § 2204 (a) (Purdon's Supp. 1988).

4. See, e.g., Ariz. Rev. Stat. § 13–3620 (A) (West Supp. 1989).

5. See, e.g., Ala. Code § 26–14–3(a) (Supp. 1988); La. Rev. Stat. Ann. § 14:403(C)(1) (West 1986).

6. See, e.g., *Groff v. State*, 390 So.2d 361 (Dist. Ct. of App., 2nd Dist., Fla, 1980) and *State v. Groff*, 409 So.2d 44 (Dist. Ct. of App., 2nd Dist., Fla., 1981), ultimately dismissed on the ground that Florida's reporting mandate was limited to "any person . . . serving children" and, therefore, did not apply to the defendant psychiatrist who was treating the father, not the child, whom he had never met.

7. N.Y. Social Services Law § 413 (West Supp. 1989).

8. M. Paulsen, "The Legal Framework for Child Protection," *Columbia Law Review 66* (1966), pp. 679, 713.

9. See, e.g., American Association for Protecting Children, *Highlights of Official Child Neglect and Abuse Reporting* (1984) (Denver, Colo.: American Humane Association, 1986), p. 32, Table 11; New York State Department of Social Services, *State Central Register Reporting Highlights: 1974–1988* (1989), Table 9.

10. See, e.g., Cal. Penal Code § 11167(e) (West Supp. 1989).

11. *Wisconsin v. Boggess*, 340 N.W.2d 516, 519 (Wisc. 1983).

12. See, e.g., U.S. National Center on Child Abuse and Neglect, *National Analysis of Official Child Neglect and Abuse Reporting* (1978) (1979), p. 20, Table 7. New York State Department of Social Services, Table 9, *supra* n. 9. See generally W. Adams, N. Barone, and P. Tooman, "The Dilemma of Anonymous Reporting in Child Protective Services," *Child Welfare 61* (January 1982), p. 3.

13. See generally, D. Besharov, "The Need to Narrow the Grounds for State Intervention," in D. Besharov, *Protecting Children from Abuse and Neglect: Policy and Practice* (Springfield, Ill.: Charles C Thomas, 1988), pp. 47, 50 *et seq.*

14. Act of January 31, 1974, codified as amended at 42 U.S.C. § 5102(1) (Supp. 1989).

15. Cf. National Center on Child Abuse and Neglect, *Study of National Incidence and Prevalence of Child Abuse and Neglect: 1988* (1988), p. 3–11, Table 3–5; and National Center on Child Abuse and Neglect, *National Study of the Incidence and Severity of Child Abuse and Neglect* (1981), p. 18, Table 4–1.

16. Reflecting the need to specify the level of severity, the National Center on Child Abuse and Neglect provides the following definitions:

   "Physical injury" means death, or permanent or temporary disfigurement or impairment of any bodily organ or function.

   "Mental injury" means an injury to the intellectual or psychological capacity of a child as evidenced by an observable and substantial impairment in his ability to function within his normal range of performance and behavior, with due regard to his culture.

   National Center on Child Abuse and Neglect, *Child Protection: A Guide for State Legislation* (draft) (1983), subsecs. 4(h) and 4(i).

17. For the definitive exposition of how the severity of the injury affects—and should affect—decision making in child protective cases, *see* J. M. Giovannoni and R. M. Becerra, *Defining Child Abuse* (New York: Free Press, 1979).

18. Wyo. Stat. Ann. § 14–3–202(a) (iii) (1989).

19. The statutes in another three or four states remove reporting obligations for children under age eighteen who are married or otherwise emancipated from parental control, again because they are presumed capable of protecting themselves. (Even in the absence of a statute, this is the usual practice.)

20. Both federal studies of the incidence of child abuse found that more than half the cases in which child protective agencies take jurisdiction involve situations in which the child has not yet suffered serious injury. See National Center on Child Abuse and Neglect (1988), p. 6–5, Table 6–2, *supra* n. 15; and National Center on Child Abuse and Neglect (1981), p. 16, Table 3–5, *supra* n. 15.

21. A. Kadushin, "Emotional Abuse." Unpublished paper presented at the joint Workshop on Emotional Maltreatment of the U.S. National Center on Child Abuse and Neglect and The National Institute on Mental Health, Houston, Tex., April 1976.

22. See, e.g., V. DeFrancis and C. Lucht, *Child Abuse Legislation in the 1970's*, rev. ed. (Denver, Colo.: American Humane Association, 1974), pp. 9–10.

23. See, e.g., N.Y. Fam. Ct. Act § 119(b) (1983).

24. See, e.g., N.Y. Fam. Ct. Act § 1012(g) (1983).

25. See, e.g., *In the Matter of Roman*, 94 Misc.2d 796, 405 N.Y.S.2d 899 (Fam. Ct., Onondaga Co., 1978).

26. See, e.g., R. S. Kempe and C. H. Kempe, *Child Abuse* (Cambridge, Mass.: Harvard University Press, 1978), p. 23.

27. *In the Matter of Scott G.*, 124 A.D.2d 928, 508 N.Y.S.2d 669, 670 (3rd Dept., 1986).

28. *In the Matter of Shane T.*, 115 Misc.2d 161, 453 N.Y.S.2d 590, 594 (Fam. Ct., Richmond Co., 1982).

29. *Doe v. County of Suffolk*, 494 F.Supp. 179, 180, n. 1 (E.D.N.Y 1980).

30. *In the Matter of Sara X*, 122 A.D.2d 943, 505 N.Y.S.2d 681, 682 (2nd Dept., 1986).

31. N. Rindfleisch and J. Rabb, "How Much of a Problem Is Resident Mistreatment in Child Welfare Institutions?" *Child Abuse and Neglect* 8 (1984), pp. 33–40. See generally U.S. National Center on Child Abuse and Neglect, *Preventing Child Abuse and Neglect: A Guide for Staff in Residential Institutions* (1980); and U.S. National Center on Child Abuse and Neglect, *Child Abuse and Neglect in Residential Institutions: Selected Readings on Prevention, Investigation and Correction* (1978).

32. *Doe v. New York City Department of Social Services*, 649 F.2d 134, 137 (2nd Cir. 1981) and 709 F.2d 782 (2nd Cir. 1983), *cert. denied*, 104 S.Ct. 195 (1983).

33. In states in which the child protective agency is administratively linked to day care or residential institutions, an investigation by the child protective agency, like one by the institution itself, might be perceived as something less than independent and objective. To provide assurance that the investigation will be thorough and fair and that it also will appear to be fair, it is essential that an administratively separate agency conduct it.

Chapter 4
Liability for Failing to Report

1. For example, the failure to report may be misprision of a felony. Cf. *Pope v. State*, 38 Md. App. 520, 382 A.2d 880 (1978); *modified*, 284 Md. 309, 396 A.2d 1054 (1979), dismissed because the state's child abuse law did not apply and because there was no crime of misprision of felony in Maryland.

2. "Doctor, Parents Charged in Death of Abused L.A. Child," *Los Angeles Times*, December 3, 1983, Pt. 1, p. 1, col. 5; and "MD Charged with not Reporting Child Abuse," *Toronto Star*, June 2, 1983, p. A16, col. 1.

3. E.g., *Groff v. State*, 390 So.2d 361 (Dist. Ct. of App., 2nd Dist., Fla., 1980), and *State v. Groff*, 409 So.2d 44 (Dist. Ct. of App., 2nd Dist., Fla., 1981), ultimately dismissed on the ground that Florida's reporting mandate was limited to "any person . . . serving children" and, therefore, did not apply to the defendant psychiatrist who was treating the father and had never met the child.

4. *People v. Poremba* (Denver County Court, 12/17/80), 7 *Family Law Reporter* (January 1, 1981), p. 2142.

5. E.g., *People v. Sok* (for punching and pushing two children) and *People v. Molitor* (for not reporting the abuse) mentioned in "Monk Seeks $60 Million Damages for Lawsuit's Allegations of Racism," *Los Angeles Times*, June 23, 1982, Pt. 2, p. 12, col. 1. According to the Los Angeles district attorney, both cases resulted in convictions.

6. E.g., "People v. Noshay," *NASW News*, February 1984, p. 21, and April 1984, p. 7, a case, later dismissed, charging the social worker for failing to report "immediately" because she worked with the victim's family for five weeks before a report was made by the family.

7. E.g., "2 Found Guilty of not Reporting Child-Abuse Case," *Providence Journal*, December 4, 1981, p. A–3, col. 3. On appeal, the case was dismissed on procedural grounds (the case was tried in the wrong court). *State v. Boucher and Flinkfelt*, 468 A.2d 1227 (R.I., 1983).

8. E.g., *Pope v. State, supra* n. 1.

9. E.g., "Principal Fined for Failure To Report Abuse Suspicion," *Denver Post*, March 10, 1982, p. A–1, col. 1; and "PTA Backs Fine in Failure to Report Alleged Abuse," *Denver Post*, March 11, 1982, p. A–1, col. 1.

10. Depending on the circumstances, the accused may raise the usual defenses to criminal liability, including ignorance, mistake, necessity, and coercion. See generally, J. Hall, *General Principles of Criminal Law* (New York: Bobbs-Merrill, 1960), chaps. 11 and 12.

11. *People v. Poremba*, p. 2144, *supra* n. 4.

12. All information and quotations from "Doctor, Parents Charged in Death of Abused L.A. Child," *supra* n. 2.

13. *Los Angeles Times*, December 1, 1984, Metro Section, p. 1.

14. J. Aaron, "Civil Liability for Teacher's Negligent Failure to Report Suspected Child Abuse," *Wayne Law Review* 28, pp. 183 and 207, n. 164, citing an interview with Steven Matz (January 22, 1981), the attorney who brought the action against the school personnel in *Beuning v. Waun*, discussed at *infra* n. 18.

15. *Borgerson v. Minnesota*, Nos. 3-78-228, 4-81-14, slip opinion (U.S.D. Ct. of Minn., 3d Div., June 12, 1981). This case is cited as an example of the claims that can be made. Minnesota does not have a civil liability statute.

16. It is not clear what effect, if any, these laws have on the preexisting common law tort actions for the failure to report that are described later in the chapter. The primary legislative intent seems to have been to remove any ambiguity over the plaintiff's right to sue. However, these statutes, by the narrower test of liability that they set forth (and the commentary associated with them) also seem to be an attempt to limit the grounds of liability to

"knowing" and "willful" failure to report. See U.S. National Center on Child Abuse and Neglect, *Model Child Protection Act* (draft), Comment to Section 12 (1977), stating: "This standard was adopted as a *specification* and a limitation on the situations in which liability may arise."

17. The "willful misconduct" standard is usually defined to mean that "the actor has intentionally done an act of an unreasonable character in disregard of a known or obvious risk that was so great as to make it highly probable that harm would follow." *Prosser and Keeton on the Law of Torts*, 5th ed. (St. Paul, Minn.: West, 1984), p. 213.

18. *Beuning v. Waun*, No. 80–214188, (Cir. Ct., Oakland, Co., Mich., filed November 7, 1980).

19. *Landeros v. Flood*, 40 Cal. App.3rd 189, 123 Cal. Rptr. 713, 719 (1975), *vacated*, 17 Cal.3d 399, 131 Cal. Rptr. 69, 551 P.2d 389, n. 13 (Sup. Ct. 1976).

20. *See Prosser and Keeton*, p. 220, *supra* n. 17. However, jurisdictions differ over whether proof of the statute's violation is the equivalent of proof of negligence, whether it raises a rebuttable inference of negligence, or whether it is merely some evidence of negligence. Violation of the statute may raise a claim of liability under the Federal Civil Rights Act (§ 1983), but so far such claims have been rejected by the courts when the failure to report is not a governmental action or policy. See, e.g., *Davis v. Casey*, 493 F. Supp. 117 (D. Mass. 1980).

21. See D. Besharov, Appendix C: "Materials on Liability for Failure to Report Suspected Child Maltreatment," *The Vulnerable Social Worker: Liability for Serving Children and Families* (Silver Spring, Md.: National Association of Social Workers, 1985).

22. *Robinson v. Wical, MD, et al.*, Civil No. 37607, Calif. Superior Ct., San Luis Obispo, filed Sept. 4, 1970. All case details from R. Brown and R. Truitt, "Civil Liability In Child Abuse Cases," *Chicago-Kent Law Review* 54 (1978), pp. 753, 762–63.

23. See *Time*, November 20, 1972, p. 74, col. 2.

24. *Landeros v. Flood*, *supra* n. 19.

25. U.S. National Center on Child Abuse and Neglect, *Curriculum on Child Abuse and Neglect: Resource Materials* (1979), p. 78.

26. *Landeros v. Flood*, pp. 397–398, *supra* n. 19, 551 P.2d. But see Annotation, "Failure to Report Suspected Case of Child Abuse," 6 *Proof of Facts* 2d 345, 357 (Rochester, N.Y.: Lawyer's Institute, 1975) stating:

> Thus, the reporting statutes generally require a report where there is reasonable cause to believe that child abuse has occurred. There are two possible interpretations of what constitutes a violation. Under one interpretation, the statute is violated if the reporter should have recognized child abuse but did not, whereas the other interpretation would require

a willful failure to report for a violation. It has been argued that the first interpretation is preferable, since it applies a reasonable person standard, while still allowing room for judgment, and since a willful violation would be extremely difficult to prove.

27. *Landeros v. Flood*, 551 P.2d, p. 393, *supra* n. 19.

28. See, e.g., *Doran v. Priddy*, 534 F.Supp. 30, 33 (D. Ken. 1981) (dicta). See also Besharov, *supra* n. 21; and Annotation, p. 358, *supra* n. 26.

29. *Prosser and Keeton*, pp. 185–86, *supra* n. 17.

30. *Standards for Social Work Practice in Child Protection* (Silver Spring, Md.: National Association of Social Workers, 1981), Standards 37 and 38.

31. See, e.g., *Groff v. State*, *supra* n. 3.

32. *Tarasoff v. Regents of University of California*, 17 Cal.3d 425, 551 P.2d 334, 131 Cal. Rptr. 14 (1976).

33. D. Wexler, "Victimology and Mental Health Law: An Agenda," *Virginia Law Review* 66 (1980), pp. 681, 682.

34. *Tarasoff v. Regents of University of California*, *supra* n. 32, 17 Cal.3d, p. 431; 551 P.2d, p. 340; 131 Cal. Rptr., p. 20.

35. For critical as well as supportive commentary, see Besharov, *supra* n. 21, at Appendix A, "Materials on the Liability of Mental Health Professionals."

36. See, e.g., *Hicks v. United States*, 511 F.2d 407 (D.C. Cir. 1975) (mental hospital); *Beck v. Kansas University Psychiatry Foundation*, 580 F.Supp. 527 (D. Kansas 1984) (mental health center, staff physicians, director of security services, and director of emergency room); *Hasenei v. United States*, 541 F.Supp. 999 (D. Md. 1982) (psychiatrist); *Vu v. Singer Company*, 706 F.2d 1027 (9th Cir.), *cert. denied*, 104 S. Ct. 350 (1983) (operator of job corps center); *Lipari v. Sears, Roebuck & Co. v. United States*, 497 F.Supp. 185 (D. Nebraska 1980) ("psychotherapist"); *Rodriguez v. Inglewood Unified School District*, 152 Cal. App. 3rd 440, 199 Cal. Rptr. 524 (2nd Dist., Div. 3, 1984) (school district); *Sinacore v. The Superior Court of Santa Clara County*, 81 Cal. App.3rd 198, 144 Cal. Rptr. 893 (1st Dist., Div. 2, 1978) (applied to social worker to lift confidentiality); *Bradley Center v. Wessner*, 250 Ga. 199, 296 S.E.2d 693 (1982) (mental health hospital); *Durflinger v. Artiles*, 234 Kan. 484, 673 P.2d 86 (1983) (therapist); *Manageris v. Gordon*, 580 P.2d 481 (Nev. 1978) (massage parlor); *McIntosh v. Milano*, 168 N.J. Super. 466, 403 A.2d 500 (1979) (psychiatrist); *Furr v. Spring Grove State Hospital*, 53 Md. App. 474, 454 A.2d 414 (Md. App. 1983) (state psychiatrist and director of admissions of state mental hospital); and *Coath v. Jones*, 419 A.2d 1249 (Pa. Super. 1980) (employer). See also, *Prosser and Keeton*, § 32, *supra* n. 17; and *Restatement on Torts 2d*, § 319.

37. Such vicarious liability is based on the legal doctrine of "respondeat superior," under which the tortious conduct of a staff member may be imputed

to the employer. See generally, *Prosser and Keeton*, chap. 12, *supra* n. 17. See also, Note, "Agency: Liability of a Hospital for Negligent Acts of a Physician–Employee," *Oklahoma Law Review* 18 (1965), p. 77; and Annotation, *American Law Reports 2d* 69 (1960), p. 30.

38. In some states, there are significant exceptions to these generalizations. For example, there is sometimes a more limited tolling of the statute of limitations in medical malpractice cases. A full discussion of these issues can be found in R. Horowitz, "The Child Litigant," in Horowitz and H. Davidson, eds., *The Legal Rights of Children* (Colorado Springs, Colo.: Shepards-McGraw, 1984), § 3.04, "Statutes of Limitation"; and *American Jurisprudence 2d* 51 (1970 and Supp. 1981), §§ 181–85, "Limitations of Actions."

39. The questions that can arise under the concept of proximate cause are too complex to discuss here. For example, what if the subsequent injury occurs many months or many years later? Also, can the failure to report be considered the proximate cause of an injury to a sibling? See generally, N. Lehto, "Civil Liability for Failing to Report Child Abuse," *Detroit College of Law Review* (1977), pp. 135, 161–62.

Chapter 5
Protections for Those Who Report

1. Some laws grant immunity to those who report in "good faith," while others deny immunity to those who report with "malice" or in "bad faith." But the effect is the same: Persons who report in good faith are legally protected from liability. *Black's Law Dictionary*, 4th ed. (1951) defines "good faith" as "honesty of intention, *and* freedom from knowledge of circumstances which ought to put the holder upon inquiry." (Emphasis added.)

   In at least Massachusetts, a distinction is made between permissive/voluntary reporters (who enjoy only good-faith immunity) and mandated reporters (who enjoy absolute immunity). Mass. Gen. Laws Ann., ch. 119, §§ 51A (West Supp. 1988). In addition, federal court decisions have also granted qualified, or good-faith, immunity for reporting to persons who are sued under the Federal Civil Rights Act. See, e.g., *Roman v. Appleby*, 558 F.Supp. 449 (E.D. Pa., 1983).

2. Actually, such provisions are technically redundant, at best. Under most reporting laws, good faith is not an affirmative defense that must be raised and proved by the reporter. Rather, the plaintiff must allege and prove the reporter's bad faith. Thus, the burden is already on the person suing to disprove the reporter's good faith. Furthermore, under the so-called Thayer Rule concerning the rebuttal of presumptions, the presumption of good faith could be rebutted by some credible evidence suggesting that the report was made maliciously. However, the question remains: If the

presumption is successfully rebutted, does the plaintiff still have the burden of proving bad faith by a preponderance of the evidence? Perhaps the best thing to say is that the presumption of good faith is a public relations provision, designed to soothe potential reporters; it does not take into account how presumptions operate in the law. See J. Thayer, *Preliminary Treatise on Evidence* (Seaman, OH: Kelley Publications [1898], p. 336). For a discussion of the development and present statement of the Thayer rule, see generally, E. Cleary, *McCormick's Handbook of the Law of Evidence*, 2d ed. (St. Paul, Minn.: West Publishing Co., 1972), §345, p. 821.

3. See, e.g, La. Rev. Stat. Ann. § 14:403(E)(West 1986).

4. Colorado's statute is typical of the broad immunity often granted:

> Any person . . . participating in good faith in the making of a report or in a judicial proceeding . . . the taking of photographs or x-rays, or the placing in temporary protective custody of a child pursuant to this article or otherwise performing his duties or acting pursuant to this article shall be immune from any liability, civil or criminal, or termination of employment that otherwise might result by reason of such reporting. For the purpose of any proceedings, civil or criminal, the good faith . . . shall be presumed. [Colo. Rev. Stat. § 19–10–110 (1986).]

5. See, e.g., *Roman v. Appleby, supra* n. 1.

6. *Austin v. French*, Civ. Action No. 80–0114, 0115(D), U.S. Dist. Ct., West. Dist. of Va., Danville Div., 1980.

7. Ibid., p. 4.

8. Cal. Penal Code § 11172(c) (West Supp. 1989).

9. See generally *Wigmore on Evidence* 8 (1981 Supp.), §2380; and Cleary, §95, *supra* n.2.

10. See, e.g., *Minnesota v. Andring*, Sup. Ct. of Minn., filed January 13, 1984.

11. Actually, a specific law abrogating confidentiality in judicial proceedings is necessary only in those rare situations in which someone who is subject to a privilege is called to testify *and* (1) that person is not required or authorized to report child abuse and neglect, (2) the information in the projected testimony is not made reportable by the reporting law, or (3) the privilege covering that person does not contain an exemption when a crime has been or will be committed.

12. Family Educational Rights and Privacy Act of 1974, codified at 20 U.S.C. § 1232(g)(1983).

13. Public Health Service Act, § 527, codified at 42 U.S.C. 290ee–3 (1988).

14. Ibid., § 523, codified at 42 U.S.C. 290dd–3 (1988).

15. For a further discussion of these issues, see U.S. Public Health Service, "Proposed Regulations on Confidentiality of Alcohol and Drug Abuse Patient

Records," *Federal Register* 48 (August 25, 1983), pp. 38758, 38767 *et seq*, codified at 42 C.F.R. 2 (1985); U.S. National Center on Child Abuse and Neglect, *Impact of Federal Law on Provision of Child Protective and Related Services* (1981), p. 16 *et seq.*; "Iowa Attorney General Issues Opinion on Dilemma in Child Abuse Reporting," *Family Law Reporter* 10 (January 3, 1984), p. 1123, discussing Iowa Attorney General's Opinion No. 83–11–3, November 9, 1983.

16. Maine mandates reports from therapists but requires the child protective agency to meet with the therapist and to consider the abuser's willingness to seek treatment before deciding what to do. [Maine Revised Statutes, Title 22, § 4011 (1–A) (C) (Supp. 1988).] Before deciding not to report, the professional must determine that there is "little threat of serious harm to the child," a difficult decision in many cases and, by the way, one that creates the threat of criminal and civil liability for not reporting. Maryland's exemption is limited to health practitioners who specialize in psychiatric treatment of pedophilia. A report is not required if the report would be based solely on the statement of an abuser made while in treatment for past abuse. [See also Maryland Code Annotated, FL, § 5–704 (Supp. 1988).] See also Ore. Rev. Stat. § 418.750 (1987), stipulating that mental health professionals, clergy, and attorneys are not required to report if such a report would disclose privileged communications, and Utah Code Ann. § 78–3c–4 (1987), abrogating the privilege between a victim and a sexual assault counselor, at the counselor's discretion, as established by statutory guidelines.

17. Under the Model Child Protection Act, for example, the local child protective agency, though still responsible for handling cases, is authorized to

> waive a full child protective investigation of reports made by agencies or individuals specified in the local plan if, after an appropriate assessment of the situation, it is satisfied that (i) the protective and service needs of the child and the family can be met by the agency or individual, (ii) the agency or individual agrees to do so, and (iii) suitable safeguards are established and observed. Suitable safeguards shall include a written agreement from the agency or individual to report periodically on the status of the family, a written agreement to report immediately to the local services at any time that the child's safety or well-being is threatened despite the agency's or individual's efforts, and periodic monitoring of the agency's or individual's efforts by the local service for reasonable period of time. [U.S. National Center on Child Abuse and Neglect, *Model Child Protection Act*, (draft) (August 1977), sec 16(d), p. 49.

18. Confidential material on file with the author.

19. See, e.g., "Virginia, Massachusetts Agencies Draw Sanctions," *NASW News* 28 (October 1983), p. 18. See generally, N. Rindfleisch and J. Rabb,

"How Much of a Problem Is Resident Mistreatment in Child Welfare Institutions?" *Child Abuse and Neglect* 8 (1984), p. 33.

20. Confidential material on file with the author.

21. See generally, H. Perritt, *Employee Dismissal Law and Practice* (New York: Wiley Law Publications, 1984); D. Cathcart and S. Kruse, "The New American Law of Wrongful Termination," *International Business Lawyer* (February 1984), p. 73; and T. Moore, "Individual Rights of Employees Within the Corporation," *Corporation Law Review* 6 (Winter 1983), p. 39.

22. See, e.g., Pa. Stat. Ann. tit.11, sec. 2204(d) (Purdon's Supp. 1988). See also, Tenn. Code Ann. sec. 37–1–410 (Michie 1984).

23. Minn. Stat. Ann. sec. 626.556(4a)(c) (West Supp. 1989).

24. Although most agencies probably have inherent administrative authority to make such deletions, to remove any residual question, many states have enacted legislation that authorizes the withholding of information that identifies the person who reported if its release would "be detrimental to the safety of such person." [Pa. Stat. Ann. tit. 11, §2215(c) (Purdon's Supp. 1988).]

Chapter 6
Sources of Suspicion

1. Although there is a small, technical difference between the two phrases, most legal authorities have concluded that they are fundamentally equivalent and have the same impact on reporting decisions. [See, e.g., Op. Ill. Attorney General, S-1298 (Oct. 6, 1977); Op. Mass. Attorney General 74/75–66 (June 16, 1975).] Since "reasonable cause to suspect" is the more common phraseology, it is used in this book.

2. Quoted in New York State Assembly Select Committee on Child Abuse, *Report* (April 1972), p. 93.

3. M. McLaughlin, "A Girl, 2, Dies—Victim of Abuse . . . and Red Tape," *New York Daily News*, December 3, 1971, p. 3, col. 1.

4. *In the Matter of Rose "B,"* 79 A.D.2d 1044, 435 N.Y.S.2d 185 (3rd Dept., 1981).

5. *Nelson v. Missouri Division of Family Services*, 706 F.2d 276, 277 (8th Cir. 1983).

6. U.S. National Center on Child Abuse and Neglect, *We Can Help: A Curriculum on Child Abuse and Neglect: Resource Materials* (1979), p. 71.

7. Ibid., p. 116.

8. B. Schmitt, "The Physician's Evaluation," in Schmitt, ed., *The Child Protection Team Handbook* (New York: Garland Press, 1978), pp. 39–40.

9. *In the Matter of S.*, 46 Misc. 2d 161, 259 N.Y.S.2d 164, 165 (Fam. Ct., Kings Co., 1965).

10. Ill. Ann. Stat. ch.37 § 802–18(2)(e) (Smith-Hurd Supp. 1989); N.Y. Fam. Ct. Act § 1046(a)(ii) (1985).

11. *In the Matter of L.E.J.*, 465 A.2d 374, 378 (D.C. Ct. of Appeals 1983); and *People v. Henson*, 33 N.Y.2d 63, 304 N.E.2d 358, 349 N.Y.S.2d 657, 665 (1973).

12. See *Prosser and Keeton on the Law of Torts*, 5th ed. (St. Paul, Minn.: West, 1984), § 39, pp. 221–24.

13. N. Dembitz, "Child Abuse and the Law—Fact and Fiction," *Record of the Bar Association of the City of New York* 24 (1969), pp. 613, 620.

14. Ibid., pp. 616–17.

15. See generally 45 Code of Federal Regulations 1340.14(i) (2) (1987)—the federal regulations concerning confidentiality of child abuse records.

16. *Wilder v. Sugarman*, 385 F.Supp. 1013 (S.D.N.Y. 1974).

17. *Hanson v. Rowe*, 18 Ariz. App. 131, 500 P.2d 919 (1972).

18. Quoted in "Legal Defense Fund Aids in Test Case in Confidentiality," *NASW News* 27:6 (June 1982), p. 22.

Chapter 7
Physical Abuse

1. Thirty-three jurisdictions have specific provisions excluding reasonable corporal punishment from their definitions of child abuse or neglect. U.S. National Center on Child Abuse and Neglect, *Analysis of State Child Abuse and Neglect Laws, 1984* (1986), Table II. In other states, the defense is established by court decision. See, e.g., *Bowers v. State*, 283 Md. 115, 389 A.2d 341, 348 (1978).

2. N. Dembitz, "Child Abuse and the Law—Fact and Fiction," *Record of the Bar Association of the City of New York* 24 (1969), pp. 613, 620.

3. Proverbs 13:24.

4. *In the Matter of M.*, 91 A.D.2d 612, 458 N.Y.S.2d 413, 414–415 (2nd Dept. 1982).

5. *In re Rodney C.*, 91 Misc. 2d 677, 682, 398 N.Y.S.2d 511, 516 (Fam. Ct., Onondaga Co., 1977).

6. W. LaFave and A. Scott, *Criminal Law* (St. Paul, Minn.: West, 1972), p. 390.

7. C. H. Kempe, F. N. Silverman, B. F. Steele, W. Droegemueller, and H. K. Silver, "The Battered Child Syndrome," 181: 1 *Journal of The American Medical Association* (1962), pp. 17–24.

8. See, e.g., Ill. Ann. Stat. chap. 37, § 802–18(2)(a) (Smith-Hurd Supp.

1989). Cf. D.C. Code § 16–2316(c) (1981); N.Y.Fam.Ct. Act § 1046(a)(ii) 1985).

9. See, e.g., *In the Matter of Rose "B,"* 79 A.D.2d 1044, 435 N.Y.S.2d 185, 186–187 (3rd Dept. 1981).

10. *People v. Henson,* 33 N.Y.2d 63, 74, 304 N.E.2d 358, 349 N.Y.S.2d 657, 665 (1973).

11. See, e.g., D.C. Code § 16–2316(c) (1981); N.Y.Fam.Ct. Act § 1046(a)(ii) (1985); Ill. Ann. Stat. Chap. 37, § 802–18(2)(e) (Smith-Hurd Supp. 1989).

12. Cf. *In the Matter of Tashyne L.,* 53 A.D.2d 629, 384 N.Y.S.2d 472, 474 (2nd Dept., 1976); *In the Matter of Young,* 50 Misc.2d 271, 270 N.Y.S.2d 250, 253 (Fam. Ct., Westchester Co., 1966), holding that the injuries must be "substantial in character."

13. B. Schmitt, ed., *The Child Protection Team Handbook: A Multidisciplinary Approach to Managing Child Abuse and Neglect* (New York: Garland Press, 1978), p. 44.

14. See, e.g., D. G. Gil, *Violence Against Children: Physical Child Abuse in the United States* (Cambridge, Mass.: Harvard University Press, 1970), p. 113.

15. See, e.g., N. Ellerstein, ed., *Child Abuse and Neglect: A Medical Reference* (New York: Wiley, 1981); Schmitt, esp. chap. 2, *supra* n. 13.

16. *Prosser and Keeton on the Law of Torts,* 5th ed. (St. Paul, Minn.: West, 1984), §39, p. 217.

17. Cf. Note, "Evidence—Child Abuse—Expert Medical Testimony Concerning 'Battered Child Syndrome' Held Admissible," *Fordham Law Review* 42 (1974), p. 935; Annotation, "Admissibility of Expert Medical Testimony on Battered Child Syndrome," *American Law Reports 3d* 98 (1980), p. 306.

18. *In the Matter of Young, supra* n. 12.

19. Derived from U.S. National Center on Child Abuse and Neglect, *We Can Help: A Curriculum on Child Abuse and Neglect: Resource Materials* (1979), p. 25.

Chapter 8
Sexual Abuse

1. Telephone conversation with Robin Alsop, American Humane Association, July 7, 1989.

2. See generally, J. Bulkley, ed., *Child Abuse and the Law,* 5th ed. (Chicago: American Bar Association, 1985), p. 4, n. 25.

3. See, e.g., New York Penal Law § 130.00(2) (1987).

4. Compiled and written by Kee MacFarlane, Children's Institute International, 1982. From "Child Sexual Abuse," Navy Family Advocacy Program, Training 1982, pp. 40–41.

5. Typically, state laws call them "molestation," "lewd and lascivious" acts, or "indecent liberties" with children. A common phrase is "the handling, feeling, or fondling of the genitals or intimate parts of a child." See, e.g., Kan. Stat. Ann. § 60–3102(c) (2) (1983) ("any lewd fondling or touching . . . with the intent to arouse"); N.M. Stat. Ann. § 30–9–13 (1984) ("unlawfully and intentionally touching or applying force to the intimate parts of a minor"); Fla. Stat. Ann. § 800.04(1) (Harrison's Supp. 1988) ("handles, fondles or makes an assault upon any child under the age of 16 years in a lewd, lascivious, or indecent manner"); Iowa Code Ann. § 709.8(1) (West 1979) ("fondle or touch the pubes or genitals of a child").

6. See, e.g., New York Penal Law at § 130.00(3) (1987).

7. Cal. Penal Code § 311.4(b) (West 1989).

8. Utah's law, for example, explains that:

> the sexual exploitation of minors is excessively harmful to their physiological, emotional, social, and mental development; that minors cannot intelligently and knowingly consent to sexual exploitation; that regardless of whether it is classified as legally obscene, material that sexually exploits minors is not protected by the First Amendment of the United States Constitution . . . and may be prohibited; and that the prohibition of and punishment for the distribution, possession, possession with intent to distribute, and production of materials that sexually exploit minors is necessary and justified to eliminate the market for those materials and to reduce the harm to the minor inherent in the perpetuation of the record of his sexually exploitive activities. [Utah Code Ann. § 76–5a–1 (Supp. 1989).]

9. See, e.g., Colo. Rev. Stat. § 18–6–403(1.5) (Supp. 1988).

10. See, e.g., Cal. Penal Code § 11166(c) (West Supp. 1989). These laws usually apply only when the processors are acting "in their professional capacity."

11. In the Matter of Dawn B., 114 Misc. 2d 834, 452 N.Y.S. 2d 817, 818 (Fam. Ct., Queens Co., 1982).

12. See generally, Bulkley, supra n. 2; see, e.g., N.Y. Fam.Ct. Act § 1012(e) (iii) (1983).

13. In re Hawkins, 76 Misc.2d 738, 351 N.Y.S.2d 574 (Fam. Ct., N.Y. Co., 1974).

14. T. Heeney, "Coping With 'The Abuse of Child Abuse Prosecutions': The Criminal Defense Lawyer's Viewpoint," The Champion: Journal of Trial Lawyers (August 1985), pp. 12–13.

15. V. Fontana, "The Maltreated Children of Our Times," *Villanova Law Review* 23 (1978), p. 450.

16. Heeney, p. 14, *supra* n. 14.

17. *In the Matter of Tonita R.*, 74 A.D.2d 830, 425 N.Y.S.2d 172 (2nd Dept., 1980).

18. *Child Abuse and Neglect Decisions Handbook* (Springfield: Illinois Department of Children and Family Services, 1982), Appendix E, p. 6.

19. See, e.g., *Lantrip v. Commonwealth of Kentucky*, 713 S.W.2d 816 (1986). See also, Note, "The Unreliability of Expert Testimony on the Typical Characteristics of Sexual Abuse Victims," *Georgetown Law Journal* 74 (1985), p. 395; Annotation, "Admissibility at Criminal Prosecution of Expert Testimony on Rape Trauma Syndrome," *American Law Reports 4th* 42 (1986), p. 879.

20. *In the Matter of Cynthia V.*, 94 A.D.2d 773, 462 N.Y.S.2d 721, 723 (2nd Dept., 1983).

21. R. D. Ruddle, ed., *Missouri Child Abuse Investigator's Manual* (Columbia: Institute of Public Safety Education, College of Public and Community Services, University of Missouri, 1981), p. 65. See generally, D. Finkelhor, *Sexually Victimized Children* (New York: Free Press, 1979).

22. See, e.g., Special Issue on Medical Evidence, *Child Abuse and Neglect: The International Journal* 13 (1989), p.2.

23. MacFarlane, pp. 45–46, *supra* n. 4.

24. For a comprehensive description of medical examinations for suspected sexual abuse, see W. Canavan, "Sexual Child Abuse," in N. Ellerstein, ed., *Child Abuse and Neglect: A Medical Reference* (New York: Wiley, 1981), p. 233.

Chapter 9
Physical Neglect

1. American Association for Protecting Children, *Highlights of Official Child Neglect and Abuse Reporting: 1984* (Denver, Colo.: American Humane Association 1986), p. 16, Table 6.

2. *Trends in Child Abuse and Neglect: A National Perspective* (Denver, Colo.: American Humane Association, 1984), p. 24, Table IV–3 and p. 97, Table A–IV–7. (1984). See generally, D. Besharov, "How Child Abuse Programs Hurt Poor Children," *Clearinghouse Review* 22 (1988), p. 218.

3. J. M. Giovannoni and A. Billingsley, "Child Neglect Among the Poor: A Study of Parental Adequacy in Families of Three Ethnic Groups," *Child Welfare* 49 (1970), pp. 196, 204.

4. Author's estimate based on *Social Security Bulletin's* (1984) report that in 1983, 3,721,000 families received Aid to Families with Dependent Children.

5. D.C.Code § 16–2301(9) (B) (1981) and § 16–2301(24)(Supp. 1988).

6. See, e.g., N.Y. Fam.Ct.Act § 1012(f) (i) (A)(1988).

7. D. Besharov, Practice Commentary to *McKinney's New York Family Court Act*, section 1012(f) (i), p. 241 of the main volume (St. Paul, Minn.: West, 1983).

8. V. DeFrancis, *The Fundamentals of Child Protection: A Statement of Basic Concepts and Principles* (Denver, Colo.: American Humane Association, 1955), p. 26.

9. This aspect of medical neglect is discussed in the section entitled "Failure to Treat a Child's Psychological Problems," in Chapter 11, this volume.

10. *In the Matter of Jerry M.*, 78 Misc.2d 407, 357 N.Y.S.2d 354, 358 (Fam. Ct., N.Y. Co., 1974).

11. *In the Matter of Hofbauer*, 47 N.Y.2d 648, 655, 419 N.Y.S.2d 936, 940, 393 N.E.2d 1009, 1013 (1979).

12. As in all forms of child maltreatment, the result of the medical neglect must be that the child's "physical, mental or emotional condition has been impaired or is in imminent danger of becoming impaired." N.Y. Fam.Ct.Act § 1012(f) (i) (1988).

13. Compare *In the Matter of Seiferth*, 309 N.Y. 80, 84, 127 N.E.2d 820, 822 (1955), refusing to order cosmetic surgery because the child was well liked, had good grades and a newspaper route, *with In the Matter of Sampson*, 37 A.D.2d 668, 323 N.Y.S.2d 253 (3rd Dept., 1971), ordering cosmetic surgery because the child's facial disfigurement prevented him from attending school and leading a normal life.

14. Compare *Custody of a Minor*, 375 Mass. 733, 379 N.E.2d 1053 (1978), ordering that the parents of a child with acute lymphocytic leukemia allow him to undergo traditional chemotherapy, which the doctors recommended, and discontinue their preferred, but useless treatment involving laetrile injections, with *In the Matter of Hofbauer*, *supra* n. 11, holding that the parents of a child with Hodgkin's disease exercised a minimum degree of care in supplying adequate medical care when they followed a physician's laetrile treatment for their son, rather than traditional medical care.

15. Cal. Welf. and Inst. Code § 16509 (West Supp. 1989).

16. See, e.g., *Prince v. Massachusetts*, 321 U.S. 158, 166–167 (1944), stating: "[T]he right to practice religion freely does not include liberty to expose . . . the child . . . to . . . ill health or death." Cf. *Wisconsin v. Yoder*, 406 U.S. 205 (1972).

17. Mo. Rev. Stat. § 210.115(3) (Vernon's 1983).

18. Child Abuse Prevention and Treatment and Adoption Reform, codified as amended at 42 USCA § 5106(g) (10) (Supp. 1989).

Chapter 10
Endangerment and Abandonment

1. B. Schmitt, "Child Neglect," in N. Ellerstein, ed., *Child Abuse and Neglect; A Medical Reference* (New York: Wiley, 1981), pp. 277, 301.

2. *In the Matter of Lydia K.*, 123 Misc.2d 41, 472 N.Y.S.2d 576, 578 (Fam. Ct., Queens Co., 1894), stating: "An isolated injury does not constitute neglect."

3. See, e.g., *In the Matter of Terry S.*, 55 A.D.2d 689, 389 N.Y.S.2d 55, 56–57 (3rd Dept., 1976).

4. However, many foster care agencies require adult supervision of children left at home until they are age ten. See, e.g., 18 NYCRR Section 7.6(f).

5. See, e.g., *Stoops v. Perales*, 117 A.D.2d 7, 501 N.Y.S.2d 489, 490 (3rd Dept., 1986), stating: "Assuming that the six-year-old was capable of caring for herself, the Commissioner properly concluded that [under the particular facts of the case] she was too young to be left alone with her one-year-old brother."

6. See, e.g., *Augustine v. Berger*, 88 Misc. 2d 487, 388 N.Y.S.2d 537 (Sup. Ct., Spec. Term, Suffolk County, 1976), holding that a mother's one-time leaving of two children, aged one and two, at home and unattended for half an hour while going to a nearby supermarket was not neglect.

7. Schmitt, p. 301, *supra* n. 1.

Chapter 11
Psychological Maltreatment

1. See generally, J. Garbarino and A. Garbarino, *Emotional Maltreatment of Children* (Chicago: National Committee for Prevention of Child Abuse, 1980).

2. See generally, *Diagnostic and Statistical Manual of Mental Disorders*, 3rd ed. (Washington, D.C.: American Psychiatric Association, 1980).

3. See, e.g., *Juvenile Justice Standards Relating to Child Abuse and Neglect*, (Chicago: American Bar Association/Institute on Judicial Administration, 1977), tentative draft Standard 2.1(C).

4. See, e.g., J. Goldstein, A. Freud, and A. J. Solnit, *Before the Best Interests of the Child* (New York: Free Press, 1979), pp. 75–86.

5. See, e.g., N.J. Stat. Ann. § 9:6–8.21(c) (4) (Supp. 1989) ("whose physical, mental, or emotional condition has been impaired or is in imminent danger of becoming impaired"); Del. Code Ann. tit 11, § 1103(b) (1987) ("whose physical, mental or emotional health and well-being is threatened or impaired"); Louis. Rev. Stat. Ann. § 4:403(B) (3) (West 1986) ("health or moral or emotional well-being is endangered"); and Ind. Code Ann. § 31–

6–4–3 (Burns 1987) ("physical or mental condition is seriously impaired or seriously endangered").

6. Child Protection Act of 1977, South Carolina Code § 20–7–490(G) (1)–(3) (1985).

7. See J. Egan, I. Chatoor, and J. Rosen, "Non-organic Failure to Thrive: Pathogenesis and Classification," *Clinical Proceedings: Children's Hospital National Medical Center* 36 (July/August 1980), p. 173.

8. The Mississippi juvenile court act recognizes the importance of such professional judgments by providing that:

> abuse encompasses a situation in which a child's mental health has been adversely affected in some substantial way as determined by examination by *competent mental health professionals.* [Miss. Code Ann. § 43-23-3(i) (1981). Emphasis added.]

9. Derived from U.S. National Center on Child Abuse and Neglect, *The Educator's Role in the Prevention and Treatment of Child Abuse and Neglect* (1979), Chart I.

10. Goldstein, Freud, and Solnit, pp. 76–77, *supra* n. 4.

11. U.S. National Center on Child Abuse and Neglect, p. 19.

12. L. Whiting, "Emotional Neglect of Children," found in *Child Abuse and Neglect: Issues on Innovation and Implementation: Proceedings of the Second National Conference on Child Abuse and Neglect* (U.S. Department of Health, Education & Welfare, 1978), pp. 209–10. The American Bar Association/Institute on Judicial Administration's project on Juvenile Justice Standards has taken a similar position; it would authorize intervention when the child is "suffering permanent emotional damage, evidenced by severe anxiety, depression or withdrawal, or untoward aggressive behavior toward self or others, *and the parents are not willing to provide treatment. . . .*" [*Juvenile Justice Standards Relating to Child Abuse and Neglect, supra* n. 3, emphasis added.]

13. *Roman v. Appleby*, 558 F.Supp. 449, 458–459 (E.D.Pa., 1983).

14. See, e.g, *In the Matter of Darlene T.*, 28 N.Y.2d 391, 393, 322 N.Y.S.2d 231, 232, 271 N.E.2d 215, 216 (1971), citing a petition that alleged that the mother "did entertain men in her apartment in the presence of Darlene"; *In the Matter of Anonymous*, 37 Misc.2d 411, 413, 238 N.Y.S.2d 422, 423–424 (Fam. Ct., Rensselaer Co., 1962), in which the mother "frequently entertained male companions in the apartment and in the presence of the children. In fact, on occasion, these male companions not only spent considerable parts of the day there but ate meals with her and the children and, on at least one occasion, one of them spent the night with the respondent and, in fact, slept with her, to the knowledge of the children."

15. Cf. *Bunim v. Bunim*, 393 N.Y. 391, 298 N.Y.S. 391, 83 N.E.2d 848 (1949), in which the appellate court reversed an award of custody to the

mother because she "admitted numerous deliberate adulteries"; with *Sheil v. Sheil*, 29 A.D.2d 950, 951, 289 N.Y.S.2d 86, 87 (2nd Dept., 1968), stating that in a determination of custody rights, "one act of adultery is not a justifiable basis upon which the mother may be denied custody."

16. M. Holmes, *Protective Services for Abused and Neglected Children and Their Families* (U.S. Department of Health, Education & Welfare, 1977), p. 25.

17. *In the Matter of Michael J. M.*, 61 A.D.2d 1056, 402 N.Y.S.2d 473 (3rd Dept., 1978).

18. *Matter of Tammie "Z"*, 105 A.D.2d 463, 480 N.Y.S.2d 786 (3rd Dept., 1984).

19. *Wisconsin v. Yoder*, 406 U.S. 205 (1972).

20. *In the Matter of Baum*, 61 A.D.2d 123, 401 N.Y.S.2d 514 (2nd Dept., 1978); *In the Matter of Skipwith*, 14 Misc.2d 325, 180 N.Y.S.2d 852 (Fam. Ct., N.Y. Co., 1958).

21. *Pierce v. Society of Sisters*, 268 U.S. 510 (1925).

22. See, e.g., *People v. Turner*, 277 A.D.2d 317, 98 N.Y.S.2d 886 (4th Dept., 1950).

Chapter 12
Parents with Severe Mental Disabilities

1. See, e.g., *U.S. National Center on Child Abuse and Neglect, Child Protective Services: Inservice Training for Supervisors and Workers*, Module III (1981).

2. See generally, J. Cocozza and H. Steadman, "The Failure of Psychiatric Predictions of Dangerousness: Clear and Convincing Evidence," *Rutgers Law Review* 29 (1976), p. 1084; Cocozza and Steadman, "Some Refinements in the Measurement and Prediction of Dangerous Behavior," *American Journal of Psychiatry* 131 (1974), p. 1012.

3. See generally, U.S. National Center on Child Abuse and Neglect, *Review of Child Abuse Research: 1979–1981* (1981), pp. 42–105.

4. J. Garbarino and S. H. Stocking, "The Social Context of Child Maltreatment," in Garbarino, Stocking, and Associates, *Protecting Children from Abuse and Neglect* (San Francisco: Jossey-Bass, 1980), p. 7, referring to R. Helfer, *Report on the Research Using the Michigan Screening Profile of Parenting (MSPP)* (Washington, D.C.: National Center on Child Abuse and Neglect, 1978).

5. R. Helfer, "Basic Issues Concerning Prediction," in Helfer and C. H. Kempe, eds., *Child Abuse and Neglect: The Family and the Community* (Cambridge, Mass.: Ballinger, 1976), p. 363.

6. See, e.g., *Roberts v. State*, 1941 Ga. App. 268, 233 S.E. 2d 224 (1977), in which a baby born to a mentally retarded, fourteen-year-old mother was placed in foster care immediately after birth. Despite the absence of any "history of deprivation," the court held that, under the circumstances, parental rights could be terminated on the ground that the child would suffer deprivation if the mother were given custody of him.

7. *In re Eugene G.*, 76 A.D.2d 781, 429 N.Y.S.2d 17, 18 (1st Dept., 1980).

8. *In the Matter of Daniel C.*, 47 A.D.2d 160, 164–165, 365 N.Y.S.2d 535, 539 (1st Dept., 1975).

9. *Department of Social Services v. Joan R.*, 61 A.D. 2d 1108, 403 N.Y.S.2d 368, 369 (3rd Dept., 1978).

10. *In the Matter of Carlton, Karen and Joseph W.*, N.Y.L.J., Feb. 11, 1976, p. 12.

11. See generally, *Diagnostic and Statistical Manual of Mental Disorders*, 3rd ed. (Washington, D.C.: American Psychiatric Association, 1980).

12. See J. Goldstein, A. Freud, and A. Solnit, *Before the Best Interests of the Child* (New York: The Free Press, 1979), p. 64.

13. M. Holmes, *Child Abuse and Neglect Programs: Practice and Theory* (U.S. Department of Health, Education & Welfare, 1977), p. 116.

14. *In the Matter of Jason B.*, 117 Misc.2d 480, 458, N.Y.S.2d 180, 181–182 (Fam. Ct., Richmond Co., 1983).

15. N. Polansky, C. De Saix, and S. Sharlin, *Child Neglect: Understanding and Reaching the Parent* (New York: Child Welfare League of America, 1973), pp. 32–33.

16. Telephone conversation with David Bateman, MD, Harlem Hospital, March 22, 1989.

17. Data from the New York City Human Resources Administration, Office of Management Analysis, December 15, 1989.

18. See D. Besharov, *The Children of Addicts: Unrecognized and Unprotected* (New York State Assembly, 1972).

19. Quoted in J. Nolan, "Babies of Addict Moms Begin Life Against Long Odds," *New York Post*, May, 9, 1988.

20. D. Clement, "Babies in Trouble," *Minnesota Monthly*, March 1989, p. 49.

21. M. A. Farber, "Killing of a Child: How the System Failed," *New York Times*, January 19, 1989, p. A1, col. 3.

22. S. Daley, "Agency Said to Fail Children Placed in Relatives' Care," *New York Times*, February 23, 1989. p. B1, col. 2.

23. M. S. Green, "Children Tangled in Drug Net," *Washington Post*, September 26, 1988, p. A8, col. 2.

24. See, e.g, N.Y. Family Court Act 1046(a) (iii) (McKinney 1988), providing

that "proof that a person repeatedly uses a drug, or drugs or alcoholic beverages, to the extent that it has or would ordinarily have the effect of producing in the user thereof a substantial state of stupor, unconsciousness, intoxication, hallucination, disorientation, or incompetence, or a substantial impairment of judgment, or a substantial manifestation of irrationality, shall be prima facie evidence that a child" is neglected.

25. *In the Matter of John Children*, 61 Misc.2d 347, 353, 306, N.Y.S.2d 797, 805 (Fam. Ct., N.Y. Co., 1969).

26. According to a telephone conversation with Gordon Avery, MD, of Children's Hospital, Washington, D.C., March 27, 1989, "cocaine babies are at risk for respiratory failure, sudden infant death syndrome, and preterm delivery and some have actual brain infarctions, which could cause a reaction similar to a stroke in old people." See also B. Whitaker, "Tiniest Tragedies of Drugs," *Newsday*, July 11, 1988, p. 9.

27. Mass. Gen. Laws Ann. ch. 119 § 51A (West Supp. 1986).

28. *In the Matter of Vanesa F.*, 76 Misc.2d 617, 620, 351 N.Y.S.2d 337, 340 (Surr. Ct., N.Y. Co., 1974).

29. U.S. National Center on Child Abuse and Neglect, *National Study of the Incidence and Severity of Child Abuse and Neglect* (1981), p. 25, Table 5–2.

30. B. Schmitt, "The Physician's Evaluation," in Schmitt, ed., *The Child Protection Team Handbook* (New York: Garland Press, 1978), pp. 39, 50–51.

31. See, e.g., C. H. Kempe, "Approaches to Preventing Child Abuse: The Health Visitors Concept," *American Journal of Diseases of Childhood* 130 (September 1976), p. 942.

Chapter 13
Interviewing Parents

1. U.S. National Center on Child Abuse and Neglect, *The Educator's Role in the Prevention and Treatment of Child Abuse and Neglect* (1979), p. 25.

2. U.S. National Center on Child Abuse and Neglect, *We Can Help: A Curriculum on the Identification, Reporting, Referral and Case Management of Child Abuse and Neglect* (1976), pp. 14–43 and 14–44.

3. Derived from U.S. National Center on Child Abuse and Neglect, *The Nurse's Role in the Prevention and Treatment of Child Abuse and Neglect* (1979), p. 25.

4. R. D. Ruddle, ed., *Missouri Child Abuse Investigator's Manual* (Columbia: Institute of Public Safety Education, College of Public and Community Services, University of Missouri, 1981), p. 51.

5. B. Schmitt, ed., *The Child Protection Team Handbook* (New York: Garland Press, 1978), p. 40.

6. New York State Assembly Select Committee on Child Abuse, *Report* (Albany, N.Y., 1977), pp. 24–25.

7. See, e.g., *In the Matter of Baby Boy Santos*, 71 Misc.2d 789, 336 N.Y.S.2d 817, 819 (Fam. Ct., N.Y. Co., 1972), describing how the child "was brought to the hospital because a friend of the mother noticed the depressed area in the child's skull. Respondent mother explained this was the first time she saw the injury and believed it occurred when the child fell back in her crib on to the mattress, striking her head on a toy. The doctor testified, as does the hospital record indicate, that there was no pericranial swelling. This, in the doctor's opinion, suggests an 'old process' which could not have occurred in the manner described by the mother."

8. Ruddle, p. 46, *supra* n. 4.

9. Schmitt, pp. 42–43, *supra* n. 5.

10. *People v. Henson*, 33 N.Y.2d 63, 304 N.E.2d 358, 349 N.Y.S.2d 657, 664 (1973).

11. *In the Matter of Rose "B,"* 79 A.D.2d 1044, 435 N.Y.S.2d 185, 186–187 (3rd Dept., 1981).

12. Derived from B. Schmitt, *Child Abuse/Neglect: The Visual Diagnosis of Non-Accidental Trauma and Failure to Thrive* (Elk Grove Village, Ill.: American Academy of Pediatrics, 1979), p. 3.

13. Schmitt, pp. 40–41, *supra* n. 5.

14. *People v. Eisenman*, 39 N.Y.2d 810, 351 N.E.2d 429, 385 N.Y.S.2d 762, 763 (1976).

15. B. Schmitt, "Child Neglect," in N. Ellerstein, ed., *Child Abuse and Neglect: A Medical Reference* (New York: Wiley, 1981), p. 302.

16. See generally, R. Starr, ed., *Child Abuse Prediction: Policy Implications* (Cambridge, Mass.: Ballinger Publishing Co., 1982). See also the sections entitled "Endangered Children" in Chapters 3 and "The Child's Behavior" in Chapter 7, this volume.

17. Schmitt, p. 41, *supra* n. 5.

18. Ibid.

19. Derived, in part, from U.S. Head Start Bureau and U.S. National Center on Child Abuse and Neglect, *Child Abuse and Neglect: A Self-Instructional Text for Head Start Personnel* (1977), pp. 61–62.

20. See, e.g., *In the Matter of JR*, 87 Misc.2d 900, 386 N.Y.S.2d 774, 776 and 777 (Fam. Ct., Bronx Co., 1976), in which a three month old had "subdural hematomas on both sides of the head; linear fracture of the skull; retinal hemorrhage; and bruises on both cheeks and the lower left portion of the abdomen. The only explanation of these injuries was the possibility that Virgin (three years old), in a fit of jealousy, threw him to

the floor and beat him." The court concluded: "No direct evidence of abuse is before the court. The injuries are consistent only with sustained widespread assault and by themselves negate the possibility of a 'single-fall' or a 'flash-beating' administered by a jealous three-year-old's physical capabilities. Moreover, even conceding the mother's explanation and assigning unwarranted credibility to it, her sheer act of leaving the baby in a position where this or similar injuries could be proximately anticipated shows her actions wanting of that standard of care required by law."

Chapter 14
Preserving Evidence

1. See, e.g., R. Ford and B. Smistek, "Photography of the Maltreated Child," in N. Ellerstein, *Child Abuse and Neglect: A Medical Reference* (New York: Wiley, 1981), p. 315.

2. V. Fontana, "The Maltreated Children of Our Times," *Villanova Law Review* 23 (1978), pp. 445, 452.

3. *Child Abuse Investigations* (Austin: Texas Department of Human Resources 1978), p. 11.

4. U.S. National Center on Child Abuse and Neglect, *Guidelines for the Hospital and Clinical Management of Child Abuse and Neglect* (1979), p. V-2.

5. Source: *Child Abuse Investigations*, p. 13, *supra* n. 3.

Chapter 15
Emergencies

1. Derived from U.S. National Center on Child Abuse and Neglect, *Treatment for Abused and Neglected Children* (1979), p. 4; and *Child Abuse and Neglect Investigation Decisions Handbook* (Springfield: Illinois Department of Children and Family Services, 1982), p. 77.

2. See generally, D. Besharov, "Protecting Children from Abuse and Neglect: The Need to Narrow the Ground for State Intervention," *Harvard Journal of Law and Public Policy* 8 (1985), pp. 539, 584.

3. A well-explained example of a court's refusal to grant an agency request for a child's removal is *In the Matter of Adrian J.*, 119 Misc.2d 900, 464 N.Y.S.2d 631 (Fam. Ct., Onondaga Co., 1983).

4. Cf. *Warden v. Hayden*, 387 U.S. 294 (1967).

5. E.g., N.Y. Family Court Act § 1024 (1983).

6. See D. Besharov, *The Vulnerable Social Worker: Liability for Serving Children and Families* (Silver Spring, Md.: National Association of Social Workers, 1985), chap. 3.

7. See *Prosser and Keeton on the Law of Torts*, 5th ed. (St. Paul, Minn.: West, 1984), § 20, pp. 129–130.

8. See, e.g., Iowa Code Ann. § 232.21 (West 1985).

9. E.g., Ala. Code § 26–14–6 (1977) (seventy-two hours); Conn. Gen. Stat. Ann. § 17–38a(e) (West 1989) (ninety-six hours); Minn. Stat. Ann. § 260.171 (2) (1982) (twenty-four or thirty-six hours depending on the circumstances); N.Y. Fam. Ct. Act § 1021 (McKinney Supp. 1983) (three court days); and Utah Code Ann. § 78–3a–30(2) (1987) (forty-eight hours).

10. Derived from U.S. National Center on Child Abuse and Neglect, *Child Protective Services: A Guide for Workers* (1979), p. 42.

11. E.g., Ga. Code Ann. § 19–7–5(c) (1982); Kan. Stat. Ann. § 38–1522(c) (1986); Iowa Code Ann. § 232.70(2) (West 1985); and K.Y. Rev. Stat. § 199.335(3) (Baldwin's 1987).

12. J. G. Collins, "The Role of the Law Enforcement Agency," in R. Helfer and C. H. Kempe, eds., *The Battered Child* (Chicago: University of Chicago Press, 1968), pp. 179, 183.

13. Attorney General's Task Force on Family Violence, *Final Report* (U.S. Department of Justice, September 1984), pp. 10, 17.

14. See, e.g., *Wong Sun v. United States*, 371 U.S. 471 (1963); and *Jones v United States*, 363 U.S. 257 (1960).

Chapter 16
Making a Report

1. See, e.g., Md. Code Ann. FL § 5–704 (Supp. 1988).

2. See, e.g., N.Y. Social Services Law § 413 (Supp. 1989).

3. *People v. Noshay*, NASW News, February 29, 1984, p. 21, and April 29, 1984, p. 7.

4. Iowa Attorney General, Opinion No. 78–9–12, September 28, 1978, cited in *Family Law Reporter* 5 (November 7, 1978), p. 2015.

5. *Mammo v. Arizona*, 138 Ariz. 528, 675 P.2d 1347 (Ariz. Ct. App. 1983).

6. *Association of Trial Lawyers of America Reporter* (Washington, D.C., 1981), p. 76.

7. Derived from D. Besharov, *The Vulnerable Social Worker: Liability for Serving Children and Families* (Silver Spring, Md.: National Association of Social Workers, 1985), p. 60.

8. It could also lead to a lawsuit claiming bad faith, as illustrated by the case of *Austin v. French*, in Chapter 5, n. 6.

9. U.S. National Center on Child Abuse and Neglect, *The Educator's Role in the Prevention and Treatment of Child Abuse and Neglect* (1979), p. 25.

10. U.S. National Center on Child Abuse and Neglect, *Guidelines for the Hospital and Clinical Management of Child Abuse and Neglect* (1979), p. V–4.

11. U.S. National Center on Child Abuse and Neglect, p. 25, *supra* n. 9.

12. H. Leake and R. Holbrook, "Medical Testimony," in N. Ellerstein, *Child Abuse and Neglect: A Medical Reference* (New York: Wiley, 1982), pp. 327, 331.

Chapter 17
Monitoring Interventions

1. See Chapter 2, n. 18.

2. "Mistreating Child Abuse," *Boston Globe*, October 14, 1982, p. 16.

3. Count 2 (of the indictment).

4. W. Holder, "A Personal View of Casework Liability," in W. Holder and K. Hayes, eds., *Malpractice and Liability* (Longmont, Colo.: Bookmakers Guild, 1984), pp. 95–96.

5. The caseworker's conviction was overturned because she had been compelled to testify (against the supervisor) before her sentencing (*Steinberger v. District Court*, 596 P.2d 755 [Colo. 1979]). The supervisor's conviction was overturned on the ground that the official misconduct statute was "void for vagueness" (*People v. Beruman*, 638 P.2d 789 [Colo. 1982]).

6. U.S. National Center on Child Abuse and Neglect, *Child Protective Services: In-Service Training for Supervisors and Workers* (1982), p. II–24.

Chapter 18
Being Prepared

1. See, e.g., Fla. Stat. Ann. § 415.509(2) (1985).

2. Cal. Penal Code § 11166.5(a) (West Supp. 1989).

3. Fla. Stat. Ann. § 395.0205 (West Supp. 1988).

4. Fla. Stat. Ann. § 232.50 (West Supp. 1985).

5. See D. Bross, R. Krugman, M. Lenherr, D. Rosenberg, and B. Schmitt, *The New Child Protection Handbook* (New York: Garland Press, 1988); and B. Schmitt, *The Child Protection Team Handbook: A Multidisciplinary Approach To Managing Child Abuse and Neglect* (New York: Garland Press, 1978). Sometimes also called "Suspected Child Abuse and Neglect" ("SCAN") teams.

6. H. Thomas, *Child Abuse: Neglect and Deprivation* (Toronto: Registered Nurses Association of Ontario, 1983), p. 44.

7. About sixteen mandate teams and twelve permit them.

8. V. Fontana, "The Maltreated Children of Our Times," *Villanova Law Review* 23 (1978), pp. 445, 452.

9. Derived from Thomas, p. 44, *supra* n. 6.

10. See National Center on Child Abuse and Neglect, *A Community Approach: The Child Protection Coordinating Committee* (1979).

Chapter 19
Is Your Child Abused?

1. *Questions Parents Ask About Child Sexual Abuse and the Service System's Response* (Madison, Wisc.: City-County Committee on Sexual Assault, January 1985), p. 1.

2. Ibid., p. 9. Originally entitled "The Feelings a Mother in an Incestuous Family May Have When She Finds Out About the Abuse."

3. Ibid., p. 1.

4. DePamfilis, "Clients Who Refer Themselves to Child Protective Services," *Children Today* (March–April 1982), pp. 21, 23.

5. Derived from M. Brassard and S. Hart, *Emotional Abuse: Words Can Hurt* (Chicago: National Committee for Prevention of Child Abuse, 1987), pp. 12–13.

6. Derived from Carol A. Johnston, *Families in Stress* (Washington, D.C.: U.S. National Center on Child Abuse and Neglect, 1979).

Chapter 20
If You Are Reported

1. Compare *People v. Sutton*, 134 Cal. Rptr. 921, 65 Cal. App. 3d 341 (1976), approving an entry based on a report of "small children left alone," *with Dennison v. Vietch*, 560 F. Supp. 435 (D. Minn., 4th Div. 1983), finding no exigent circumstances because the police were given no information suggesting that the child was in immediate danger.

2. If the police perform the investigation, most, but not all, states subject them to the rules established in *Miranda v. Arizona*, 384 U.S. 436 (1966). Cf. *Harris v. City of Montgomery*, 435 So. 2d 1207 (Ala. 1983). The same is not true for social workers: "To require such a warning would frustrate the State's performance of its duty as *parens patriae* to investigate and protect the welfare of children. In any event, there appears to be no precedent for the requirements of a warning in connection with a civil proceeding." [*In the Matter of Diana A.*, 65 Misc. 2d 1034, 1040, 319 N.Y.S. 2d 691, 698 (Fam. Ct., N.Y. Co., 1971). Cf. *People v. Yanus*, 92 A.D. 2d 674, 460 N.Y.S. 2d 180 (3rd Dept., 1983).]

3. S. Reynolds and J. Strickland, "The New Untouchables: Risk Management of Child Abuse in Child Care," *Child Care Information Exchange*, No. 63 (October 1988), p. 19.

4. Ibid.

5. See, e.g., *In re Vulon*, 56 Misc.2d 19, 288 N.Y.S.2d 203 (Fam. Ct., Bronx Co., 1968).

6. Rates for substantiated cases are about twice as high. U.S. National Center on Child Abuse and Neglect, *National Analysis of Official Child Neglect and Abuse Reporting* (1978) (1979), p. 36, Table 28.

7. *Harris v. City of Montgomery*, p. 1210, *supra* n. 2.

8. *Hale v. City of Virginia Beach*, U.S. Dist. Ct., E. D. of Va., Norfolk Div., Civ. SO-151-N. Complaint, pars. 6.A. and 9 (emphasis added).

9. *E. Z. v. Coler*, 603 F.Supp. 1546 (N.D.Ill., 1985), Complaint par. 9(c).

10. Derived from E. Greb, *What's Happening to My Family?: A Guide for Families Receiving Child Protective Services* (San Diego: County of San Diego Department of Social Services, undated), p. 3.

11. See "Confidentiality of Records as to Recipients of Public Welfare," *American Law Reports 3rd* 54 (1973), p. 768. See also, National Legal Resource Center on Child Advocacy and Protection, *Access to Child Protective Records—A Basic Guide to Law and Policy* (Chicago: American Bar Association, April 1979); and R. Levin, "Child Protective Records: Issues of Confidentiality," *Social Work* 21(4) (July 1976), p. 323.

12. See, e.g., Wash. Rev. Code Ann Sec. 26.44.070(8) (Supp. 1988).

13. For example, Nebraska's law directs the agency "not release data that would be harmful or detrimental or that would identify or locate a person who, in good faith, made a report or cooperated in a subsequent investigation." [Neb. Rev. Stat. Sec. 28–722 (1985).]

14. See generally, D. Besharov, "Putting Central Registers to Work: Using Modern Information Management Systems to Improve Child Protective Services," *Chicago-Kent Law Review* 54 (1978), pp. 687, 733 *et seq.*

15. For example, Utah's statute provides that

> (1) The Division shall establish a statewide central register for child abuse or neglect reports made pursuant to this chapter. (2) The central register shall contain, but is not limited to: (a) all information in the written report; (b) record of the final disposition of the report, including services offered and services accepted; (c) the plan for rehabilitative treatment; (d) the names and identifying data of the child and the reported abuser; (e) dates and circumstances of any persons requesting or receiving information from the register; and (f) any other information that might be helpful in furthering the purposes of this chapter [Utah Code Ann. Sec. 78–3b–12(1) and (2) (1987).]

16. South Carolina's procedure reflects a common approach:

> The names, addresses and all other identifying characteristics of all persons named in all unfounded reports shall be destroyed one year from the date that the last report has been determined to be unfounded; *provided,*

however, that all information in any such report which is unnecessary for auditing purposes shall be destroyed immediately upon a determination that such report is unfounded and the remaining information shall be kept confidential except for auditing purposes. [Code of Laws of S.C. 1976 Ann., § 20–7–650 (F) (1985).]

17. The parents' right to appointed counsel is mandatory in thirty-four jurisdictions and permissive in sixteen. U.S. National Center on Child Abuse and Neglect, *Analysis of State Child Abuse and Neglect Laws, 1984* (1986), Table DD.

18. Derived from E. Krasnow and J. MacNeice, *101 Ways to Cut Legal Fees and Manage Your Lawyer: A Practical Guide For Broadcasters and Cable Operators* (Washington, D.C.: National Chamber of Commerce, 1986), Appendix A. Used with permission.

19. Derived from Ibid., § 18. Used with permission.

Index